Constitutional Law in Singapore

Constitutional Law in Singapore

Fourth Edition

Kevin Y.L. Tan

This book was originally published as a monograph in the International Encyclopaedia of Laws/Constitutional Law.

Founding Editor: Roger Blanpain
General Editor: Frank Hendrickx
Volume Editors: André Alen & David Haljan

Wolters Kluwer

Published by:
Kluwer Law International B.V.
PO Box 316
2400 AH Alphen aan den Rijn
The Netherlands
E-mail: lrs-sales@wolterskluwer.com
Website: www.wolterskluwer.com/en/solutions/kluwerlawinternational

Sold and distributed by:
Wolters Kluwer Legal & Regulatory U.S.
7201 McKinney Circle
Frederick, MD 21704
United States of America
Email: customer.service@wolterskluwer.com

ISBN 978-94-035-4671-1

e-Book: ISBN 978-94-035-4432-8
web-PDF: ISBN 978-94-035-4862-3

The Author

Prof. Dr Kevin Y.L. Tan was born and educated in Singapore. He graduated with LLB (Hons) from the Faculty of Law of the National University of Singapore in 1986 and joined the teaching staff of the same faculty the same year. Subsequently obtained his LLM (Master of Laws) and JSD (Doctor in the Science of Law) at Yale Law School, New Haven, United States. From 1986 to 2000, he taught at the Law Faculty, specializing in Constitutional and Administrative Law, Law and Government, Law and Society and International Human Rights. He resigned in 2000 to start Equilibrium Consulting Pte Ltd, a boutique consultancy specializing in historical research and publications. He continues to teach part-time and is currently Adjunct Professor at the Faculty of Law, National University of Singapore and Visiting Professor at the S Rajaratnam School of International Studies, Nanyang Technological University, Singapore. Kevin has published widely in the fields of constitutional law, human rights, legal history and the Singapore legal system and is the author and editor of over fifty books.

The Author

Table of Contents

List of Abbreviations

AC	Appeal Cases (United Kingdom)
AG	Attorney General
AGC	Attorney General's Chambers
All ER	All England Law Reports
CDC	Community Development Council
Ch	Chancery (United Kingdom)
CLR	Commonwealth Law Reports (Australia)
CNW	Cruises to Nowhere
Cox CC	Cox's Criminal Cases
CPA	Council for Presidential Advisors
FC	Federal Court (Malaysia)
GPC	Government Parliamentary Committee
GRC	Group Representation Constituency
HDB	Housing and Development Board
ICLQ	International and Comparative Law Quarterly
ICON	International Review of Constitutional Law
ISA	Internal Security Act
JA	Judge of Appeal
LegCo	Legislative Council
Mal LR	Malaya Law Review
MLJ	Malayan Law Journal
MP	Member of Parliament
MRHA	Maintenance of Religious Harmony Act
NCMP	Non-Constituency Member of Parliament
NMP	Nominated Member of Parliament
NPPA	Newspapers and Printing Presses Act
ORD	Order for the Review of Detention
OSA	Official Secrets Act

List of Abbreviations

PAP	People's Action Party
PBS	Parti Bersatu Sabah
PCA	Prevention of Corruption Act
PEC	Presidential Elections Committee
PMO	Prime Minister's Office
PP	Public Prosecutor
PSA	Port of Singapore Authority
QB	Queen's Bench
QC	Queen's Counsel
SALJ	Singapore Academy of Law Journal
SDP	Singapore Democratic Party
SGCA	Singapore Court of Appeal
SGD	Singapore Dollar
SGDC	Singapore District Court
SGHC	Singapore High Court
SICC	Singapore International Commercial Court
Sing LR	Singapore Law Review
SJICL	Singapore Journal of International and Comparative Law
SJLS	Singapore Journal of Legal Studies
SLR	Singapore Law Reports
SMC	Single-Member Constituency
US	United States
USNO	United Sabah National Organisation
WLR	Weekly Law Reports (United Kingdom)

General Introduction

§1. An Outline of Singapore Constitutional History[1]

I. The Straits Settlements Period (1819–1942)[2]

1. Singapore's modern constitutional development began with the arrival of Sir Thomas Stamford Raffles in Singapore on 29 January 1819. He concluded a treaty with Tengku Hussein allowing the British to establish a trading post on the island. In 1824, the British signed two further treaties under which Sultan Hussein and Temenggong Abdul Rahman ceded Singapore to the British. The British treated the island as *terra nullius* and administered an elementary version of British law (1819–1827). Raffles himself promulgated an illegal set of Regulations (1823)[3] that appeared to have been enforced till 1827. In 1826, Singapore, Malacca and Penang became the Straits Settlements, and were controlled by the East India Company from India. Legal chaos prevailed until 1827 when the Second Charter of Justice (1826) arrived, establishing the Court of Judicature for Prince of Wales Island (Penang), Malacca and Singapore[4] and brought English common law into the three territories.

2. Under the Charter, a Recorder travelled on circuit. His Court was charged to 'give and pass judgment and sentence according to justice and right' (English common law). Due to severe budgetary constraints and the lack of an institutional infrastructure, the first few decades of judicial administration were fraught with

1. *See* Kevin Y.L. Tan, *A Short Legal and Constitutional History of Singapore, in The Singapore Legal System* 26–66 (Sing. U. Press 2d ed. 1999). *See also* C.M. Turnbull, *Constitutional Development 1819–1968, in Modern Singapore* (Ooi Jin Bee & Chiang Hai Ding eds, U. Singapore 1969); and R.H. Hickling, *The Origins of Constitutional Government in Singapore, in Essays in Singapore Law* 1–51 (Peladuk Publication 1992).
2. *See* generally, Sir Walter Napier, *An Introduction to the Study of the Law Administered in the Colony of the Straits Settlements* (Fraser & Neave 1898) reproduced with an introduction in 16 Mal LR 4–51 (1974); Sir Roland St. John Braddell, *The Law of the Straits Settlements: A Commentary* (Kelly & Walsh 1915), reprinted with an introduction by M.B. Hooker by Oxford University Press in 1982; R.O. Winstedt, *The Constitution of the Colony of the Straits Settlements and of the Federated and Unfederated Malay States* (Royal Inst. Intl. Affairs 1931).
3. *See* Thomas Stamford Raffles, *Singapore Regulations – 1823*, reprinted in 10 Mal LR 248 (1968), with an introduction by M.B. Hooker.
4. *See* James William Norton Kyshe's, *A Judicial History of the Straits Settlements 1786–1890*, which was originally published as the Preface of his four-volume work Cases Heard and Determined in Her Majesty's Supreme Court of the Straits Settlements, 1808–1890, reprinted with an introduction by M.B. Hooker, 11 Mal LR (1969).

administrative and financial problems. On 1 April 1867, after much local agitation, the Straits Settlements became a Crown Colony and was placed under London's direct control and granted a colonial constitution. Legislative authority was vested in the Legislative Council (LegCo) which comprised two classes of members: the Official Members and the Unofficial Members, with the latter taking precedence over the former. There were always more Official Members than Unofficial Members, and the Governor held a casting vote. In 1867, the LegCo consisted of the Governor, the Chief Justice, the Officer Commanding the Troops, the Lieutenant Governor of Penang, the Colonial Secretary, the Attorney General (AG), the Colonial Engineer and four unofficial Europeans. By 1871, the Lieutenant Governor of Malacca, the Judge of Penang, the Treasurer, the Auditor-General and two more Unofficial Members were added to the Council.

3. In 1868, the Court of Judicature was abolished and replaced by the Straits Settlements Supreme Court presided over by the Chief Justice with two puisne judges, one for Penang and another for Singapore and Malacca. In 1877, an Executive Council was introduced to advise the Governor.[5] Thereafter, the structure of government remained largely unchanged until World War II. In the interim sixty-five years, the only noteworthy changes to the Constitution were those made by Governor Laurence Guillemard in the 1920s: Two Unofficial Members of the LegCo were to be nominated to sit on the Executive Council, and the LegCo was enlarged to comprise twenty-six members, with equal numbers of unofficials and officials with the Governor retaining his or her casting vote. The Penang and Singapore European chambers of commerce could each nominate one Unofficial, while the Governor nominated the rest on a racial basis: five Europeans including one each from Penang and Malacca, three Chinese British subjects, one Malay, one Indian and one Eurasian.

II. The Japanese Occupation (1942–1945)[6]

4. The structure of the Constitution remained almost intact till the Japanese invaded Singapore in February 1942. At first, there was much confusion as to who has proper legislative authority. Several government or military bodies had the power to make laws. At the top was the Supreme Command of the Southern Army Headquarters, then came the twenty-fifth Army Headquarters, the Military Administration Department and then the Malai Malayan Military Administration Headquarters and the City Government of Tokubetsu-si. Most of these bodies issued streams of regulations, laws and notices through the Tokubetsu-si without adhering to the normal chain of command. Often these laws and regulations were contradictory, but the problem usually resolved itself since the body higher up on the hierarchy always prevailed. All existing courts ceased to function and a Military Court of Justice of the Nippon Army was established by a Decree. On 27 May 1942, the

5. *Ibid.*
6. *See* generally, Goh Kok Leong, *Legal History of the Japanese Occupation in Singapore*, 1 MLJ xx (1981).

civil courts were reopened, and all former British laws were administered so long as they did not interfere with the Military Administration. At the apex of this judicial administration was the Syonan Supreme Court or the Syonan Koto-Hoin which opened on 29 May 1942. Although a Court of Appeal was constituted, it never sat.

III. The Colony of Singapore (1946–1958)[7]

5. When the Japanese surrendered in September 1945, Singapore came under the British Military Administration (BMA). When civilian rule returned a year later, the Straits Settlements was disbanded and Singapore became a Crown Colony with its own constitution.[8] Malacca and Penang became part of the new Malayan Union. The Constitution preserved the Governor's veto and reserved powers over legislation and set up an advisory Executive Council comprising six officials and four nominated unofficials. The LegCo comprised four ex officio members, seven officials and up to four nominated unofficials, and nine elected members.

6. In 1946, Governor Sir Franklin Gimson convened a Reconstitution Committee to consider the Constitution, and it recommended a revamped LegCo comprising four ex officio members, five officials, four nominated unofficials, three chamber of commerce representatives (representing the Singapore, Chinese and Indian Chambers of Commerce) and six popularly elected members. The new constitution came into effect on 1 March 1948, and elections were held for the first time on 20 March 1948. Most of the seats in the first election were won by the Progressive Party which dominated Singapore politics till the late 1950s. The judicial structure and hierarchy of courts remained unchanged.

IV. The Rendel Constitution (1955)[9]

7. From 1948 to 1953, Singapore's constitutional development was slow and leisurely, the Government being occupied with having to deal with communist front activities. In 1950, the Progressive Party demanded three additional elected seats in the Council, and in 1951, this change was implemented in time for the triennial elections. Other than this amendment, the basic constitutional structure remained intact. In the second general election, the Progressive Party won six of the nine seats. However, political development still proceeded at a snail's pace.

---

7. The most detailed published treatment of the post-war period of developments to Singapore's constitution is Kevin Y.L. Tan, *The Evolution of Singapore's Modern Constitution: Developments from 1945 to the Present Day*, 1 SALJ 1 (1989). *See also* Kevin Y.L. Tan, *The Development of Constitutional Development in Singapore: 1945–1995*, unpublished JSD dissertation (Yale L. Sch. 1995); and Philip N. Pillai & Kevin Tan Yew Lee, *Constitutional Development*, in *Management of Success: The Moulding of Modern Singapore* 647–668 (K.S. Sandhu & Paul Wheatley ed., ISEAS 1989).
8. C.M. Turnbull, *British Planning for Post-War Malaya*, 5 J. Southeast Asian Stud. 239 (1974).
9. On the period leading up to the crafting of the Rendel Constitution, *see* Yeo Kim Wah, *Political Development in Singapore 1945–1955* (Sing. U. Press 1973).

8. To increase widespread participation in government, more changes in the Constitution were necessary. To this end, a Constitutional Commission headed by Sir George Rendel was set up in 1953. The Rendel Commission was asked to conduct a comprehensive review of the Constitution. The Commission recommended automatic registration of voters and a new LegCo of thirty-two members. Of these thirty-two members, twenty-two would be Elected Unofficial Members, three ex officio Official Members holding ministerial posts and four would be Nominated Unofficial Members. The Commission also recommended the creation of a Council of Ministers comprising three ex officio Official Members and six elected members appointed by the Governor on the recommendation of the 'Leader of the House', who would be the leader of the largest party in the Assembly or of a coalition of parties assured of majority support.

9. These recommendations were implemented under the 1955 Constitution, and seventy-nine candidates contested the twenty-five seats at the general elections that followed. The Labour Front, led by David Marshall, won ten seats; the Progressives four seats; the People's Action Party (PAP) three seats; and the Democratic Party two seats. Marshall became Singapore's first Chief Minister.[10] One major problem with the Rendel Constitution was that the ministers' powers, especially those of the Chief Minister, were not well defined. Furthermore, the retention of the portfolios of Finance, Administration and Internal Security and Law in the hands of the British proved to be a major impediment to the development of self-government. Marshall was determined to wield real power and found himself on a collision course with Governor Sir John Nicoll.

10. In July 1955, Marshall demanded the right to appoint four assistant ministers. When the new Governor Sir Robert Black refused, Marshall immediately threatened to resign unless Singapore was given immediate self-government. The Colonial Office was appalled by Marshall's demands but feared that his resignation would pave the way for a more radical and irresponsible government or a possible communist takeover. The Governor was therefore instructed to act on the Chief Minister's advice, and the British agreed to hold constitutional talks the following year to discuss self-government for the Colony.

V. Constitutional Talks and Self-Government (1956–1958)

11. In 1956, a thirteen-member all-party delegation representing all the parties in the Assembly held constitutional talks in London with officials of the Colonial Office. Marshall demanded full internal self-government by 1 April 1957, leaving foreign policy and external defence in British hands but allowing Singapore a veto on defence and rights of consultation on foreign affairs. The British rejected his proposal, insisting that their High Commissioner hold the casting vote in the proposed

10. *See* Kevin Y.L. Tan, *Marshall of Singapore: A Biography* (Inst. S.E. Asian Stud. 2008); Chan Heng Chee, *A Sensation of Independence – David Marshall: A Political Biography* (Oxford U. Press 1984); and Alex Josey, *David Marshall's Political Interlude* (Eastern U. Press 1982).

Internal Security Council. Marshall refused to concede this point and the talks broke down. Marshall resigned on his return, and Lim Yew Hock (his deputy in the Labour Front) replaced him as Chief Minister.

12. In March 1957, Lim led a second all-party delegation to London to renew discussions on self-government. This time, the British agreed that in the seven-member Internal Security Council, Britain and Singapore would each have three representatives, while the seventh member would be appointed by the soon-to-be independent Federation of Malaya. The delegation accepted these terms, and in 1958, a third all-party mission went to London to settle the final terms for the new constitution.[11]

13. On 1 August 1958, the British Parliament passed the State of Singapore Act which converted the Colony into a self-governing state. By the Singapore Constitution Order in Council 1958, the post of Governor was abolished and the office of the Yang di-Pertuan Negara (Head of State) was established. At the same time, the post of Chief Minister was renamed that of Prime Minister. The Yang di-Pertuan Negara would appoint as Prime Minister the person who was most likely to command the authority of the Assembly, and the ministers were also appointed on the Prime Minister's advice. The new Legislative Assembly had fifty-one elected members, and the structure of the judiciary was left very much intact, with the Chief Justice being appointed by the Yang di-Pertuan Negara on the Prime Minister's advice. Responsibility for the external affairs was placed in British hands. In the 1959 general elections that followed, the PAP won forty-three out of the fifty-one seats, and its Secretary General Lee Kuan Yew became Singapore's first Prime Minister.

VI. Merger and Separation (1963–1965)[12]

14. The PAP government sought merger with the Federation of Malaya as a matter of urgency to achieve political independence and to guarantee Singapore's economic survival. The pro-communist elements within the PAP opposed this plan as they feared being proscribed by the Federation of Malaya's fiercely anti-communist government. The campaign for merger led to a split within the PAP, between the so-called moderates and their left-wing radical colleagues. This led to the expulsion of thirteen Assemblymen who went on to establish the opposition Barisan Sosialis (Socialist Front) with Lim Chin Siong as its secretary general. After much prevarication, Malaya's Prime Minister, Tunku Abdul Rahman ('the Tunku'), agreed to the merger plan.

---

11. *See* Singapore (Constitution) Order in Council, 1958; *see also* O. Hood Phillips, *The Constitution of the State of Singapore*, Pub. L. 50 (1960); and L.A. Sheridan, *Singapore's New Constitution*, MLJ xxv (1959).
12. On Singapore's constitutional position in Malaysia, *see* Harry E. Groves, *The Constitution of Malaysia* (Malay. Publ'n Ltd. 1964). This was a much expanded version of his article *The Constitution of Malaysia*, 5 Mal LR 245 (1963).

15. Under the Malaysia Agreement, the former British territories of North Borneo (Sabah), Sarawak and Singapore, together with the Federation of Malaya, were amalgamated to form the Federation of Malaysia. Singapore left control over foreign affairs, defence and internal security to the central government but maintained considerable powers over finance, labour and education. She was allocated 15 of the 127 seats in the new federal legislature and retained her own executive government and Legislative Assembly.[13] The day-to-day administration of Singapore was the responsibility of the Singapore State government, and Singapore was to pay 40% of her income from taxes to the federal government. A new State Constitution (1963) was granted to Singapore to effect this change in status.[14]

16. The internal politics of the Federation and the PAP's abortive attempt at federal politics proved fatal to the merger. Soon, personal suspicions, fuelled by the increasing communist and communalist threats and the failure of the proposed common market, brought relations between the central government and Singapore on a steadily downhill path. Singaporeans began to resent the strains and irritations which merger involved, and this was worsened by incidents created by the Indonesian Confrontation (Konfrontasi). In August 1965, Prime Minister Lee was summoned to Kuala Lumpur and informed of the Tunku's decision to expel Singapore from the Federation, and on 9 August 1965, Singapore's independence was proclaimed.

VII. Post-1965 Developments

A. *The Aftermath of Independence*[15]

17. Immediately after separation, Singaporeans were promised a new constitution but this document did not materialize. On 22 December 1965, Parliament adopted a makeshift Constitution comprising three separate documents: (1) the Constitution of the State of Singapore 1963; (2) the Republic of Singapore Independence Act 1965; and (3) portions of the Malaysian Federal Constitution imported through the Republic of Singapore Independence Act. In 1980, the AG issued a *Reprint* of the Constitution, incorporating all amendments to 31 March 1980. For the first time since 1965, all the provisions of Singapore's Constitution could be found in one single composite document.

---

13. *See* Ahmad Ibrahim, *The Position of Singapore in Malaysia*, MLJ cxi (1964).
14. *See* L.A. Sheridan, *Constitutional Problems of Malaysia*, 13 ICLQ 1349 (1964); Emma Sadka, *Singapore and the Federation: Problems of Merger*, 1 Asian Survey 17–25 (1962).
15. *See* generally L.A. *Sheridan, Constitutional and Legal Implications and Problems in the Separation of Singapore from Malaysia*, 1 Fiat Justitia 47 (1966); and L.A. Sheridan, *From the Federation of Malaya to Malaysia*, 14 J. du Droit Int'l 543 (1965).

B. The Wee Chong Jin Commission

18. One of the Government's most important concerns was how to protect and safeguard minority rights and interests. To this end, a Constitutional Commission (only Singapore's second), headed by then Chief Justice Wee Chong Jin, was set up in December 1965 and charged with seeing how these interests could be safeguarded. The Commission issued their Report in 1966 and made a number of important recommendations:

(a) Constitutional provisions relating to fundamental liberties, the judiciary, the legislature, general elections, minority rights and the special position of Malays, and the amendment procedures themselves should be entrenched. This was to be done by making these provisions amendable only if the amendment secures a vote of two-thirds majority in Parliament and two-thirds majority at a national referendum.
(b) Creation of a Council of State whose main function would be to 'consider all proposed legislation, except all Supply Bills or a Bill presented on a Certificate of Urgency, and to report thereon to Parliament'. The Council would be a purely advisory body and would not be part of the legislature. It would offer Parliament 'serious and weighty advice' on impending legislation and their effects on racial, linguistic, religious or cultural minorities.
(c) Creation of the office of an Ombudsman or Parliamentary Commissioner for Administration to ensure 'that civil servants carry out their administrative duties according to law so that citizens may feel that, apart from the ministerial responsibility for the acts of civil servants which is a feature of our parliamentary system in Singapore, there is also an independent check on the acts and decisions of civil servants'.
(d) Entrenching of judicial offices to maintain the independence of the judiciary and a more appropriate method of appointing members of the Public Service Commission.

19. Following a brief debate in Parliament, Parliament rejected most of these recommendations and only pursued the Council of State proposals which were sent to Select Committee. This body was constitutionally created and named the Presidential Council.[16]

20. As constituted under the 1969 constitutional amendments, the Presidential Council comprised a Chairman, ten permanent members and ten non-permanent members appointed by the President on the advice of the Cabinet. Its general function was 'to consider and report on such matters affecting any racial or religious communities in Singapore as may be referred to the Council by Government',[17]

16. *See* Thio Su Mien, *The Presidential Council*, 1 Sing LR 2 (1969).
17. Article 77, Constitution of the Republic of Singapore.

while its particular function is 'to draw attention to any Bill to any subsidiary legislation if that Bill or subsidiary legislation is in the opinion of the Council a differentiating measure or otherwise inconsistent with the fundamental liberties of the subject'.[18]

C. Changes to the Judiciary

21. Singapore's judicial structure was altered by its merger with Malaysia. The 1955 Courts Ordinance – the last Ordinance to refer back to the jurisdiction of the English High Court – was replaced by the federal Courts of Judicature Act 1964. Under this Act, the High Court of Malaysia in Singapore replaced the old Supreme Court of the Colony of Singapore. Under this new system, the Singapore branch of the Malaysian High Court was part of the larger national system of courts that included the two sister High Courts of Malaya and Borneo. At the top of the judicial hierarchy was the Federal Court.

22. At independence, Singapore's Parliament did not change the judicial system to reflect her independent status, and the Singapore High Court remained part of the Federal Court structure. This situation was remedied only in 1969 with the passing of the Constitution (Amendment) Act 1969 and the Supreme Court of Judicature Act. This amendment was necessary to constitute the Singapore judiciary because the 1963 State Constitution did not provide separately for judicial system and all matters involving the judiciary were dealt with at federal level. The amending act also made the Judicial Committee of Her Britannic Majesty's Privy Council, Singapore's final Court of Appeal.

23. The shortage of High Court judges led to an amendment to Article 94 of the Constitution in 1971 to permit the appointment of *supernumerary judges*. Judges of the Supreme Court who were compelled by the Constitution to retire at the age of 65 were permitted to stay on as 'contract judges', usually for terms of between one and three years. Difficulties in persuading senior practitioners to accept appointments to the bench led to a constitutional amendment in 1979 to create the position of Judicial Commissioner.[19] Judicial Commissioners can be appointed on a temporary basis, and this allowed practitioners who take up such appointments to return to private practice when their terms are up. Appointments as Judicial Commissioner, like those of supernumerary judges, are for periods ranging between six months and three years, and is often viewed as a prelude to a full judgeship. In 1993, then Chief Justice Yong Pung How announced that he would appoint Judicial Commissioners for very short terms and to hear long cases which would otherwise disrupt normal court hearing schedules. These intentions were manifested in the

---

18. Article 78(2), Constitution of the Republic of Singapore.
19. The first Judicial Commissioner to be appointed under this scheme was Chan Sek Keong, the former managing partner of the firm Shook Lin & Bok. Chan subsequently became a puisne judge, Attorney General of Singapore and was, in April 2006, appointed Chief Justice of Singapore. He retired in 2012.

insertion of Article 94(5) in the Constitution.[20] As of 2021, no Judicial Commissioner has been appointed to hear specific cases on a 'one-off' basis.

24. In 1989, the Constitution was amended to restrict appeals to the Privy Council. Appeals would only proceed to the Privy Council if both parties to the litigation agreed prior to their Court of Appeal hearing (in civil cases) or where the death penalty was involved and there was no unanimity among the judges in the Court of Criminal Appeal. In 1993, all appeals to the Privy Council were abolished,[21] and a constitutional amendment was passed to constitute a permanent Court of Appeal and to create a new class of judges known as Justices of Appeal who would rank above puisne judges and sit on appeals in the new court.[22]

25. The Court of Appeal is presided over by the Chief Justice as the court's President. In September 1994, a new Article 100 was inserted into the Constitution, establishing a *Special Tribunal* consisting of not less than three Judges of the Supreme Court. The President may refer to this tribunal 'for its opinion any question as to the effect of any provision' of the Constitution. The tribunal is under a duty to 'consider and answer the question so referred as soon as may be and in any case not more than sixty days after the date of such reference'.[23]

26. This amendment was not only significant but also foretold things to come. The then Deputy Prime Minister, Lee Hsien Loong, pointed out that unlike in Malaysia, the 'Singapore Constitution does not have any provisions for referring questions of interpretation of the Constitution to the Courts for an advisory ruling'. Lee explained that having such a tribunal will be useful in resolving interpretation of the complex provisions of the elected presidency scheme, and that an issue with respect to the interpretation of Article 22H relating to the President's veto powers had already arisen. This *Special Tribunal* determined its first reference in early 1995 in *Constitutional Reference No. 1 of 1995*.[24]

D. Entrenching Singapore's Sovereignty

27. During the 1972 general elections, a number of politicians argued for a return to the Malaysian Federation as part of their political agenda. This prompted the Government to amend the Constitution to protect Singapore's sovereign status.

---

20. This provision has since been renumbered as Art. 95(5)(a).
21. Judicial Committee (Repeal) Act 1994 (No. 2 of 1994).
22. Section 29, Supreme Court of Judicature Act (Cap 322).
23. Article 100(2), Constitution of the Republic of Singapore.
24. [1995] 2 SLR 201. For an excellent account of events leading up to this reference, *see* Li-ann Thio, *Working Out the Presidency: The Rites of Passage*, December SJLS 509 (1995); for a rebuttal to Thio, *see* Chan Sek Keong, *Working Out the Presidency: No Passage of Rites – In Defence of the Opinion of the Constitutional Tribunal*, July SJLS 1 (1996).

A new Part III was added to preclude any surrender or transfer of Singapore's sovereignty by merger, federation or otherwise, unless it was supported by at least two-thirds of the electorate during a national referendum. The amendment also prohibits the relinquishing of control over the Singapore Police Force and, or the Singapore Armed Forces, under the same terms.

E. Changes to the Parliamentary System[25]

28. From 1965 to 1981, the PAP won every general election and occupied every single seat in Parliament. This was, in no small way, aided by the fact that the leading opposition party, the Barisan Sosialis, decided to abandon Parliament and take their struggles to the streets in 1966. In 1981, veteran Worker's Party Secretary General J.B. Jeyaretnam defeated the PAP's candidate in the Anson constituency by-elections and broke the PAP's stranglehold on power. To quell demands for more opposition members in Parliament, a constitutional amendment was passed in 1984 to 'ensure the representation in Parliament of a minimum number of Members from a political party or parties not forming the government'.

29. Under the original scheme, the three best 'losers' in the general elections (on the basis of percentage votes cast) would be appointed as Non-Constituency Members of Parliament (NCMPs). The NCMPs have all rights and privileges as regular Members of Parliament (MPs) but cannot vote on Bills to amend the Constitution, Supply or Money Bills or on a motion of no confidence in the Government.[26] The scheme came into operation after the 1984 general election. As two opposition members were directly elected to Parliament, only one NCMP seat would be offered. There were no takers for this offer. Over the years, several persons, including veteran opposition leader Lee Siew Choh (1917–2002), were appointed NCMPs.

30. The NCMP scheme proved controversial as a number of MPs felt that it was a way into Parliament 'through the back-door'. As a result, the scheme had a 'sunset clause' under which it would expire at the end of each Parliament, and the new Parliament would have to consciously endorse the scheme for its term. In 2016, the scheme was made permanent and NCMPs were given exactly the same rights as elected MPs. In the following years, the maximum total number of NCMPs was increased from three to six, and then nine. In 2016, it was increased from nine to the present twelve. However, the actual number of NCMPs is determined by section 52 of the Parliamentary Elections Act which provides the formula for the appointment of NCMPs as 12-B (where B is the total number of opposition MPs

25. *See* Kevin Y.L. Tan, *Parliament and the Making of Law*, in *The Singapore Legal System* 123–159 (Kevin Y.L. Tan ed., Sing. U. Press 2d ed. 1999); Li-ann Thio, *Choosing Representatives: Singapore Does It Her Way*, in *The People's Representatives: Electoral Systems in the Asia-Pacific Region* 38–58 (Graham Hassell & Cheryl Saunders eds., Allen & Unwin 1997); and Li-ann Thio, *The Post-Colonial Constitutional Evolution of the Singapore Legislature*, July SJLS 80 (1993).

26. *See* V.S. Winslow, *Creating a Utopian Parliament*, 28 Mal LR 268 (1984).

elected into Parliament in the preceding general election). Based on this formula, only two NCMPs were appointed in the aftermath of the 2020 general election since the opposition Workers' Party, who won ten electoral seats.

31. One of the most important constitutional amendments took place just before the 1988 general election. This amendment introduced the Group Representation Constituency (GRC). Under this new scheme, three single-member constituencies (SMCs) would be clustered into one GRC. Each GRC would have at least one candidate from a minority race, that is, Malay or Indian or other (non-Chinese) race. The amendment was prompted by the Government's observation that there was a 'voting trend which showed young voters preferring candidates who were best suited to their own needs without being sufficiently aware of the need to return a racially balanced slate of candidates'. The Government was concerned that if this trend continued, there was a danger that Singapore might have a Parliament with no ethnic minority MPs. This amendment was thus intended to entrench the multiracial component of politics in Singapore's Constitution.[27]

32. The GRC scheme was expanded in each subsequent general election. In 1991, the number of MPs in a GRC was increased from three to four. The reason offered was that as the populations grew in these constituencies, the workload for MPs grew correspondingly, and it would need more MPs to help shoulder the burden. In 1996, it was increased from four to between four and six members. In the 1997 general election that followed, Singapore was divided into fifteen GRCs of between four and six members each and nine single-seat wards. While all the single-seat wards were contested, only six GRCs were contested.[28] While no constitutional amendments were made, the Government has, since 2015, adopted a policy reducing the maximum size of GRCs. In the 2020 general election, there were no six-member GRCs, while there were eleven five-member, and six four-member GRCs.

33. In 1990, the Constitution was amended to introduce yet another class of MP – the Nominated Member of Parliament (NMP). The Government felt that there should be alternative views on policies different from those espoused by the political parties represented in Parliament, and that this would best be achieved by nominating non-political persons who have distinguished themselves in their respective professions or fields of endeavour to serve as NMPs. The first two Nominated MPs, Dr Maurice Choo and Mr Leong Chee Whye, were sworn into office. Originally, the maximum number of NMPs allowed under the Constitution was six, but this was increased to nine in a 1997 constitutional amendment.

---

27. *See* Eugene K.B. Tan, *Multiracialism Engineered: The Limits of Electoral and Spatial Integration in Singapore*, 4 Ethnopolitics 413–428 (2005).
28. For a critique of these changes, *see* Kevin Y.L. Tan, *Constitutional Implications of the 1991 Singapore General Election*, 13 Sing LR 1 (1992); and Kevin Y.L. Tan, *Is Singapore's Electoral System in Need of Reform*, 14 Commentary 109–117 (1997).

F. The Elected President[29]

34. At the National Day Rally in 1988, Prime Minister Lee Kuan Yew mooted the idea of transforming the office of President into an elected one. While the significance of this suggestion manifested itself only eight years down the road, that speech started a string of debates and discussions on the need to protect Singapore's foreign reserves. After much debate, the Constitution was amended in 1991 to provide for a popularly elected Head of State. The purpose was to institutionally safeguard Singapore's massive foreign reserves and the integrity of its civil service from a profligate and populist government. Under this complicated scheme (which we shall deal with in Part II), the popularly elected President would hold the 'second key' to the reserves and have veto power on the appointment of top civil servants. At the same time, the amendments gave the elected President veto powers over the continued preventive detention of prisoners and the issuing of prohibition orders against extremist religious proselytes.

35. There are several notable features of the new presidency:

(a) provisions relating to the elected presidency cannot be amended without the President's concurrence unless it is supported at a referendum by a two-thirds majority;
(b) the qualifications for candidacy are extremely stringent, with a three-man Presidential Elections Committee (PEC) determining who is or is not eligible to run for President;
(c) the Constitution requires any candidate wishing to run for office to be non-partisan in that he or she cannot be a member of any political party; and
(d) under the Presidential Elections Act, if there was only one candidate for the elections, there would be no need for formal elections and that candidate would be deemed elected as President.

36. The first Presidential Elections were held on 29 August 1993. Ong Teng Cheong, a former Deputy Prime Minister, Chairman of the PAP and long-time trade union leader and politician, defeated retired banker and former Accountant-General Chua Kim Yeow to become Singapore's first elected President. A series of amendments have been made to the elected presidency provisions in the last decade. These are dealt with in greater detail in Part II.

---

29. The most complete and thorough studies of the Elected Presidency are *Managing Political Change in Singapore: The Elected Presidency* (Kevin Y.L. Tan & Lam Peng Er eds, Routledge 1997), and *Constitutional Change in Singapore: Reforming the Elected Presidency* (Jaclyn L Neo & Swati Jhaveri eds, Routledge, 2021); *see also* Kevin Y.L. Tan, *The Elected Presidency in Singapore: Constitution of the Republic of Singapore (Amendment) Act 1991*, SJLS 179–194 (1991). *See also* Kevin Y.L. Tan, *The Presidential Executive System in Singapore: Problems and Prospects, in The Powers and Functions of Executive Government: Studies from the Asia Pacific Region* 37–53 (Graham Hassell & Cheryl Saunders eds, Ctr. Comp. Constitutional Stud., The U. Melbourne 1994).

G. Amendment to Citizenship Laws

37. In 1985, an amendment was passed to consolidate the provisions relating to citizenship under the Constitution. Under the new Article 135, the Government is empowered to deprive a citizen of Singapore of his or her citizenship if he or she 'voluntarily claimed and exercised any rights … available to him under the law of any country' or if he or she has 'applied to authorities of a place outside Singapore for the issue or renewal of a passport or used a passport issued by such authorities as a travel document'. A major change to the citizenship provisions was the inclusion of a new ground for deprivation, that is, where a citizen has been 'ordinarily resident outside Singapore for a continuous period of ten years'. In 2004, the citizenship provisions were again amended to allow citizenship by descent to be conferred on children of Singapore women.

VIII. Conclusion

38. Compared to other Third World nations with a colonial past, the history of Singapore's constitutional development is uncharacteristic in at least two significant ways. First, the tutelage system worked out by the British to effect a gradual and peaceful transition of power was in many respects far more successful in Singapore than in other countries, and there were none of the convulsions and revolutions that plagued other post-independence administrations. Of course, the Singapore Government has had its share of infighting, riotous situations and crises, but in general the constitutional process has prevailed and the Constitution has always provided the basic framework within which government was run.

39. Second, alterations that have been made to the constitutional system have taken Singapore further and further away from the Westminster model which it inherited. Changes to the parliamentary system which served to accommodate what has been called the 'legislative gaps' that have emerged with the rise of a single-party dominant system of government have clearly set us apart from those countries still operating under the Westminster model. The GRC system is an important innovation in the attempt to accommodate pluralistic societies and in entrenching minority representation in Parliament. At the same time, the system has also been used to cleverly stump the opposition parties as changes are made close to election time. The elected presidency is clearly the most important constitutional change we have had to date and a clear departure from the British notion of a nominal Head of State with little but ceremonial powers.

40. Whether the changes that have been made to date will bring about more accountable governance and a better life for Singaporeans is difficult to tell since options and alternatives are few and far between. At the end of the day, constitutions should ultimately serve the aspirations of the people in whose names they are drafted and legitimized. What then are the ends of the Singaporean state? Thus far, all changes that have been made to the Constitution are premised on the idea that it would bring about better governance, and make Singapore more racially tolerant, and prosperous. Law is thus viewed formalistically, and the state's notion of the *rule of law* is that everything should be done in accordance with the law, in other words purely positive law. Law is an instrument of the state, to be used by its leaders, to be moulded and shaped to further what they perceive to be the state's interests. Law is thus not a limiting factor. In that sense, as one scholar has remarked, it is 'an idea of rule *through* law rather than rule *of* law'[30].

41. Ideally, a constitution must organize, separate and control the arbitrary exercise of power. Given the political realities of a single-party dominant system of government in Singapore, the Constitution's limitation powers are weak. Other than the sovereignty provisions under Part III and the elected president provisions – which require a two-thirds majority in a national referendum – the rest of the Constitution is amendable by a two-thirds majority in Parliament. This special majority has been easy to obtain since 1968 when the PAP secured an almost hegemonic grip on power. The party system with its Whip-enforced discipline was inherited from the British and lovingly cherished by the PAP. This allows the ruling party to change the Constitution almost at will, save where amendments might destroy the *basic structure* of the Constitution (e.g., where the right is removed).[31]

§2. Form of Government

I. General

42. Singapore operates a parliamentary system of government modelled on the British Westminster system. The current Constitution is based on the State Constitution of Singapore 1963, enacted when Singapore was a constituent state of the Federation of Malaysia. After independence in 1965, the Constitution was amended regularly to adapt the Westminster model to what the Government perceived were the needs of the state. Most of these institutional changes pertained to the structure of the legislature, with different types of members of Parliament being created. This is dealt with in greater detail in Part II. In 2021, there were 104 seats (made up of 93 elected MPs, 2 NCMPs and 9 NMPs) in the unicameral legislature called the Parliament. Members are popularly elected for five-year terms. Since 1959, the PAP has won every single general election.

43. Like in Britain, members of the executive (Cabinet) are drawn from the members of the legislature. The Prime Minister is the most important and powerful member of the executive and presides over all Cabinet meetings. At the time of writing, the Singapore Cabinet comprises twenty members. Assisting the Prime Minister is the Deputy Prime Minister. In addition, there are two Senior Ministers in the Prime Minister's Office (PMO): Teo Chee Hean and Tharman Shanmugaratnam.

30. Kanishka Jayasuriya, *The Rule of Law and Capitalism in East Asia*, 9 The Pac. Rev. 367 at 384 (1996).
31. *See Yong Vui Kong v. Public Prosecutor* [2015] 2 SLR 1129, at [68]–[72] (Court of Appeal, Singapore).

There are currently sixteen ministries in Government: Culture, Community and Youth; Defence; Education; Finance; Foreign Affairs; Health; Home Affairs; Communications & Information; Law; Manpower; National Development; Sustainability and the Environment; Trade & Industry; Transport; and the PMO. Ministers can be reassigned by the Prime Minister at will, and some portfolios are in fact split between two different ministers. There is also nothing to prevent one Minister from having two or more portfolios.

44. Each Minister is assisted by two secretaries – one for parliamentary and political affairs, and another for administrative affairs. Parliamentary or Political Secretaries are typically elected Members of Parliament, whereas the administrative secretary is the highest-ranking civil servant in the Ministry – the Permanent Secretary. The PMO is a ministry in charge of various departments, including the Elections Department and the Corrupt Practices Investigation Bureau.

45. The constitutional Head of State is the President. From 1965 to 1991, the President played a mainly ceremonial role in state affairs. In almost all cases, the President would act on the advice of the Prime Minister and his or her Cabinet. He was elected by Parliament for a renewable four-year term. The office was also used as a symbolic representation of the various races in Singapore.[32] The first President, Yusof bin Ishak, was a Malay, and he was succeeded by Benjamin Henry Sheares, a Eurasian, and C.V. Devan Nair, an Indian. In 1991, the office of President was transformed into an elected office with significant veto powers.[33] This will be discussed in greater detail in Part II.

II. Separation of Powers[34]

46. Singapore is a unitary state and as such, there is no separation of powers between a central federal authority and the regions. Neither is there a division between central and local government authorities even though municipal matters are administered by Town Councils.[35] Like most states operating under a Westminster-style constitution, there is no strict separation of powers between the legislative and executive branches of government even though the judiciary is independent. As a result, members of the Cabinet are necessarily drawn from the serving Members of Parliament. Under this system of government, there is little by way of checks and balances between the legislative and executive branches of government. This problem is exacerbated by the fact that in Singapore, all political parties adhere to a strict

32. *See* Huang Jianli, *The Head of State in Singapore: An Historical Perspective*, in *Managing Political Change in Singapore: The Elected Presidency* 9–51 (Kevin Y.L. Tan & Lam Peng Er eds, Routledge 1997).
33. *See* Kevin Tan, *The Presidency in Singapore: Constitutional Developments*, in *Managing Political Change in Singapore: The Elected Presidency* 52–87 (Kevin Y.L. Tan & Lam Peng Er eds, Routledge 1997).
34. *See* generally, Li-ann Thio, *The Constitutional Framework of Powers*, in *The Singapore Legal System* 67–122 (Kevin Y.L. Tan ed., 2d ed., Sing. U. Press 1999).
35. *See* the Town Councils Act (Cap 329A).

regime of party discipline, and anti-hopping laws exist to prevent disgruntled Members of Parliament from crossing the floor – that is leaving their own parties to join the opposition. In the absence of a strong opposition, the executive is thus able to control the entire machinery of government by controlling the Cabinet and the central executive committee of the ruling party.

47. The judiciary is established and protected under the Constitution and comprises the Supreme Court and a whole battery of subordinate courts.[36] At the apex of the legal system is the Court of Appeal, headed by the Chief Justice, who is also President of the court. Up to 1994, Singapore still allowed for final appeals to be brought before the Judicial Committee of the Privy Council in the United Kingdom, but this facility has since been abolished.[37]

§3. State Territory

48. Singapore is a small island city state lying at the southern tip of the Malayan Peninsula between Malaysia and Indonesia, less than 100 km north of the Equator. It is separated from the Malaya Peninsula by the Johore Strait and from Indonesia by the Singapore Strait. Originally made up of a main island and some fifty-four islets, the area of Singapore has grown from its original 582 sq km in 1960 to 728 sq km in 2021 through intensive land reclamation. Reclamation works continue apace, and geographers expect Singapore's land mass to grow by another 100 sq km by 2030. Much of the central core of Singapore island is formed by igneous granite, while the north-western portion of the island is dominated by reserves of sedimentary rocks, and the north-eastern portion of the island was formed by metamorphic rocks (mainly quartzite). Because of its proximity to the Equator, Singapore enjoys a tropical rainforest climate with uniformly high temperatures and rainfall throughout the year.

49. Because of its unique geographical position, Singapore has, since ancient times, been a major port and commercial centre as well as an important military and shipping node. Throughout its history, Singapore had always been part of a larger political entity.[38] The earliest record, the Javanese *Negara-Kertagama* of 1365, noted that the island of Singapore was a dependency of the great Majapahit Empire based in Java, while the seventeenth-century account of Singapore in the *Serjarah Melayu* or *Malay Annals* described Singapore as being part of the Srivijaya Empire.

50. The lack of reliable historical evidence on the early sovereign status of Singapore made it a prime target in the European race for trade supremacy in Southeast Asia. When Thomas Stamford Raffles landed on Singapore on 28 January 1819

---

36. *See* Supreme Court of Judicature Act (Cap 322) and the State Courts Act (Cap 321).
37. *See* Judicial Committee Repeal Act, No. 2 of 1994.
38. *See* Benedict C.W. Teo, *The Historical Evolution of Singapore's Status in International Law*, in *Encounters with Singapore Legal History: Essays in Memory of Geoffrey Wilson Bartholomew* 129–159 (Kevin Y.L. Tan & Michael Hor eds, Singapore Journal of Legal Studies 2009).

to claim the island for the British, he capitalized on a succession feud between Tengku Hussien (Tengku Long) and his brother Tengku Abdul Rahman, installed the former as Sultan of Singapore, and signed a Treaty of Friendship enabling the British to establish a trading post on the island. This action was complicated by the fact that the Dutch had earlier laid claim to the island by virtue of a 1787 treaty it signed with the Sultan of Johore.[39]

51. In August 1824, after the British and the Dutch concluded Anglo-Dutch Treaty of the same year, Singapore's British Resident, John Crawfurd, signed a Treaty of Friendship and Alliance with Sultan Hussien and Temenggong Abdul Rahman (not to be confused with Sultan Hussien's brother by the same name). In exchange for increased pensions to the Malay chiefs and for cash, the Sultan and Temenggong ceded Singapore to the East India Company and its successors in perpetuity.[40]

52. With this cession of the island, the British East India Company established Singapore, Malacca and the island of Penang (or Prince of Wales' Island) as the Straits Settlements. With the collapse of the East India Company in 1858, the British Crown took possession of all its assets, including the territories of the Straits Settlements. From 1819 to 1867, Singapore, along with the other territories of the Straits Settlements, was administered from Calcutta by the Government of India. In 1867, after much agitation from the local merchants, the Straits Settlements was transferred to the direct control of the Colonial Office in London. The British thus enjoyed sovereignty over Singapore till 1942 when the Japanese invaded the island.

53. Japan controlled Singapore – which it renamed *Syonan-to* or Light of the South – from February 1942 to August 1945 during what is known as the 'Japanese Occupation'. Japan's occupation of Singapore was procured by the illegal use of armed force which means that the title it acquired in 1942 was illegal and title over the island reverted to British control in 1945. By this time, the British had decided to amalgamate the territories of Malacca and Penang with the rest of the Malay states to form the Malayan Union. Singapore would become a stand-alone colony to be administered directly by the Colonial Office.

54. The British granted Singapore limited self-government under the Rendel Constitution of 1954 under which responsibility for running the island came under a newly formed Legislative Assembly and Council of Ministers. Under the Rendel Constitution, the portfolios of Finance, Internal Security and Defence remained in the hands of the British, while portfolios such as Commerce and Industry, Education and Labour and Welfare were run by locally elected Assemblymen. Further devolution of control came in 1958 with the new constitution (Order in Council)

39. *See* A.P. Rubin, *International Personality of the Malay Peninsula* 180 (Penerbit Universiti Malaya 1974).
40. Article 2 of the Treaty provided that title to Singapore and all islands within ten miles of her shore would be ceded to the British.

under which the British retained control over Defence and Foreign Affairs but shared responsibility for internal security with representatives of Singapore and Malaya in the Internal Security Council.

55. A clear break from Britain occurred only with the merger of Singapore with the Federation of Malaysia on 16 September 1963. This new federation was made up of the old Federation of Malaya, the British territories of Sabah and Sarawak, and Singapore. Under the Malaysia Agreement, concluded in July 1963, Singapore gained its independence from Britain to become a constituent state in a federation. Singapore's membership in Malaysia lasted less than two years due to fundamental differences over racial and economic policy. On 7 August 1965, the Malaysian Government signed the Independence of Singapore Agreement with the Government of the State of Singapore, and Singapore seceded from the Federation to become an independent unitary state. This Agreement was later enshrined in the Malaysian Constitution, and a copy was registered with the United Nations under Article 80 of the Vienna Convention on the Law of Treaties. On 9 August 1965, Singapore became an independent, sovereign state and was immediately recognized by Britain, Australia, New Zealand and the United States of America. On 21 September 1965, Singapore was admitted to the United Nations as its 117th member.

§4. Population[41]

56. Singapore has a population of 5.45 million (2021) and a population density of some 7,800 persons per sq km, making it one of the most densely populated countries in the world. Of these, 3.52 million are Singapore citizens, while the rest are permanent residents or expatriates and foreign workers. Almost all of Singapore island is urbanized, and Singapore's highly successful public housing programme has transformed the city state into a modern metropolis, with some 80% of the population living in public housing. As is symptomatic in most developed urban populations, population growth is extremely small.

57. The population of Singapore is largely of immigrant stock, with Chinese making up the bulk of the population (74.1%). The largest group of minorities is the Malays (13.4%), many of whom are descendants of indigenous inhabitants of Singapore island and its surrounding lands. South Asians, classified as 'Indians', make up 9.2% of the population. The remaining 3.2% of population is made up of Eurasians, Europeans and other races.[42]

58. The bulk of the Singapore population professes to be Buddhists (33.3%) or Taoists (10.9%). Almost all Malays are by definition also Muslims, thus making up the bulk of the 14.7% who profess Islam as their religion. Christians make up the next most significant religious group in Singapore, with 18.3%. Hindus make up

---

41. Census of Population 2020: Demographic Characteristics, Education, Language and Religion (Singapore: Department of Statistics, 2021).
42. *Ibid.*, at ix

5.1% of the population, while the remaining 0.7% comprises Sikhs and other religions. A significant 17.0% of the Singapore population profess no religion.[43]

59. The national language of Singapore is Malay although it is not the most commonly spoken language in Singapore. Other than Malay, the other official languages are English, Mandarin Chinese and Tamil. All Singaporean children are schooled in English as their first language, and must also study a second language which is their 'mother-tongue' (based on the ethnicity of the child's father). Most Singaporean Chinese speak either Mandarin or a Chinese dialect (the most popular being Hokkien, Teochew and Cantonese) at home (52%), while about 48.3% of the population speak English at home. Among the Malays, about 60.7% speak Malay at home, and among Indians, 27.4% speak Tamil at home.[44]

43. *Ibid.*, at x.
44. *Ibid.*, at 27–28.

Part I. Sources of Constitutional Law

Chapter 1. Treaties[45]

60. As an independent state, Singapore has capacity to enter into treaties with any other state or international organization. Like in the United Kingdom, the power to enter into treaties vests in the executive branch of government.[46] There are no constitutional provisions stipulating or regulating the treaty-making powers of the state; neither are there any provisions that allow treaties to which it is party, automatically create rights or obligations enforceable in Singapore courts. The process for the entering into treaties and their ratification is not specified by law. However, state practice in Singapore follows British convention and the executive branch retains the prerogative of treaty-making with no requirement that the legislature ratifies treaties entered into by the executive. The classic statement of this practice is found in the Privy Council decision of *AG for Canada v. Attorney-General for Ontario* (1937) which held:

> Within the British Empire there is a well-established rule that the making of a treaty is an executive act, while the performance of its obligations, if they entail alteration of the existing domestic law, requires legislative action ... Parliament, no doubt ... has a constitutional control over the executive: but it cannot be disputed that the creation of the obligations undertaken in treaties and the assent to their form and quality are the function of the executive alone. Once they are created, while they bind the State as against the other contracting parties, Parliament may refuse to perform them and so leave the State in default. In a unitary State whose Legislature possesses unlimited powers the problem is simple. Parliament will either fulfil or not treaty obligations imposed upon the State by its executive. The nature of the obligations does not affect the complete authority of the Legislature to make them law if it so chooses.[47]

45. *See* Chao Hick Tin, *Singapore and International Law: A Brief Survey of the Questions Relating to Singapore's Membership of International Organisations, State Succession and the Law of the Sea*, 1 MLJ lcxxxv (1979); and S. Jayakumar, *Singapore and State Succession: International Relations and Internal Law*, 19 ICLQ 398 (1970).
46. *See Attorney-General for Canada v. Attorney-General for Ontario* [1937] AC 326.
47. *Ibid.*, at 347–348.

61. Unlike some constitutions – for example, that of Germany – Singapore's Constitution privileges its sovereignty, so international treaties and customary international law do not automatically apply unless they have been explicitly transformed into local legislation. At the same time, there is no notion of a hierarchical structure that prefers international law over municipal law. Again, British practice is adopted in the Singapore situation:

> Unlike some other countries, the stipulations of a treaty duly ratified do not within the Empire, by virtue of the treaty alone, have the force of law. If the national executive, the government of the day, decide to incur the obligations of a treaty which involve alteration of law they have to run the risk of obtaining the assent of Parliament to the necessary statute or statutes. To make themselves as secure as possible they will often in such cases before final ratification seek to obtain from Parliament an expression of approval. But it has never been suggested, and it is not the law, that such an expression of approval operates as law, or that in law it precludes the assenting Parliament, or any subsequent Parliament, from refusing to give its sanction to any legislative proposals that may subsequently be brought before it.[48]

62. This executive prerogative to enter into treaties has never been challenged either in Parliament or in the courts of law. However, since treaties and other international obligations are not self-executing, Parliament must legislate to incorporate the treaty obligations and rights into Singapore law since it is only Parliament that has legislative competence.[49]

63. When Singapore became independent in 1965, the Agreement Relating to the Separation of Singapore from Malaysia as an independent and sovereign state provided for the devolution of treaty obligations that formerly attached to Singapore as a constituent state of the Federation of Malaysia. The relevant portions of Clause 13 of Annex B to the Agreement read as follows:

> Any treaty, agreement or convention entered into before Singapore Day between the Yang di-Pertuan Agong or the Government of Malaysia and another country or countries, including those deemed to be so by Article 169 of the Constitution of Malaysia shall in so far as such instruments have application to Singapore, be deemed to be a treaty, agreement or convention between Singapore and that country or countries, and any decision taken by an international organisation and accepted before Singapore Day by the Government of Malaysia shall in so far as that decision has application to Singapore be deemed to be a decision of an international organisation of which Singapore is a member.

---

48. *Ibid.*
49. *See* Art. 38, Constitution of the Republic of Singapore.

64. At least one commentator has doubted the effectiveness of this devolution clause on the grounds that it cannot establish any treaty relation between the successor state and third states.[50]

50. Chao Hick Tin, *Singapore and International Law: A Brief Survey of the Questions Relating to Singapore's Membership of International Organisations, State Succession and the Law of the Sea*, 1 MLJ cxxxv, at cxxxviii (1979).

Chapter 2. The Constitution

§1. Typification

65. The present-day Constitution is really an aggregate of three separate legal documents – the State of Singapore Constitution 1963, the Republic of Singapore Independence Act 1965 and the provisions of the Federal Constitution of Malaysia that were imported into Singapore via the Republic of Singapore Independence Act. These various provisions were consolidated and published as the Reprint of the Constitution of the Republic of Singapore 1980 by the AG.

66. The Constitution proclaims itself to be the supreme law of Singapore (Article 4), and also that any law that is inconsistent with the Constitution 'shall, to the extent of its consistency, be void'.

67. The Singapore Constitution may be classified as a formal and rigid document in the sense that its provisions are fairly well entrenched and amendment of the Constitution requires a two-thirds majority in Parliament, and in some cases, a two-thirds majority in a national referendum.

§2. Procedure for Amending the Constitution

68. Most provisions of the Constitution are amendable by a two-thirds majority in Parliament. The main provision governing the amendment of the Constitution is Article 5(2) of the Constitution that provides that 'A Bill seeking to amend any provision of the Constitution shall not be passed *unless it has been supported on Second and Third Readings by the votes of not less than two-thirds of the total number of the elected Members of Parliament*' (emphasis added).

69. There are, however, some provisions of the Constitution which are more difficult to amend. Under Article 8, for example, an amendment to Part III of the Constitution (Protection of the Sovereignty of Singapore) 'shall not be passed by Parliament unless it has been supported, at a national referendum, by not less than two-thirds of the total number of votes cast by the electors registered under the Parliamentary Elections Act'.

70. In 2016, Article 5(2A) – which was inserted into the Constitution in 1991 but was never brought into force – was repealed, to be replaced by Articles 5A, 5B and 5C. The old Article 5(2A) provided that the President's concurrence was required for certain amendments. In the absence of such assent, such amendments can only be passed by Parliament after it has received the endorsement of two-thirds of the total number of electors in a national referendum. Amendments requiring Presidential Assent included changes to: Article 5A (President's right to refuse assent to constitutional changes); any provision under Part IV (Fundamental Liberties); any provision in Part V Chapter 1 (The President); Article 93A (Jurisdiction to determine the validity of Presidential Elections); Article 65 (prorogation and dissolution of Parliament) or 66 (conduct of parliamentary elections); or any other provision in this Constitution which authorizes the President to act in his discretion.

71. The new scheme – which is currently in abeyance – is extremely complicated providing for either parliamentary or plebiscitarian overrides where the President's concurrence is refused. The President's concurrence is required where a constitutional amendment Bill affects clauses establishing the presidency, its functions;[51] term of office;[52] immunity from suit;[53] rules for the vacation of and removal from office;[54] persons exercising the functions of President when the office is vacant;[55] temporary disability of the President;[56] as well as his discretionary powers in relation to the appointment of public officers;[57] members of statutory boards;[58] approving budgets of statutory boards;[59] appointment of directors of government companies;[60] approving budgets of government companies;[61] control over the investment of moneys in the Central Provident Fund;[62] appointment of members and alternate of the Council of Presidential Advisors;[63] exemption of transactions from Article 144 (giving of guarantees and raising of loans by the Government); and matters covered in Part XI of the Constitution (financial provisions). In addition, the President may withhold his assent to any Bill that 'directly or indirectly' seeks to circumvent or curtail his discretionary powers.

72. With respect to these changes, the President, acting in his or her personal discretion, must concur; otherwise, the Government may only submit the amendment Bill to Parliament if it obtains more than half the votes cast in a national referendum. However, if the President's refusal to concur went against the recommendations of the Council of Presidential Advisors, the Bill may be introduced in Parliament without the need for a national referendum. Where the amendment Bill is put before Parliament, it shall be passed if it is supported at the Second and Third Readings by not less than two-thirds of the total number of Members of Parliament (excluding NMPs).

73. While it is theoretically difficult to amend most provisions of the Constitution, the fact that the PAP, who has governed Singapore since 1959, has, since 1965, held such an overwhelming majority in Parliament that the two-thirds majority

51. Article 17(1) and 17(2).
52. Article 20(1) and 20(2).
53. Article 22K.
54. Article 22L.
55. Article 22N.
56. Article 22O.
57. Article 22.
58. Article 22A.
59. Article 22B.
60. Article 22C.
61. Article 22D.
62. Article 22E.
63. Article 37B and 37C.

requirement has never acted as any kind of a real impediment. Indeed, between 1965 and 2017, the Constitution was amended over forty times.

§3. HIERARCHY

74. The Constitution declares itself to be the 'supreme law' of the land and any law that is inconsistent with the Constitution 'shall, the extent of its inconsistency, be void'.[64] The courts have always reserved the right to pronounce on the constitutionality of legislation, but this judicial review power was only used in one instance since Singapore's independence in 1965. This occurred in the case of *Taw Cheng Kong v. Public Prosecutor,*[65] when the High Court ruled section 37 of the Prevention of Corruption Act (PCA) unconstitutional. This decision was subsequently reversed by the Court of Appeal.[66]

64. Article 4, Constitution of the Republic of Singapore.
65. [1998] 1 SLR 943.
66. [1998] 2 SLR 410; [1998] SGCA 37.

Chapter 3. Legislation

75. Ordinary legislation is passed by the Singapore Parliament under its general legislative powers.[67] When first introduced, they are known as Bills, and become Acts after being duly passed by Parliament and being assented to by the President. Legislation is passed during parliamentary sessions by a simple majority. Under Article 59 of the Constitution, any member of the House may introduce any Bill.

76. Like most modern administrative states, Parliament in Singapore no longer holds exclusive right to legislate. Many statutes provide for the delegation of legislative powers to the executive. This is necessary since it would be much too cumbersome to summon Parliament every time a minor regulatory matter needed to be legislated on. Acts of Parliament are thus primary legislation, while all other laws made by the executive under their delegated powers are known as subsidiary legislation, or orders.

77. Under section 2 of the Interpretation Act (Cap 1), 'subsidiary legislation' is defined as 'any order-in-council, proclamation, rule, regulation, order, notification, by law or other instrument made under any Act, Ordinance or other lawful authority and having legislative effect'. These are thus formal rules with binding force and are to be distinguished from other forms of informal rules such as executive circulars or administrative guidelines.[68]

78. Under section 36 of the Interpretation Act, the Minister who has been given subsidiary legislative powers may, with the President's approval and by notification in the *Government Gazette*, subdelegate his or her powers to another official.

67. *See* Art. 58, Constitution of the Republic of Singapore.
68. *See Cheong Seok Leng v. Public Prosecutor*, [1988] 2 MLJ 481 (1988).

Chapter 4. Case Law as Judicial Precedent

79. English common law was received into Singapore by virtue of the Second Charter of Justice 1826.[69] Since then, these judge-made rules have formed the bedrock of Singapore's legal system which continues to adhere to the common law practice of treating previously determined cases as important legal precedents and a key source of law.

80. The Second Charter of Justice, that established the Court of Judicature (1826–1867), did not observe the historical separation that existed between the common law courts and courts of equity in England. As such, the Court of Judicature, and then the Supreme Court of the Straits Settlements (1867–1942), exercised jurisdiction over both common law and equity. Subsequently, the fusion of common law and equity was legislatively adopted through the Straits Settlements Civil Law Ordinance of 1878, and is retained under the present Civil Law Act. As such, Singapore courts practise both common law and equity, applying the most appropriate solution and remedy to each case.

81. A judicial precedent is a decision of a court. Each case, which a court decides and is reported, becomes a judicial precedent. When deciding disputes, courts make pronouncements on the law. This can either be an interpretation of a statutory provision, or the clarification or extension of a common law principle. From the thirteenth century, most of the important cases have been recorded by either private or official law reporters, and are published in a series of *law reports*. Technically, all cases are judicial precedents, but not all cases are necessarily sources of law. This is because some cases are far more important than others in that they either formulate or elaborate substantive principles of law.

---

69. *See Regina v. Willans* (1858) 3 Kyshe 16. *See also* Andrew B.L. Phang, *The Reception of English Law*, in *Essays in Singapore Legal History* 7–26 (Kevin Y.L. Tan ed., Sing. Acad. L. & Marshall-Cavendish 2005).

Chapter 5. Unwritten Law

§1. Custom

82. Beyond statute law and case, there is an extremely small body of unwritten law or custom that might qualify as a source of law. Chinese customary law was habitually applied by the Singapore courts especially in the colonial era in matters relating to marriage, divorce and succession. Most of these laws have fallen into disuse as a result of statutes regulating the same areas, chief of which is the Women's Charter.[70]

83. The Administration of Muslim Law Act[71] establishes a Syariah Court with jurisdiction to hear and determine 'all actions and proceedings in which all the parties are Muslims or where the parties were married under the provisions of the Muslim law' and which involves disputes relating to marriage, divorces, betrothal, disposition of property on divorce or nullification of marriage, or the payment of maintenance or marriage expenses.[72]

§2. Customary International Law

84. Singapore courts have always operated on the assumption that customary rules of international law are applicable in Singapore even though it was only in 2005 that the Court of Appeal had occasion to articulate these principles in the case of *Nguyen Tuong Van v. Public Prosecutor.*[73] The Court of Appeal considered the question as to whether the imposition of the death penalty under the Misuse of Drugs Act (Cap 185) was in violation of customary international law. The court held that there was no general customary international law rule that forbade death by hanging as a cruel and unusual punishment.

85. A second matter considered by the Court of Appeal was whether the rules contained in the Vienna Convention on Consular Relations applied to Singapore as part of customary international law. At the time of the case, Singapore was not a party to the Convention and was thus not bound by treaty rules. The Court of Appeal held that as the Government of Singapore did not object to the rules contained in the Vienna Convention and since the Convention codified customary international law rules, the same applied to Singapore notwithstanding the fact that Singapore was not a party to the Convention.

---

70. Cap 353, Singapore Statutes. *See also* M.B. Hooker, *Chinese Customary Law in Contemporary Malaysia and Singapore*, 1 Austl. J. Asian L. 34 (1991); and Leong Wai Kum, *Common Law and Chinese Marriage Custom in Singapore*, in *The Common Law in Singapore and Malaysia* 177–194 (A.J. Harding ed., Mal LR., 1985).
71. Cap 3, Singapore Statutes.
72. *See* s. 35(2), Administration of Muslim Law Act (Cap 3).
73. *See Nguyen Tuong Van v. Public Prosecutor*, [2005] 1 SLR 103.

Chapter 6. Administrative Regulations and Orders

86. See discussion of subsidiary legislation in paragraphs 76–78 above.

Part II. Form of Government

Chapter 1. General

87. Singapore's constitutional system is based on the British Westminster system it inherited from its former colonial masters, the United Kingdom. While there is a technical separation of powers between the legislative and executive branches, neither of these bodies acts as an effective check against the other since members of the executive (in this case, the Cabinet) are drawn from the ranks of the legislature (in this case, Parliament). The judicial arm of government is independent of both other branches.

88. In the years since Singapore became independent in 1965, numerous constitutional amendments have been made to the structure of government. In particular, provisions relating to the legislature have been significantly amended. At the same time, Parliament transformed the office of the President from a ceremonial one into an executive position with limited veto powers.

89. Following in the British tradition, the powerful state bureaucracy provides the administrative backbone of the state. Indeed, so important is the civil service that the whole Part IX of the Constitution is devoted to safeguarding its integrity and functioning.

90. The legislature is voted in during regular elections, and there are fifteen registered political parties in Singapore. Since 1959, the PAP has been the dominant party in Singapore, and it has won every single general election since. So dominant was the PAP that between 1968 and 1981, it won every single seat in Parliament. Since 1981 to the present time, there have been no more than ten opposition parliamentarians in the House. The other significant political parties are the Workers' Party and the Singapore Democratic Party (SDP).

Chapter 2. Head of State

§1. Introduction

91. In the Westminster system of government, real power rests in the hands of Prime Minister and his or her Cabinet rather than the Head of State. The Head of State – usually the President – is a titular office and his or her role is largely ceremonial. This quirk was an accident of history since the English monarch did in fact have much real power before the Glorious Revolution of 1688. Indeed, many of these former British colonies soon abandoned the Westminster model in favour of a limited Presidential Executive where the Head of Government and Head of State reposed in a single office, and where the President, as Head of Government, wielded more effective power.

92. Among post-colonial states, Singapore was unique in refusing to follow this trend. From independence in 1965–1991, Singapore's non-executive President had very limited powers; his or her functions were largely ceremonial and real power resided in the Prime Minister and his or her Cabinet. However, in 1991, a major constitutional amendment was made to make the post of President an elected one.

§2. Singapore's Presidential Executive: A Short History[74]

I. Introduction

93. During the colonial era, Singapore's chief executive was the Governor. He was appointed by the Crown and acted on its behalf. In 1959, when Singapore was granted self-governing status, the office of the Governor was transformed into that of the Yang di-Pertuan Negara (Malay for 'Head of State'). Like the Governor, the Yang di-Pertuan Negara was appointed by the Queen, but only after consultation with the Government.

94. During the transition from colony to self-governing state, the then-Governor of Singapore, Sir William Goode (1907–1987), became the first Yang di-Pertuan Negara. At the same time, he was also appointed by the Queen as the first United Kingdom Commissioner. To complete the transition, Goode resigned his office as Yang di-Pertuan Negara six months later and Yusof bin Ishak (1910–1970), a former journalist, succeeded him to the post. Yusof thus became the first and only Malayan-born Yang di-Pertuan Negara of Singapore.

---

74. *See Managing Political Change in Singapore: The Elected Presidency* (Kevin Y.L. Tan & Lam Peng Er eds, Routledge 1997); *see also* Kevin Y.L. Tan, *The Elected Presidency in Singapore: Constitution of the Republic of Singapore (Amendment) Act 1991*, SJLS 179–194 (1991); and Kevin Y.L. Tan, *The Presidential Executive System in Singapore: Problems and Prospects*, *in The Powers and Functions of Executive Government: Studies from the Asia Pacific Region* 37–53 (Graham Hassell & Cheryl Saunders eds, Ctr. Comp. Constitutional Stud., The U. Melbourne 1994).

95. When Singapore joined the Federation of Malaysia in 1963, Yusof remained as Yang di-Pertuan Negara and upon Singapore's independence in 1965, the post of Yang di-Pertuan Negara was abolished and replaced by the office of President. Yusof thus became Singapore's first President. He died in office in 1970 and was succeeded by world-renowned Eurasian gynaecologist Benjamin Henry Sheares (1907–1981) who also died in office in 1981. Singapore's third President was former trade unionist C.V. Devan Nair (1923–2005) who resigned in 1985 and was replaced by former journalist Wee Kim Wee (1915–2005) who was President from 1986 to 1993. Wee was Singapore's last non-executive President and Singapore's first 'elected' President. He was succeeded by another former unionist and architect Ong Teng Cheong (1936–2002) in 1993. SR Nathan (b 1924), a former senior civil servant, served as President from 1993 to 2011. In 2011, an electoral contest with four candidates saw Tony Tan Keng Yam, a former Deputy Prime Minister, elected by a very slim margin. In 2016, following constitutional amendments to provide for 'reserved' elections (*see* paragraph 141 below), the sole candidate, Halimah Yacob – a former Speaker of Parliament – was 'elected' as President.

II. The Elected President: The Proposals

96. In 1984, then Prime Minister Lee Kuan Yew mooted the idea of converting the office of President into an elected one. However, it was only in 1988 that the first White Paper on this subject was issued. In August 1990, a second White Paper outlining the specific proposals was issued with an accompanying Constitution Amendment Bill. Following lengthy debates in Parliament, a Select Committee was appointed. Several amendments were made to the original Bill, and it was finally passed into law in January 1991.

97. The rationale for the proposal was outlined in the first White Paper as follows:

(a) Many irresponsible governments mismanaged and economically ruined their countries by providing handouts and heavy subsidies to buy votes.
(b) Singapore has so far been fortunate to have a responsible government, but with over USD 30 billion in the national reserves, the temptation for a future irresponsible government will be very great. A future irresponsible government may spend this hard-earned money on short-term vote-buying and on popular measures.
(c) A cornerstone of Singapore's success has been its public service. Key appointment holders in the public service and statutory boards are persons of integrity and ability. But this may be destroyed through nepotism and corruption.
(d) Nothing in the Constitution prevents any government from squandering all the nation's reserves, leaving it economically ruined. Nor is there any safeguard against the irresponsible appointment of key civil servants. The Prime Minister and his or her Cabinet have untrammelled power.

(e) It is therefore necessary to have some constitutional safeguard to secure the future for Singaporeans and to prevent an irresponsible Government from ruining Singapore.

98. In designing a constitutional safeguard, the White Paper also found the following considerations vital:

(a) The parliamentary system of government should be preserved and the Prime Minister and his or her Cabinet should retain governmental initiative.
(b) The safeguard mechanism must enable quick action to control a potentially disastrous situation.
(c) The person must have moral authority gained through an election.
(d) The person must have ministerial, High Executive or Administrative experience to 'balance the demands of political expediency and the public interest'.
(e) The Constitution should require Presidential candidates to have such experience and qualities.

99. The Government considered several options, such as 'creating an upper legislative body, reposing the power of the veto in the Presidential Council for Minority Rights or some other body analogous to the Federal Reserve Board, or requiring decisions on financial assets to be subject to the approval of the electorate in a referendum' but found them unsuitable. It was thus decided to transform the office of President into an elected one with the President holding the 'second key' to the nation's financial reserves. His or her powers were to be confined to two specific areas – government spending and the appointment of key posts in the public service.

100. In the Second White Paper issued in 1991, several additional considerations were brought into play. First, the President would be required to check against possible executive abuse of power in preventive detention cases under the Internal Security Act (ISA). Second, the President's discretion was extended to the making of prohibition orders under the Maintenance of Religious Harmony Act (MRHA); and third, in the interests of upholding the integrity of the Cabinet, the Director of the Corrupt Practices Investigation Bureau was to report directly to the President.

101. A fourth change related to the President's advisory panel. The original 'Presidential Committee for the Protection of Reserves' was renamed Council for Presidential Advisors (CPA) and would comprise six members instead of the original five. The President, the Chairman of the Public Service Commission and the Prime Minister would nominate two members each. In addition, the role of the CPA was defined as giving the President advice on all matters in which he or she has discretionary powers, although the President is legally obliged to consult the Council only on questions involving the budgets of the Government, statutory boards and key government companies.

102. Finally, a new provision allowed Parliament to override the Presidential veto. In addition to these changes, other provisions relating to the qualification and disqualification of candidates, terms of office, specific government statutory boards and companies to be included under the President's purview were specifically spelt out.

103. Parliament debated the Bill vociferously during the Second Reading before committing it to Select Committee. The Select Committee's Report was presented to Parliament on 18 December 1990. A month later, the Bill and its amendments were passed into law. Set out below is the scheme that emerged in 1991.

III. The Final Scheme

104. Under the final scheme, candidates for the presidency must:

(a) be a Singapore citizen;
(b) be aged 45 and above;
(c) not be a member of any political party on the date of nomination for election;
(d) have his or her name appear on the current register of electors;
(e) be a resident of Singapore at the time of nomination, and have been a resident for a period amounting in aggregate of not less than ten years; and
(f) not be subject to any disqualification under Article 45.

105. In addition, he or she had to satisfy the PEC that 'he is a person of integrity, good character and reputation', and has for a period of not less than three years held office in one of the numerous capacities laid down under Article 19(2)(g). Specifically, these offices are:

(a) Minister.
(b) Chief Justice.
(c) Speaker.
(d) Attorney General.
(e) Chairman of the Public Service Commission.
(f) Auditor-General.
(g) Permanent Secretary.
(h) Chairman or chief executive officer of one of the statutory boards referred to in Article 22A read with Schedule 5 (viz., Board of Commissioners of Currency, Singapore, Central Provident Fund Board, Housing and Development Board (HDB), Jurong Town Corporation, Monetary Authority of Singapore and the Post Office Savings Bank of Singapore).

(i) Chairman of the board of directors or chief executive officer of a company incorporated or registered under the Companies Act with a paid-up capital of at least SGD 100 million or its equivalent in foreign currency;[75] or
(j) In any other similar or comparable position of seniority and responsibility in any other organization or department of equivalent size or complexity in the public or private sector which, in the opinion of the PEC, has given him or her such experience and ability in administering and managing financial affairs as to enable him or her to carry out effectively the functions and duties of the office of the President.

§3. Presidential Elections[76]

106. Article 17(2) of the Constitution provides that the President 'shall be elected by the citizens of Singapore in accordance with any law made by the Legislature', in this case, the Presidential Elections Act 1991. Under the Act, elections will be held within six months after the office of the President becomes vacant, but not more than three months before the expiration of the incumbent.

107. After the notice of election and at least two clear days before Nomination Day, each candidate must apply to the PEC for a certificate stating that the PEC was satisfied that he or she is a qualified candidate under Article 19 of the Constitution. If there is only one candidate in a Presidential Election, that candidate will be declared elected as President (*see* section 15, Presidential Elections Act). In the first Presidential Election in 1993, Ong Teng Cheong defeated Chua Kim Yeow for the post. However, in both the 1993 and 1999 'elections', there was only one candidate – SR Nathan – who was duly declared elected as President. Four candidates vied for the post of President in the 2011 elections, and Tony Tan Keng Yam defeated his nearest opponent, Tan Cheng Bock, by securing 35.2% of the votes against the latter's 34.85%, a difference of some 3,300 votes.

108. Following the 2016 amendments to the Constitution and Presidential Elections Act (*see* below paragraphs 123–125), the 2016 Presidential Election was thus declared to be 'reserved' for persons of the Malay community as no Malay had served as President in the preceding five terms. This election proved controversial largely because of disputes over the application of the constitutional definition of who was or was not a member of the Malay community, race being a social construct. Article 19B(6) provides that a member of the Malay community is 'any person, whether of the Malay race or otherwise, who considers himself to be a member of the Malay community and who is generally accepted as a member of the Malay

75. In 2016, this requirement was revised to require the candidate's company to be worth at least SGD 500 million in shareholder equity.
76. For a critique of the electoral process, *see* Li-ann Thio, *Singapore: (S)electing the President: Diluting Democracy?*, 5 Intl. Rev. Const. L. 526–543 (2007); and Valentine Winslow, *Electing The President: The Presidential Elections Act 1991*, SJLS 476–481 (1991).

community by that community'. This definition was criticized as being tautologous and arbitrary, especially since the sole candidate, Halimah Yacob, was born of an Indian father and a Malay mother.

§4. Term of Office, Powers and Immunities

109. The President's term of office is six years. Generally, he or she must exercise his or her functions, on the advice of the Cabinet or of a Minister acting under the authority of the Cabinet. However, he or she may act in his or her personal discretion in the following instances:

(a) appointment of the Prime Minister;
(b) withholding consent to a request for the dissolution of Parliament;
(c) withholding assent to any Bill under Article 22E, 22H, 144(2) or 148A;
(d) withholding concurrence under Article 144 to any guarantee or loan to be given or raised by the Government;
(e) withholding concurrence and approval of appointments and budgets of statutory boards and Government companies applicable under Article 22A and 22C;
(f) disapproving of transactions referred to in Article 22B(7), 22D(6) or 148G;
(g) withholding concurrence under Article 151(4) in relation to the detention or further detention of any person under any law or ordinance made or promulgated in pursuance of Part XII (Special Powers Against Subversion and Emergency Powers);
(h) the exercise of his or her functions under section 12 of the MRHA 1990; and
(i) any other function the performance of which the President is authorized by this Constitution to act in his or her discretion.

110. In addition, the President may consent to investigations undertaken by the Corrupt Practices Investigations Bureau even if the Prime Minister refuses to give his or her consent. When exercising his or her discretion, the President is, in some cases, bound to consult the CPA, and in others, he or she may refer these matters to them for advice. The President is immune from any court proceedings for anything he or she does or omits while acting in his or her official capacity.

§5. Removal of the President

111. Under Article 22L, the President may be removed from office if he or she 'is permanently incapable of discharging his functions of his office by reason or physical infirmity' or has been found guilty of the following:

(a) intentional violation of the Constitution;
(b) treason;
(c) misconduct or corruption involving the abuse of the powers of his or her office; or
(d) any offence involving fraud, dishonesty or moral turpitude.

112. To determine whether the President is guilty, a tribunal appointed by the Chief Justice and consisting of not less than five Judges of the Supreme Court would be constituted.

113. Before the President can be removed under Article 22L, 'Prime Minister or not less than one-quarter of the total number of the Members of Parliament' must give notice of a motion alleging his or her unsuitably under the terms of this article. If the motion has been adopted 'by not less than half of the total number of the Members of Parliament, the Chief Justice must appoint a tribunal to inquire into the allegations against the President'. If the tribunal reports to the Speaker that in its opinion the President is either permanently incapable of discharging his or her functions has been guilty of one of the allegations, Parliament 'may by a resolution passed by not less than three-quarters of the total number of the Members of Parliament remove the President from office'.

§6. Entrenchment of Office

114. The office of the President is now more tightly entrenched than most other provisions under the Constitution, including the parliamentary system of government, judiciary and fundamental liberties. Article 5A, 5B and 5C requires that any Bill to amend Articles 17–22 and 37 of the Constitution cannot be passed by Parliament unless it has been supported at a national referendum. Although enacted into law, these provisions have been held in abeyance and have not come into force. Some scholars have questioned the way in which these provisions were introduced, as well as the need to entrench these provisions so tightly in the Constitution.

§7. Subsequent Changes

115. Since 1991, provisions relating to the elected President have been amended several times. Most of these changes reflect an about-turn in the Government's thinking about the President's powers. The first major amendment came in September 1994. In moving amendments, then Deputy Prime Minister Lee Hsien Loong pointed out that the elected presidency mechanism was 'even more complex' than the Government had 'originally anticipated'. Some of the more important changes and their implications are dealt with in this section.

116. President to State Reasons for Spending Reserves. The first important amendment provides that if the President consents to the Government drawing down the reserves, he or she must publish his or her reasons in the *Gazette*. He or she must thus publish the rationale for his or her actions, whether he or she exercised his or her Presidential veto or not.

117. Transfer of Surpluses. In the 1994 amendment, transfers of surpluses from statutory boards or government companies were deemed not to be a draw on their reserves. In 2004, these provisions were again amended, this time allowing statutory boards and government companies to transfer their surpluses either to the Government or to each other without the President's scrutiny. Under the new Article 148I, the Government is now permitted to transfer its past reserves to any statutory board or a Schedule 5 government company (at present, only Jurong Town Corporation, the Monetary Authority of Singapore, the HDB and the Central Provident Fund Board) without the President's consent.

118. Advisory Capacity of the Supreme Court. A new Article 100 was added in 1994 to establish a Special Tribunal consisting of not less than three Judges of the Supreme Court. The President may refer to this tribunal 'for its opinion any question as to the effect of any provision' of the Constitution. The tribunal is under a duty 'consider and answer the question so referred as soon as may be and in any case not more than sixty days after the date of such reference'. Any dissenting opinions of any judge must accordingly be reflected in the opinion rendered to the President although the majority decision shall be considered the opinion of the tribunal and shall be pronounced in open court. The opinion is not subject to question in any court. This amendment was significant since an important question had arisen with respect to the interpretation of the President's powers under Article 22H. This was dealt with in *Constitutional Reference No. 1 of 1995*. Lee, in moving the amendment, pointed out that unlike in Malaysia, the 'Singapore Constitution does not have any provisions for referring questions of interpretation of the Constitution to the Courts for an advisory ruling.'

119. Reduction of Veto Powers. In 1994, a new Article 151A was inserted. With this change, the President no longer has a veto on 'any defence and security measure'. This is defined as 'any liability or proposed transaction which the Prime Minister and the Minister responsible for defence, on the recommendations of the Permanent Secretary to the Ministry of Defence and the Chief of Defence Force, certify to be necessary for the defence and security of Singapore'. This certificate cannot be challenged in court and is 'conclusive evidence of the matters specified therein'.

120. This amendment created an uproar in Parliament. Some MPs pointed out that the new provision could be abused by unscrupulous politicians. Nominated MP Walter Woon (who was later to become the AG) argued that it would be all too easy to circumvent the safeguards in the Constitution since 'national security' was 'such a wide thing that it would be possible to fit any sort of handouts within the rubric'. However, the Government's position was that since the Prime Minister and the Cabinet are responsible for deciding whether the country goes to war, they must have the power to execute the decision, and we cannot risk a tussle between the Prime Minister and the President over whether spending is necessary for defence and security.

121. In 1996, a 'deeming provision' was inserted under a new Article 5A(6). This provides that the President will be *deemed* to have assented to a Bill thirty days after the Bill is presented to him or her for his or her assent if he or she does nothing. New articles were added to Article 22, 22A and 22C – concerning the President's power to veto appointment of public officers, members of statutory boards and directors of government companies. This change provides that where the President acts contrary to the CPA's recommendation by refusing to make an appointment or refuses to revoke an appointment, Parliament may override the President's decision by passing a resolution of not less than a two-thirds majority.

122. Since then, a number of other amendments have been made to contain and whittle down the oversight powers of the President. The provisions relating to fiscal control are extremely complicated and technical, covering the President's oversight role in budgets of the Government, government-linked companies and even statutory boards.[77]

123. In 2016, the Government established a Constitutional Commission to review the workings of the scheme, and in particular to consider if the criteria for candidates' qualification were sufficiently stringent. At the same time, the Commission, under the Chairmanship of Chief Justice Sundaresh Menon, was asked to consider how the scheme could be modified to ensure that ethnic minorities in Singapore had a fair chance of being elected to the office.

124. The Commission, which received over a hundred representations from members of the public, held public hearings to canvass the views of representors and proposed the following:[78]

(a) Separating the President's custodial and symbolic functions by returning the office to its old ceremonial role and having its custodial functions repose in a separate body, such as an enlarged Council of Presidential Advisors or a second chamber. In such a case, the President would be elected or appointed by Parliament.
(b) If the current system is maintained, to heighten the private sector requirements for candidate qualification by requiring the candidate to have been Chairman or chief executive officer of a publicly listed company valued at a minimum of SGD 500 million in shareholder equity.
(c) Increasing the minimum period a public sector candidate must have served in the qualifying category from three years to six years.
(d) To provide for a 'reserved' election for any ethnic group who has not had one of its community members occupy the Presidential office for five consecutive terms.

125. The Government accepted proposals listed in (b) and (d) above and proceeded to amend the Constitution and the Presidential Elections Act accordingly.

77. For a comprehensive study of this, *see* Yvonne C.L. Lee, *Under Lock and Key: The Evolving Role of the Elected President as a Fiscal Guardian*, SJLS 290–322 (2007).
78. Report of the Constitutional Commission 2016 (Singapore: The Commission, 2016).

§8. The Indonesian Loan Controversy

126. In November 1997, a constitutional controversy broke out when it was announced that Singapore was to grant a USD 5 billion loan to crisis-hit Indonesia. According to newspaper reports, the decision was made by Prime Minister Goh Chok Tong in consultation with Senior Minister Lee Kuan Yew. The Workers' Party issued a two-page statement alleging that this move ran counter to the Constitution as it violated Article 144(2).[79] Finance Minister responded by saying that Workers' Party chief, Mr J.B. Jeyaretnam, had 'misread the Constitution'.

127. Then AG Chan Sek Keong gave a written opinion on the matter and concluded that there was no need to secure the President's assent for such a loan. Article 144(1) argued that the AG was to be read '*reddendo singula singulis,* that is, to render each to each, applying each verb to its appropriate subject'. Jeyaretnam then offered to refer the matter to the High Court if the state would bear the costs. When his offer was rejected by the Government, the matter was dropped and was not pursued in the courts. There is thus no authoritative pronouncement on the question of whether Presidential Assent was necessary when loans are given by the state.[80] This opinion was given legal weight by the Court of Appeal in a case in which a similar argument was made by Kenneth Jeyaretnam (JB's son) in respect of an undertaking by the Singapore Government to the International Monetary Fund.[81]

§9. Constitutional Reference No. 1 of 1995

128. In early 1995, a problem arose with respect to the interpretation of Article 22H. This problem arose mainly because Article 5(2A) was (and continues to be) held in abeyance (i.e., not in operation) and Article 22H (which is operational) refers directly to Article 5(2A). As a result, some provisions relating to the presidency are protected by Article 5(2A) while others are not. However, since Article 5(2A) was not yet operational, the question before the tribunal was whether an amendment to Article 22H circumvented or curtailed the President's discretionary powers.

129. In early 1995, President Ong Teng Cheong referred this constitutional question to the Special Tribunal under Article 100. The tribunal was asked to consider whether the President could veto a Bill to amend Article 5(2A) and Article 22H of the Constitution. The Special Tribunal ruled that the President could not.[82] This decision became the subject of an academic debate that followed.[83]

---

79. *See* Loan offer to Indonesia 'Breach of Constitution', The Straits Times (21 Nov. 1997).
80. *See* Indonesian Loan 'Does Not Go Against Constitution', The Straits Times (22 Nov. 1997).
81. *Jeyaretnam Kenneth Andrew v. Attorney-General* [2014] 1 SLR 345.
82. *See* Constitutional Reference No. 1 of 1995, 2 SLR 201 (1995).
83. *See* Li-ann Thio, *Working out the Presidency: The Rites of Passage*, SJLS 509 (1995); and Chan Sek Keong, *Working out the Presidency: No Passage of Rights – In Defence of the Opinion of the Constitutional Tribunal*, SJLS 1 (1996).

§10. The President Exercises His Discretion

130. The financial crisis that broke out in the United States in 2007 spread like a wildfire throughout the world. By 2008, Singapore was affected by the contagion and because of its open economy and heavy reliance on exports to the United States and Europe. In the fourth quarter of 2008, Singapore's economy shrank by 12.5%, while it declined 5.4% in the July-September quarter. It was the third consecutive quarterly decline in gross domestic product. Growth in the economy was only 1.5% for 2008, compared with 7.7% for 2007. By the end of 2008, the Government was predicting that Singapore's economy would contract by 2% in 2009.

131. The economy was bleeding so badly that the Government announced that it would bring forward the Budget debate from March to 22 January. Rumour was rife about the Government needing to draw down on its past reserves to meet the crisis. On 17 February 2009, President SR Nathan announced that he agreed to the first-ever draw on Singapore's past reserves.[84] Nathan's announcement, while not wholly unexpected, nonetheless attracted much interest from the public who was keen to understand the process under which the President exercised his discretion.

132. Under Article 148A(1) of the Constitution, the President may:

> acting in his discretion, withhold his assent to any Supply Bill, Supplementary Supply Bill or Final Supply Bill for any financial year if, in his opinion, the estimates of revenue and expenditure for that year … are likely to lead to a drawing down on the reserves which were no accumulated by the Government during its current term of office, except that if the President assents to any such Bill notwithstanding his opinion that the estimates, supplementary estimates or statement of excess are likely to lead to a drawing on those reserves, the President shall state his opinion in writing addressed to the Speaker and shall cause his opinion to be published in the Gazette.

133. If the President withheld his or her assent to the Supply Bill, Parliament can vote to overrule the President within thirty days by passing such a resolution with a two-thirds majority.[85] If such an overruling action was not feasible, Parliament can authorize the use of expenditure from the Consolidated Fund in an amount not exceeding the previous year's budget. This means that if President Nathan had not given his assent, Parliament – which is overwhelmingly controlled by the ruling PAP – would have had no problem overruling his decision.

134. In any case, that did not happen. Indeed, Nathan took great pains to explain to the public how the decision was made to support the Government's two new schemes to alleviate the economic hardship of Singaporeans – Jobs Credit Scheme

---

84. Sue-Ann Chia, *President SR Nathan: Why I Said Yes (on Use of Past Reserves)* 1 (The Straits Times, 18 Feb. 2009).
85. Article 148D.

and Special Risk-Sharing Initiative – especially since a number of observers were concerned that he was able to come to his decision within eleven short days. He explained that throughout 2008, he and his CPA members received regular briefings by officials from the Ministry of Trade and Industry and the Monetary Authority of Singapore and was kept apprised of the state of the global and Singapore economies.

135. On 18 January, he was approached by Prime Minister Lee Hsien Loong, who explained the dire state of the economy to him and told him that extraordinary measures were needed to give confidence to the people and to address the impact of the economic crisis on the people, especially those in the low-income bracket. In this connection, the Prime Minister underscored the severity of the situation and requested the President's assent to use the past reserves. What happened next was revealed in President Nathan's interview:

> The CPA and I were already aware of the circumstances that were prevailing and how they were impacting on us. So I agreed at that stage to give every consideration to the proposal when it was submitted to me.
> After that, the Minister for Finance came to see me and he formally made a request the next day for the specifics of the scheme and sought a meeting to discuss this in greater detail.
> So a meeting was convened with the CPA and myself and it was addressed by the Minister for Trade and Industry, Minister for Finance and it was attended by people from the Attorney-General's Chambers (and the) Accountant-General.
> The Minister for Finance and the relevant officials went through the Resilience Package of $20.5 billion with (its) focus on saving jobs, keeping companies afloat and the long-term infrastructure and capability development that have to be embarked upon.
> When the CPA was convened on my direction, two briefings were provided – first by the Minister for Trade and Industry and his officials and the Monetary Authority of Singapore, and the second by the Ministry of Finance.[86]

136. After the briefing, President Nathan left the meeting to allow the CPA to deliberate the proposals. The CPA reviewed the details of the proposal, sought legal advice on the constitutional implications of the request and agreed to a formal proposal being tabled by Minister of Finance Tharman Shanmugaratnam on 19 January. In all, the process of obtaining the President's assent took eleven days 'from the time the matter was first broached'.[87]

137. In 2020, when Singapore was hit by the Covid-19 contagion, the Singapore Government unveiled four different economic stimulus packages to support businesses and industries most affected by the pandemic, as well as ordinary citizens.

86. Kevin Y.L. Tan, *The Constitution of Singapore: A Contextual Analysis* 143 (Hart, 2015).
87. *Ibid.*

These packages come to nearly SGD 67 billion, most of which was to be funded from current budget surpluses – although about SGD 37 billion had to be drawn from Singapore's constitutionally protected past reserves. In late May 2020, President Halimah Yacob gave her consent to a drawdown on Singapore's reserve for the fourth stimulus package – the Fortitude Package. At her online press conference, the President explained that as Singapore was weathering its worst crisis since independence, she had spent 'a great deal of time' thinking about the decision to draw down on the past reserves. In reaching her decision, she consulted with the Prime Minister, the Deputy Prime Minister and her Council of Presidential Advisors before concurring with the Cabinet.[88]

§11. Some Unique Aspects of the Presidency

138. Singapore's elected President scheme is unique in a number of ways. First, unlike the American or French presidents, he or she has greatly limited powers. Indeed, these powers are of a reactive rather than a proactive nature. As such, even though the President's power to say 'No' is an extremely potent one, he or she is in no position to formulate or promote particular policies or platforms.

139. Second, the President is political but non-partisan. Unlike the American President who can hail from either the Democratic or Republican parties, the Singaporean President cannot be a member of any political party. If he or she is, he or she must resign from the party before Nomination Day. A great deal of debate was generated on this point during the Select Committee hearings as many feared that if any member of a political party should become the President, he or she might be biased towards his or her party and would therefore not be effective as a check against a deviant or unscrupulous government.

140. Third, the office of the President is now a competitive one. This represents a marked departure from the established Westminster model of government. In the past, the Head of State has often been seen as a unifying component in the Westminster constitutional set-up. The role of the ceremonial Head of State, no matter how trivial and formal, is an important one. Loyalty is owed to the state as epitomized by the President, and it is he or she who provides the rallying point for all nationalist sentiment. This function is especially important in multiracial, multireligious Singapore.

141. Previously, the President represented Singapore's multiracial and multireligious make-up. Even though Singapore's population is predominantly Chinese, the other minority races – Malays, Indians, Eurasians and other minorities – are given due recognition by having members of their communities elected as President. Singapore's first President, Yusof bin Ishak, was a Malay. He was succeeded by Dr

88. *See* Kevin Y.L. Tan, *Singapore's Regulatory Response to COVID-19*, The Reg. Rev., 15 Jun. 2020, available at: https://www.theregreview.org/2020/06/15/tan-singapore-regulatory-response-covid-19/ (accessed 1 Oct. 2021).

Benjamin Henry Sheares, an Eurasian and when Sheares died, C.V. Devan Nair, an Indian, succeeded to the post of President. The first Chinese President was Wee Kim Wee, a Peranakan or a straits-born Chinese. With the changes in 1991, this symbolic function was practically lost. This was what prompted the Government to appoint the Constitutional Commission in 2016 to study ways to ensure that minority races would have a chance of being elected President. The upshot of the 2016 constitutional changes was the 'reserved' election (*see* paragraph 123).

§12. The Head of State's Discretion

142. Under the Constitution, the President must generally act on the Cabinet's advice.[89] As such, he or she cannot impose his or her own view on any matter before him or her but must act according to the Cabinet's instruction. All acts of state are done in the name of the President, but this does not mean that he or she can personally dictate how they should be executed. There are, however, areas in which the President has a clear discretionary power: (a) the appointment and dismissal of the Prime Minister; and (b) the dissolution of Parliament.[90] Let us consider how this discretionary power can be exercised.

I. Appointment and Dismissal of the Prime Minister

143. Article 25(1) provides that the President:

> shall appoint as Prime Minister a Member of Parliament who in his judgment is likely to command the confidence of the majority of the Members of Parliament, and shall, acting in accordance with the advice of the Prime Minister, appoint other Ministers from among the Members of Parliament.

144. The keywords here *–in his judgment–* indicate the exercise of a personal discretion. However, this does not mean that the President can act in any way he or she likes. On the practical front, how should the President determine whether or not a particular MP 'is likely to command the confidence' of the House?

145. There is no local case law on this matter, but a very interesting Sabah High Court case, *Tun Datu Haji Mustapha bin Datu Harun v. Tun Datuk Haji Mohamed Adnan Robert*, Yang di-Pertua Negeri Sabah & Datuk Joseph Pairin Kitingan (No. 2)[91] may prove instructive. In 1985, Sabah's Parliament was dissolved at the request of its Chief Minister, Datuk Harris Salleh, so that a snap election could be held. The incumbent Berjaya Party had ruled Sabah for many years and in the run-up to the elections regarded the United Sabah National Organisation (USNO) party as the

89. Article 21(1).
90. Article 21(2).
91. [1986] 2 MLJ 420.

only possible competition (especially since USNO had previously governed the state under the flamboyant Tun Mustapha).

146. A new party, Parti Bersatu Sabah (PBS), led by a former Berjaya Minister, Datuk Joseph Pairin Kitingan, fielded forty-six candidates in the elections but did not expect to defeat Berjaya. On the eve of election day, media coverage revealed that PBS won more seats than either Berjaya or USNO or for that matter, the two parties put together. The leaders of the losing parties got together and decided to form a coalition. In the middle of the night, they went to the Yang di-Pertua Negeri's (Governor's) residence and insisted that Tun Mustapha, leader of USNO, be sworn in as the new Chief Minister. Under stress and with great reluctance, the Governor, Tun Datuk Haji Mohamed Adnan Robert, appointed Tun Mustapha as Chief Minister, but later revoked the appointment. Datuk Joseph Pairin Kitingan was then sworn in as the new Chief Minister.

147. Tun Mustapha commenced legal proceedings against both the Governor and Datuk Kitingan. One of the questions before the Sabah High Court was whether the Governor properly exercised his or her discretion under Article 6(3) of the Sabah Constitution by appointing Tun Mustapha Chief Minister even though he was not the leader of the party that won the elections. Justice Tan Chiaw Thong held that the Head of State could not:

> constitutionally exercise or make his judgment on the appointment of a Chief Minister without taking into account the number of elected seats secured by each and every political party and, for that matter, by the independent candidates, in the election. It is clear that, if he omits to take into account the number of seats obtained by any particular political party which participated in the election, it cannot be said that he had exercised or made his judgment under art 6(3) for, if he did so, he would be acting unlawfully and unconstitutionally by ignoring or not complying with the requirement, in particular of art 6(3). In such circumstances, it is equally clear, in my view, that he has made no judgment under art 6(3). In this connection, I see no difference between this situation and the case where the Head of State appoints as Chief Minister a person who is not a member of the Legislative Assembly, contrary to the express requirement of art 6(3).

148. Juxtaposing the Sabah situation with Singapore's context, it is clear that the President cannot act on his or her whim in determining who he or she should appoint as Prime Minister. The appointee must be someone who clearly commands the confidence of the House, and this is determined by taking into account the electoral majorities of the various parties following the general election.

149. Likewise, under Article 26(1)(b), the President may declare the office of the Prime Minister vacant if he or she is *satisfied* that the Prime Minister has ceased to command the confidence of Parliament. What does it mean for the Head of State to be 'satisfied'? Is this a purely personal discretion like: I am satisfied because it is raining today? Here again, we turn to the case law of other countries.

150. The leading case is the Privy Council decision of *Adegbenro v. Akintola*[92] from Nigeria. In this case, the Governor of Nigeria, Sir Adesoji Aderemi, received a letter signed by the members of the Nigerian legislature, stating that they had lost confidence in the Premier, Chief Samuel Ladoke Akintola. Sir Aderemi then dismissed Akintola on the grounds that he no longer commanded the support of the majority of the House and appointed Alhaji Soroye Adegbenro the new Premier. The question before the Privy Council concerned the meaning of the words 'the Premier no longer commands the support of a majority of the members'. Was this support to be determined solely by a formal vote in the legislature or could it be evidenced by other means; in this case, a letter to the Governor? The Privy Council ruled that in the Nigerian Constitution, the words used 'it appears to him' did not preclude the Governor 'from forming his opinion upon the basis of anything but votes formally given on the floor of the House'.

151. A similar situation arose in Sarawak in the case of *Stephen Kalong Ningkan v. Tun Abang Haji Openg and Tawi Sli.*[93] In this case, Stephen Kalong Ningkan was appointed Chief Minister of Sarawak in 1963. On 14 June 1966, the Legislative Assembly or Council Negri met, and apart from the Speaker, Ningkan and twenty other members were present. Bills were passed without opposition. That same day, a letter signed by twenty-one of the forty-two members of Council Negri indicated that they had lost their confidence in Ningkan as Chief Minister. This letter was never shown to Ningkan but was handed to the Governor on 16 June 1966 who then proceeded to dismiss Ningkan. The High Court distinguished *Adegbenro v. Akintola* and held that 'by the provisions of the Sarawak Constitution, lack of confidence may be demonstrated only by a vote in Council Negri'.

152. As between the two precedents, the Malaysian case of *Stephen Kalang Ningkan* offers a better and more certain method for the exercise of the President's discretion in determining if the Prime Minister has lost his support – by a formal vote on the floor of the House.

II. Proroguing and Dissolving Parliament

153. Article 65(1) of the Constitution provides that the President may prorogue Parliament by proclamation in the Gazette. It further provides that if at any time the office of Prime Minister is vacant, the President shall dissolve Parliament 'as soon as he is satisfied, acting in his discretion, that a reasonable period has elapsed since that office was last vacated and that there is no MP likely to command the confidence of a majority of the Members' in the House.

92. [1963] 3 WLR 63.
93. [1967] 1 MLJ 46.

154. The wording of Article 65 makes it clear that the President has a personal discretion in determining whether or not the office of Prime Minister has been vacated and whether any MP is likely to command the confidence of the majority in the legislature. Once he or she makes this determination, he or she must dissolve Parliament to pave the way for general elections.

155. Under Article 65(3), the President may also dissolve Parliament if the Prime Minister advises him or her to do so, but he or she must first be 'satisfied that, in tendering that advice, the Prime Minister commands the confidence of a majority of the Members of Parliament'. However, the President cannot exercise a discretion to dissolve Parliament after he or she has notice of a motion proposing an enquiry into his or her own conduct under Article 22L(3). This is to prevent the President from dissolving Parliament to pre-empt any enquiry into his or her capabilities or any offences he or she may have committed in his or her capacity as President. Naturally, if Parliament passes a resolution requesting the President to dissolve Parliament, he or she must do so.

III. Discretion During an Emergency

156. Part XII of the Constitution, entitled 'Special Powers Against Subversion and Emergency Powers', contains provisions to deal with situations warranting the declaration of a national emergency. Under Article 150 of the Constitution, a state of grave emergency exists if 'the security or economic life of Singapore is threatened'. This section further provides that if the President is 'satisfied' that such an emergency exits, he or she may issue a Proclamation of Emergency. This can happen whether Parliament is sitting or not. If Parliament is not sitting (i.e., prorogued), the President is duty-bound to summon Parliament 'as soon as practicable' and 'may, until Parliament is sitting, promulgate ordinances having the force of law, if satisfied that immediate action is required' (Article 150(2)). The key issues here concern the nature of the President's discretion, its application and whether the court may judicially review the exercise of this discretion.

157. In *Stephen Kalong Ningkan v. Tun Abang Haji Openg and Tawi Sli (No. 2) (1967)*,[94] the High Court of Malaysia held that it was not open to a court 'to enquire into the sufficiency of the reasons for a declaration of emergency provided it was made bona fide'. As such, if the Proclamation appeared on the face of it to have been made the manner required by the statute and the bona fides of the making of the declaration is not impugned, it is not open to the court to enquire into it.

94. [1967] 1 MLJ 46.

IV. Justiciability of the President's Discretion

158. The President's exercise of discretion may be legally challenged in court.[95] Generally speaking, the President's exercise of discretion is reviewable under administrative law. This was confirmed by the Court of Appeal in the landmark case of *Chng Suan Tze v. Minister of Home Affairs & Ors and Other Appeals* [1988] 2 SLR(R) 525 where the court held:

> In our view, the notion of a subjective or unfettered discretion is contrary to the rule of law. All power has legal limits and the rule of law demands that the courts should be able to examine the exercise of discretionary power.

159. This holding has been upheld and reaffirmed many times since, most notably by the Court of Appeal again in *Tan Seet Eng v. Attorney-General & Anor Matter* [2106] 1 SLR 779 as follows:

> 98 In our judgment, the following propositions flow from the foregoing passage in *Chng Suan Tze*, and continue to be relevant to this case:
>
> (a) Unfettered discretion is contrary to the rule of law. All power has legal limits and it is within the province of the courts to determine whether those limits have been exceeded.
>
> (b) It follows that if discretion is vested in the Executive branch by the Legislature, it remains a matter for the courts to decide:
>
> (i) what the boundaries are of the jurisdiction or power that is vested in the Executive; and
>
> (ii) whether the Executive has acted within the ambit of that jurisdiction or power.
>
> (c) This follows also by reason of Art 93 of the Constitution, which vests the judicial power in the courts.
>
> (d) Therefore, the courts, in the final analysis, are the arbiters of the lawfulness of actions including government actions.

160. The justiciability of the Head of State's discretion to grant pardon also came under scrutiny in the case of *Yong Vui Kong v. Attorney-General*[96] where the Court of Appeal held that while the clemency power is not justiciable on its merits, it was nevertheless subject to judicial review under the grounds of arbitrariness and bad faith.

---

95. *See Yong Vui Kong v. Attorney-General* [2011] 2 SLR 1189.
96. *Ibid.*

§13. CONCLUSION

161. Singapore's presidency is unique. While still essentially ceremonial in character, the President has fairly extensive powers to veto Government action and legislation. Even under the pre-1991 scheme, the President is vested with personal discretion in several areas, and the courts cannot generally question his or her exercise of this personal discretion unless there is a clear breach of the law. Over the last decade, Parliament seems to rethink its original intention to give the President wide scrutiny powers over government companies and actions. The amendments that have been made to the scheme since 1991 clearly evince an intention to scale down the extent of the President's power under the Constitution.

Chapter 3. The Legislature

§1. A Historical Outline

162. During the time of the Norman kings, there existed in England a Great Council or *Magnum Concilium* which was an assembly of landowning barons and ecclesiastics. Although they owed allegiance to the King, the King was forced to consult them on all matters of taxation. As time went on, a second smaller body of semi-professional advisors known as the *Curia Regis* or King's Court or Council was formed to deal with judicial problems which were beyond the scope of the ordinary law courts. Their meetings came to be known as *concilium regis in parliamento* or 'the king's council in parliament'. The word 'parliament' was from the French *parlement* and roughly translates into 'talking shop'. Both the Great Council and the King's Council sat together to discuss affairs of state. In 1254, a great advance was made in representative government when each sheriff was told to send two knights from the shires to attend Parliament as the people's delegates. During the mid-nineteenth century, Parliament consisted of representatives from the cities, the boroughs and the shires.

163. By the fourteenth century, Parliament had organized itself into two Houses: the Lords (consisting of the higher clergy and the barons) and the Commons (which was largely made up of the knights of the shires, burgesses and representatives of the lower clergy). The strong leadership of the Tudors, especially under King Henry VIII (1491–1547) and Elizabeth I (1533–1603), concentrated much power in the monarchy and it was not till the Civil War and the Glorious Revolution of 1688 that Parliament, especially the Commons, regained much of their former powers. Within the Commons, there developed two factions – the Whigs and the Tories – who were ancestors of present-day British political parties. King William III (1650–1702) initially chose his council of officers from both factions but when this became impractical, he chose them from the party in the majority. During the time of Queen Anne (1665–1714), this council became a distinctly policymaking organ and is the predecessor of the modern-day Cabinet. In the last two centuries, Parliament in England has remained largely unchanged even though the House of Lords has lost much of its powers.

164. The history of representative government in Singapore is a relatively short one.[97] From the time the British arrived in 1819 up till its transfer from the Indian Office to the Colonial Office in 1867, the administration of law and order in Singapore was haphazard and highly inadequate. There was no elected representative municipal government in the Straits Settlements until 1857 and public opinion was vent through petitions, newspapers, town meetings, the chambers of commerce and the Grand Jury. The transfer of the Straits Settlements to the Colonial Office in 1867

97. *See* Kevin Y.L. Tan, *Parliament and the Making of Law in Singapore*, in *The Singapore Legal System* 123–159 (Kevin Y.L. Tan ed., Sing. U. Press 2d ed. 1999).

made it a Crown Colony with Singapore as its capital and this brought about long-needed changes. A colonial constitution was introduced and the Colonial Office appointed a Governor who was expected to rule with the help of an Executive Council and a LegCo.

165. The Governor was empowered to convene and prorogue the Councils, initiate legislation and to assent to, veto or reserve Bills 'for the Royal pleasure'. In 1867, the Executive Council comprised the Governor, the Officer Commanding the Troops in the Straits and six senior officials. The LegCo was made up of members of the Executive Council, the Chief Justice and four non-officials nominated by the Governor. The Executive Council which formed a sort of Cabinet was not responsible to the LegCo, and Official Members were bound to support the Governor. The non-official members were not bound as such and could speak their minds and vote according to the dictates of their conscience on all matters. The Governor's executive supremacy was maintained and remained intact till the advent of World War II. Although many changes were proposed and championed, the system remained fixed, and the LegCo remained primarily an advisory body to air the views of the various communities.

166. Following the turmoil of World War II, a colonial-style Singapore Constitution was introduced. From 1946 to 1948, Singapore was ruled by the Governor with the help of an advisory Executive Council consisting entirely of officials and nominated non-officials. There were ten members in the Executive Council (six officials and four nominated members) and the LegCo did not have any non-official majority. By 1947, the movement towards self-government was already in motion and as a first step, a new constitution to be implemented in 1948 created an Executive Council with an official majority and a LegCo with nine officials and thirteen non-officials, of whom four would be nominated by the Governor, three chosen by the chambers of commerce and the remaining six elected by adult British subjects who had been resident in Singapore for one year prior to the election. This, however, excluded the bulk of the migrant population who were not granted citizen status.

167. In 1953, Sir George Rendel headed a commission to review the Constitution, and the Commission recommended keeping local government separate and proposed, for the central government, a single-chamber Legislative Assembly of thirty-two members (twenty-five elected councillors, three ex officio ministers and four nominated non-officials). They also recommended the replacement of the Executive Council by a council of nine ministers: three appointed by the Governor, and the remaining six recommended by the leader of the strongest party in the Legislative Assembly who would also enjoy many of the functions of a Prime Minister. With the implementation of the Rendel Constitution in 1955, Singapore saw, for the first time, a meaningful form of representative government, although essential matters such as external affairs, internal security and defence remained in the hands of the British.

168. These arrangements did not last long. The Constitutional Talks of 1956 and 1957 resulted in the granting of a new constitution in 1958 which provided for internal self-government and which created a Legislative Assembly of fifty-one members elected on the basis of adult suffrage.[98] The British retained control over foreign affairs and external defence but could only suspend the Constitution in an emergency.

169. When Singapore became independent as a constituent state of the Federation of Malaysia in 1963, control over foreign affairs, defence and security laid in the hands of the central government, but it retained wide-ranging powers over finance, labour and education. Singapore was accorded fifteen seats in the 159-member federal legislature but retained her own executive government, her Legislative Assembly and her own Head of State: the Yang di-Pertuan Negara. Independence and separation from Malaysia in 1965 necessitated changes in her constitution. The renaming of the Legislative Assembly as 'Parliament' was the only change insofar as the legislative branch of government was concerned, and as Singapore was no longer a part of the Federation, it ceased to have the fifteen seats in the federal legislature.

§2. The Unicameral Nature of Singapore's Parliament

170. Singapore's Parliament is unicameral in that it is made up of only one chamber. Presently, there are 104 seats in Parliament. Of these, 93 are occupied by elected MPs, while the other 11 seats are occupied by 9 Nominated MPs and 2 Non-Constituency MPs. A two-chamber house was rejected by both the Rendel Commission (1954) as well as the Wee Chong Jin Constitutional Commission (1966). Several reasons were offered: (a) Singapore's small size which obviated the need for special representation of certain provinces, tribes or communities; (b) the fear that the second chamber would only represent special interest groups; (c) a second chamber would make the structure of government overly cumbersome and complicated; (d) insufficiency of manpower; and (e) the danger that it would perpetuate racial and other differences.

§3. Qualifications of Members

171. Under the Constitution, there are two categories of MPs: (1) elected members (from both GRCs and SMCs); (2) NCMPs who are not directly elected but obtained the highest number of votes from among the defeated candidate.

172. The qualifications of candidates wishing to stand for election are set out under Article 44 of the Constitution. To qualify, a person must be: (a) a citizen of

98. *See* Singapore (Constitution) Order in Council, 1958; *see also* O. Hood Phillips, *The Constitution of the State of Singapore*, Pub. L. 50 (1960); and L.A. Sheridan, *Singapore's New Constitution*, MLJ xxv (1959).

Singapore; (b) over the age of 21; (c) resident in Singapore at the date of nomination; (d) able to take an active part in the proceedings in Parliament; and (e) unless blind, be able to read and write one of the official languages of Singapore. He or she must also be a registered voter and not be disqualified under one of the limbs of Article 45.

173. A person may be disqualified from standing in an election if he or she: (a) is of an unsound mind; (b) is an undischarged bankrupt; (c) holds an office of profit; (d) fails to lodge 'any return of election expenses'; or (e) voluntarily exercised or acquired citizenship in a foreign country. Other disqualifications include being convicted of an offence entailing a term of imprisonment of one year or more or a fine exceeding SGD 2,000 or conviction of an offence under any law relating to elections to Parliament. Such disqualifications may be removed by the President under Article 45(2), and if not so removed, shall automatically cease to apply after five years. No person can at the same time be an MP of more than one constituency.

174. An MP's seat becomes vacant when Parliament is dissolved.[99] A vacancy can also occur if a member: (a) ceases to be a citizen of Singapore; (b) ceases to be a member or is expelled from his or her political party; (c) resigns his or her seat or absents himself or herself for 'two consecutive months in each of which sittings of Parliament … are held' without the Speaker's permission.[100] In February 2012, Yaw Shin Leong, MP for Hougang Constituency was sacked from the Workers' Party and thereby lost his seat in Parliament. His sacking precipitated a constitutional challenge to the Prime Minister's discretion on calling a by-election to fill the vacancy. The Court of Appeal held that in the event a vacancy in Parliament occurs, the Prime Minister was constitutionally required to call a by-election although this may be done 'within a reasonable time', taking all relevant factors into account.[101] Resignations by the PAP's Michael Palmer in 2012 and David Ong in 2016 also led to by-elections in Punggol East and Bukit Panjang constituencies respectively.

175. The question as to whether a by-election required when a single seat in a GRC is vacated arose in *Wong Souk Yee v. Attorney-General*.[102] In that case, one member of the Marsiling-Yew Tee GRC, Mdm Halimah Yacob resigned to contest the 2016 Presidential Election. The Government took the position that there was no requirement to call a by-election in such an instance. The matter turned on the interpretation of Article 49 of the Constitution which provides:

> **49.**—(1) Whenever the seat of a Member, not being a non-constituency Member, has become vacant for any reason other than a dissolution of Parliament, the vacancy shall be filled by election in the manner provided by or under any law relating to Parliamentary elections for the time being in force.

---

99. Article 46(1).
100. Article 46(2).
101. Vellama d/o Marie Muthu v. Attorney-General [2013] 4 SLR 1.
102. [2019] 1 SLR 1223.

176. The Court of Appeal held that given that there was an apparent contradiction between Article 49(1) (which required a by-election to be held even if a single seat becomes vacant), and Article 46 (which specifies the only grounds under which a vacancy may arise), Article 49(1) must be read to apply only to vacancies in SMCs and not to GRCs. The court added that as section 24(2A) of the Parliamentary Election provided that in the case of a GRC, no writ of election shall be issued 'for an election to fill any vacancy unless all the Members for that constituency have vacated their seats in Parliament' it was Parliament's clear intent that no by-election be required unless *all* the seats in a GRC is vacated.

§4. Duties of Members

177. Elected Members of Parliament (MPs) must represent their constituents by bringing their problems and difficulties to Parliament's attention. Members are also expected to hold the Executive accountable for its actions. This duty is not an unfettered licence to criticize the Government. The Westminster system assumes a Parliament dominated by two main parties with the Opposition's Shadow Cabinet controlling the Government by holding them accountable for their actions. Opposition MPs also help curb the Government's legislative initiative by questioning them with well-prepared speeches in debate.

178. However, this ideal has no bearing on reality in Singapore. The PAP's total monopoly of Parliament from 1968 to 1981 and its continued dominance of it since does not allow for such forms of control. Indeed, the PAP was so dominant that from 1965 to 1981, backbenchers often took on the role of 'opposition members'. This form of control is both restricted and unrealistic and amounted to little more shadow boxing. Under the Westminster model, strict party discipline is taken very seriously, and no matter how critical PAP members may be of Government policy, they must vote according to the party line. At best, members who disagree vehemently with the Government's position abstain from voting or absent themselves when the vote is being taken. In this scenario, Parliament's ability to function as a restraint on the use of executive power is seriously undermined. This institutional problem is further compounded by PAP MPs' reluctance to criticize Government policies.

§5. Parliamentary Privilege

179. For MPs to perform their duties without harassment or undue influence from the public or the Government, they are given a special status carrying with it certain powers, privileges and immunities. These are contained in the Parliament (Privileges Immunities and Powers) Act and are 'the same as those of the Commons House of Parliament of the United Kingdom and of its Speaker, members or Committees at the establishment of the Republic of Singapore'.

180. Essentially, these privileges and immunities enable the members to speak and debate freely in Parliament. They protect members from repressive measures or legal actions by the Government and others. Parliament has power to summon witnesses, experts and other persons, call for records or papers to assist them in their Committee work. These powers also enable Parliament to punish recalcitrant members of the House or members of the public who abuse their parliamentary privileges.

181. The main privileges and immunities pertain to the freedom of speech and to immunity from arrest in certain cases. Under section 5 of the Parliament (Privileges, Immunities and Powers) Act, speeches made in the course of debate or in parliamentary proceedings are not 'liable to be impeached or questioned in any court, commission of inquiry, tribunal or any other place whatsoever out of Parliament'. Furthermore, a member shall not be liable to legal proceedings whatsoever only by reason of any matter or thing brought up before Parliament or committee. Neither may he or she be arrested or detained in respect of any civil proceedings if he or she is either attending, sitting or returning from any parliamentary proceedings.

182. Offences for which members may be punished include failure to comply with rules, orders or summons of Parliament, the use of violence or force on the Speaker or fellow members, publishing false reports or creating a disturbance within the precincts of the House. There are, of course, several other offences like failure to disclose pecuniary interest and corruption, but it would not be practical to list them all here. Section 20(1) allows Parliament to commit a member to a term of imprisonment 'not extending beyond the current session of Parliament' as well as to fine that member up to a maximum of SGD 50,000.

§6. Life of Parliament

183. The Constitution stipulates 'unless sooner dissolved', the life of each Parliament shall be five years.[103] The President can dissolve Parliament at any time 'if he is advised by the Prime Minister to do so' and if the Prime Minister commands the confidence of the majority of the Members of Parliament. This matter is dealt with in greater detail in Chapter 5. A general election must be held within three months of Parliament's dissolution.

184. Under Article 64(1) of the Constitution, there must be a session of Parliament 'once at least in every year', and Parliament must sit for a new session within six months of the last sitting of the previous session. Parliament is prorogued at the end of each session of Parliament.

103. Article 65(4).

§7. Principal Officers of Parliament

I. The Speaker

185. The Speaker presides over Parliament. The rules of procedure are found in the Standing Orders of Parliament. Following a general election, Parliament must elect a Speaker. The Speaker need not be a Member of the House although someone who does not qualify to stand as an MP cannot be elected. Traditionally, the Speaker is also an MP, but this has not always been the case. Singapore's first Speaker, Sir George Oehlers (1908–1968), was not a Member of the House when he was elected Speaker.

186. Generally, the Speaker's job is to preside over Parliament and to regulate the conduct of debate. He or she also tries to ensure that the voice of the minority is heard and rules on matters of procedure and order from which there are no appeals. The Speaker is the guardian of Parliament's prestige and honour and is thus empowered to mete out punishments to errant members.

187. The Deputy Speaker performs all the duties of the Speaker in the Speaker's absence. He or she is elected in the same manner as the Speaker except that the presiding officer in this instance is the Speaker himself or herself.

II. The Clerk of Parliament

188. The Clerk of Parliament is the House's chief permanent officer. He or she is appointed by the President upon consultation with the Speaker and the Public Service Commission and may only be removed by a two-thirds vote in Parliament. In such an instance, only the President on consultation with the Speaker can remove him or her.

189. The Clerk and Assistant Clerks form part of the Secretariat of Parliament. Their main duties are to assist the Speaker in the regulation and conduct of all matters connected with the business and proceedings of Parliament and its Committees; process all notices of Bills, motions, questions and other business handed in by Members of Parliament in accordance with Standing Orders; conduct research into parliamentary procedures, examine whether there are any difficulties in the working of the Standing Orders and build up memoranda to ensure uniformity of practice and procedure in Parliament; be responsible for the publication of the Votes and Proceedings and the Parliamentary Reports (often referred to as 'Hansard', after the Hansard family who used to publish parliamentary reports for the House of Commons); and attend to matters of administration relating to Parliament, its members, staff, accounts and premises.

190. The office of the Clerk of the House is a very specialized one and demands great expertise in legislative procedure and parliamentary administration. He or she has custody of all votes and proceedings, records, Bills and other documents presented to or laid before Parliament and advises the Speaker and members on matters of procedure. The Clerk also administers oaths, presides over the election of the Speaker and is responsible for the printing and circulation of all Bills and motions. When Parliament is in session, the Clerk sits at the Table in front of and below the Speaker's Chair wearing his or her traditional black gown.

III. The Whip

191. The word 'whip' is an abbreviation of an eighteenth-century fox-hunting term 'whipper-in'. The whipper-in kept the hounds from straying from the pack, and this is analogous to what Government and Opposition Whips do in Parliament. They are party disciplinarians tasked with rounding up party support during voting and ensuring that members are present during other occasions. This is essential in the parliamentary system of government that depends heavily on strong party discipline.

192. In Singapore, there is only the Government Whip as there is insufficient opposition to require an Opposition Whip. There are also two Deputy Government Whips. The Whip ensures the efficient and smooth running of the parliamentary machinery. He or she lists the speakers for each item of business and estimates the time likely to be required for each item and thereby assists the House to complete its business on time. He or she also ensures efficient communication within his or her party, and ensures that backbenchers vote in line with the party's stand. Party MPs may vote according to their conscience only after he or she has lifted the Whip.

193. The Whip is directly responsible to the Leader of the House and to the Prime Minister. His or her other duties include advising the Government on parliamentary business and procedure and maintaining a close liaison with Ministers in regard to parliamentary business which affects their departments. In carrying out his or her duties, the Whip must work closely with the Leader of the House.

IV. Leader of the House

194. Back when English Prime Ministers were also peers of the realm, they often had to be present in the House of Lords and thus were absent from the House of Commons. To represent them, they appointed a leading Minister as the Leader of the House. According to Sir William Gladstone (1809–1898), four-time Prime Minister of Britain, the Leader of the House, 'suggests, and in a great degree fixes, the course of all principal matters of business, supervises and keeps in harmony the actions of his colleagues, takes the initiative on matters of ceremonial procedure, and advises the House in every difficulty as it arises'.[104]

104. *See* William Ewart Gladstone, *Kin Beyond Sea*, in his collection, *Gleanings of Past Years 1843–1878* 241 (C Scribner's Sons 1886).

195. Under Parliament's Standing Orders, the leader is responsible for making representations to the Speaker on urgent matters of public interest that may require sittings. He or she also advises the Speaker on the sitting arrangements within the House. In the Prime Minister's absence, the leader expresses the sense of the House on formal occasions, such as in moving motions of thanks or congratulation. The Leader of the House is also responsible for arranging Government business and the legislative programme in the House (in consultation with the Government Whip), advising the House on any difficulty which may arise and moving procedural motions relating to the business of the House on formal occasions.

§8. Parliament's Committees

196. There are two types of parliamentary committees: (1) those established under the Standing Orders of Parliament, and (2) those established by the PAP and as Government Parliamentary Committees (GPCs). Parliamentary committees provide a closer and more in-depth study of government business and also act as a minor check on the executive. In the case of Select Committees, they also provide an opportunity for the public to present their views directly to Parliament.

I. Committee of the Whole House

197. A Committee of the Whole House comprises all members of the House. In fact, it is the Whole House in a less formal capacity and a Chairman (who is the Speaker) presides. Whenever the House goes into committee, the Speaker leaves the Chair, and the Mace is removed from the Table by the Serjeant-at-Arms and placed in the lower brackets. The Speaker then assumes the Chairmanship of the Committee but does not sit at the Speaker's Chair. Instead, he or she assumes his or her seat at the Table, and he or she enjoys all the powers as the Speaker except that he or she cannot inflict serious forms of punishment on members. The House may resolve itself into a Committee of the Whole House to consider any matter although they must do this when Parliament considers Bills. Usually, the Committee of the Whole House will deliberate Bills that are uncomplicated, are of a regulatory measure or are minor amendments. Major or controversial Bills or amendments like the Organ Transplant (Amendment) Act 2004 are usually committed to Select Committee for more detailed consideration.

II. Select Committees

198. Select Committees are small committees appointed by Parliament for a specific purpose. Usually, it is to scrutinize a particular piece of legislation, for example, the Copyright Bill 1986 and the Constitution (Amendment) Bill 1991. Select Committees are appointed for this purpose only if the Bill is complex, controversial or has a wide-ranging impact. They have the power to send for persons, papers and records in the fulfilling of their function and are accountable to the Whole House by way of a report in which they express their findings.

III. Sessional Committees

199. Under the Standing Orders, Sessional Committees may be established. Each sessional committee consists of a Chairman (usually the Speaker) and seven members. Membership in these committees should, as far as possible, reflect 'the balance between the Government benches and the Opposition benches in Parliament'. There are currently seven Sessional Committees: (1) Committee of Selection; (2) Public Accounts Committee; (3) Estimates Committee; (4) Standing Orders Committee; (5) House Committee; (6) Public Petitions Committee; and (7) Committee of Privileges.

200. The Committee of Selection is responsible for informing Parliament whenever any member has been appointed to any of the Committees. The job of the Public Accounts Committee is to 'examine accounts showing the appropriation of sums granted by Parliament to meet public expenditure and such accounts laid before Parliament'. The Estimates Committee is charged with the duty to 'examine any of the Estimates, to report what economies consistent with the policy implied in the Estimates might be effected' and 'suggest the form in which the Estimates might be presented'. These Estimates form the subject matter of the Finance Minister's Annual Budget which contains estimates of revenue and expenditure for the fiscal year. They also show the assets and liabilities of the country.

201. The Standing Orders Committee's duties are to consider from time-to-time matters pertaining to the Standing Orders of Parliament and to make recommendations for any necessary amendments. The House Committee's duty is to 'consider and advise the Speaker upon all matters connected with the comfort and convenience of Members of Parliament', while the Public Petitions Committee considers all petitions referred to it. Finally, the Committee of Privileges is charged with the handling of 'any complaint of breach of privilege or any matter which appears to affect the powers and privileges of Parliament' and to report on them to Parliament.

IV. Government Parliamentary Committees

202. Early in 1987, then First Deputy Prime Minister Goh Chok Tong proposed forming GPCs, each focusing on a specific area affecting the future of Singapore. These GPCs are not like parliamentary committees since they are organs of the PAP. They have no constitutional status but are instead an initiative of the PAP government. Goh cited three main reasons for setting up GPCs. First, more participation from the MPs was needed, especially in a Parliament dominated by one party; second, the public would also have a say in policies through the resource panels; and third, it would strengthen our democratic institutions and take us into the twenty-first century.

203. These GPCs are limited to MPs from the governing party, and they closely monitor the policies of particular ministries with the help of resource panels, comprising experts and interested laypersons. They provide a wider range of views in Parliament and help cabinet ministers refine policies. They also serve as sounding boards and provide valuable feedback and suggestions to the relevant ministries on issues of public interest. The number of GPCs corresponds with a government ministry, and each consists of five backbenchers, and is chaired by one senior member. Each GPC is backed by a twelve-member resource panel, and their task is to concentrate on a particular area affecting the Government of the country examining all intended Bills in that area and in some instances, they will be consulted even before the Bill is drafted.

204. The creation of GPCs was a step in the right direction given the state of oppositional representation in Parliament. Its use as simulated critics of Government legislation will definitely be far more effective than expecting backbenchers to take on the role of Opposition members. Furthermore, the level of debate and discussion on each policy has, in my opinion, reached a greater level due to the specialized nature of the GPCs and the utilization of experts outside of Parliament. This has led community leaders and professionals to participate more actively in the affairs of state, albeit behind the scenes.

Chapter 4. Making Law in Singapore

§1. Introduction

205. Under Article 58 of the Constitution, 'the power of the Legislature to make laws shall be exercised by Bills passed by Parliament and assented to by the President'. Only the people's elected representatives have power to make law since they are deemed to have the support and acquiescence of their constituents. Ideally, MPs should introduce measures and laws that reflect the aims and aspirations of society. However, this is seldom the case in Westminster-style parliaments as legislative initiative often comes from the Government.

206. In Singapore, this problem is compounded by the fact that at both formulation and actual lawmaking stages, MPs assume a muted and passive role, abdicating its once exclusive domain in favour of the executive. Chan Heng Chee's article entitled 'The Role of Parliamentary Politicians in Singapore'[105] argues that MPs lack legislative initiative and that almost all legislation comes from the Cabinet acting on its own initiative or on the advice of senior civil servants. This is borne out by the fact that only three Private Members' Bills have been enacted into law – the Titular Roman Catholic Archbishop of Singapore Bill (initiated by PAP backbencher P. Selvadurai in 1974); the Maintenance of Parents Bill (initiated by NMP Walter Woon in 1994); and the Prevention of Human Trafficking Act (moved by PAP backbencher Christopher de Souza in 2014). During the passage of Bills in Parliament, MPs are again reluctant to speak out against Bills and policies. The Government is thus able to set its goals and values for society through laws passed in Parliament. Nonetheless, Parliament performs the crucial symbolic role of legitimizing both the Government's rule and the laws it passes through established and accepted procedures.

§2. Rule Formulation

207. Bills may be introduced by individual members or by the Government. Private Member Bills are rare, as we have seen above. Government Bills typically originate in the various ministries and government departments and are drafted by the Attorney General's Chambers (AGC). Before they are drafted, the Cabinet must, in principle, agree to the Bill. Next, the Permanent Secretary of the Ministry initiating the legislation will prepare a draft of the Bill or a detailed statement of its proposed contents and refer it to the AGC. The Bill will normally contain a provision enabling subsidiary legislation to be made. Once the Bill has been printed and vetted by the AGC, a copy of the Memorandum to the Cabinet is sent to the Permanent Secretary for the Ministry of Law for approval before submission to the Cabinet.

105. Chan Heng Chee, *The Role of Parliamentary Politicians in Singapore*, 1 Legis. Stud. Q. 423–441 (1976).

I. Introduction of Bills in Parliament

208. Any member may introduce a Bill into Parliament provided sufficient notice is given to the House. The period of notice is two clear days for Government Bills, and four clear days for Private Member Bills. Bills that either directly or indirectly provide for tax collection, state expenditure involving the Consolidated Fund or matters relating to the financial obligations of the Government may not be introduced or moved unless it is recommended by the President and signified by a Minister.

209. On the actual day of the Bill's introduction, the member introducing the Bill will read aloud the long title of the Bill and then present the Bill to the Clerk at the Table. The Clerk will then read aloud the short title of the Bill. The Bill will then have been introduced into Parliament with no questions put, and this is known as the First Reading of the Bill. After this, a date will be fixed for the Second Reading of the Bill.

II. The Second Reading

210. After the Bill's First Reading, the Clerk will: (a) publish the Bill the *Gazette*; (b) print the Bill; and (c) circulate it to members. All this must be done at least seven clear days before the Second Reading. If an amendment is to be made to the Bill after the First Reading, two clear days' notice of amendment, signed by a cabinet minister, must be given to the Clerk. This does not, however, include Urgent Bills which may be read three times and passed within the day.

211. During the Second Reading, the Minister moving the Bill usually delivers a speech outlining the objectives of the Bill. Members will then debate the Bill. At the end of the debate, a motion is put 'That the Bill be now read a Second Time'. At this point, a vote is taken on which there may or may not be a division. Once the Bill passes its Second Reading, it moves on to the *Committee Stage.*

III. The Committee Stage

212. After the Second Reading, the Bill will be committed either to a Select Committee or to the Committee of the Whole House. If the Bill goes to Select Committee, a Chairman and his or her committee are appointed and given powers to call persons, records and other documents and must list their findings and recommendations in a Select Committee Report. If the Bill is not being committed to Select Committee, the House resolves itself into the Committee of the Whole House and deliberates the Bill in great detail, going through each clause. The Committee may only discuss the details of the Bills and not its underlying principles.

213. At the *Committee Stage*, amendments to the Bill may be made but the Bill cannot be rejected outright since that power is reserved for the House. After the Bill has been dealt with in Committee, a report must be made to the House. This is known as the *Report Stage*. The Chairman of the Select Committee or of the Committee of the Whole House (whichever the case may be) will report the findings of the Committee to Parliament. If amendments are made, the amendments are put to the House, and they may either be accepted or rejected although the latter alternative is rarely the case. Once the House accepts the amended Bill, a motion may be moved that 'The Bill be read a Third Time.'

IV. The Third Reading

214. The Third Reading is similar to the Second Reading although the debate is usually far more limited. Amendments to correct errors or oversights may be made with the Speaker's permission, but no amendments of a material character may be made. The Minister moving the Third Reading may again make a speech outlining the changes made and perhaps explain what repercussions the legislation would have. At the end of the debate, the Bill is put to a vote and once accepted will have been passed by Parliament. However, further steps are needed before the Bill becomes law.

V. The Presidential Council for Minority Rights and the Presidential Assent

215. After the final reading and before the Bill is presented to the President for his or her assent, the Speaker will send an authenticated copy to the Presidential Council for Minority Rights for its consideration. The Council must consider the Bill and make a report to the Speaker within thirty days. This thirty-day limit may be extended if the Bill is particularly complex or difficult. If the Council presents no report within the time limit, it is presumed that no provision of the Bill contains a differentiating measure.

216. The Presidential Council for Minority Rights is established under Part VII of the Constitution.[106] It comprises a Chairman (appointed for three years), not more than ten members appointed for life and not more than ten members appointed for three years appointed by the President on the Cabinet's advice. To qualify for membership, a person must be a Singapore citizen, resident in Singapore and at least 35 years old. He or she must not be of unsound mind, an undischarged bankrupt or have been convicted of an offence carrying a term of imprisonment lasting one year or more or a fine of SGD 2,000 or more.

---

106. *See* Thio Su Mien, *The Presidential Council*, 1 Sing LR 2 (1969); David S. Marshall, *The Presidential Council*, 1 Sing LR 9 (1969); Francis Khoo, *The Presidential Council*, 1 Sing LR 14 (1969); Gerald de Cruz, *The Presidential Council*, 1 Sing LR 20 (1969); and S. Jayakumar, *Singapore's Presidential Council – An Advisory Organ for Parliament on Human Rights*, IV (2–3) Hum. Rights J. 477–492 (1969).

217. It is the particular function of the Council 'to draw attention to any Bill or to any subsidiary legislation if that Bill or subsidiary legislation is, in the opinion of the Council, a differentiating measure'. However, three types of Bills are exempted from the Council's scrutiny: 'Money Bills', Bills on a Certificate of Urgency and Bills which affect the defence, security, public safety, peace or good order of Singapore. A 'differentiating measure' is defined in Article 68 of the Constitution as:

> any measure which is, or is likely in its practical application to be, disadvantageous to persons of any racial or religious community and not equally disadvantageous to persons of other such communities, either directly by prejudicing persons of that community or indirectly by giving advantage to persons of another community.

218. If the Council issues an adverse report, Parliament can either amend the Bill and resubmit it to the Council or proceed to present the Bill for the Presidential Assent in spite of the adverse report. The latter course of action is only feasible if Parliament passes the motion for presentation by 'an affirmative vote of not less than two-thirds of the total membership of Parliament'. If the report presented to Parliament is not adverse, then it goes to the President for his or her assent without further delay. Once the President assents to the Bill, it becomes an Act of Parliament, that is law. Of course, the President may, in areas where his or her personal discretion is invoked under the Constitution – such as budgets or the raising of loans or giving of guarantees by the Government – refuse to assent to a Bill duly passed by Parliament.

219. An Act comes into force only at the date of its publication in the *Gazette*. The publication date of a law and its commencement date are two different things. An Act may be published in the *Gazette* but may not be in force because of a clause providing for the date of commencement to be decided by the Minister. Often the date of commencement depends on the drafting of necessary subsidiary legislation.

§3. Subsidiary Legislation

220. Due to time constraints and other practical considerations, Parliament delegates legislative powers to the Executive. Many Acts contain provisions empowering the Minister in charge to promulgate necessary subsidiary legislation. To prevent abuse by the Executive, all subsidiary legislation is made pursuant to its parent Act. Under the ultra vires doctrine, the Minister cannot promulgate legislation which is not substantially or procedurally provided for in the parent act. Procedures for promulgating subsidiary legislation vary from Act to Act. Generally, subsidiary legislation is drafted by legal officers acting on behalf of the AG based on a draft prepared by the responsible Permanent Secretary.

221. All subsidiary legislation is also subject to the Presidential Council for Minority Rights' scrutiny. The Minister in charge must, within fourteen days of the legislation's publication, submit an authenticated copy to the Council. The Council has thirty days to consider it and report to the Speaker and the appropriate Minister whether the subsidiary legislation contains any differentiating measure. If, in the opinion of the Council, there appears to be a differentiating measure, then the offending provision can either be revoked or amended within six months. Alternatively, Parliament can pass a resolution confirming the provision in question. If the Council does not report within the thirty-day period, it is presumed that the Council is of the opinion that the subsidiary legislation does contain no provision that is a differentiating measure.

§4. Legislative Powers in an Emergency

222. Parliament's legislative powers are extensively amplified in an emergency. Notwithstanding anything in the Constitution, Parliament may 'make laws with respect to any matter, if it appears to Parliament that the law is required by reason of the emergency'. Parliament may also bypass the President's assent (Article 150(4)). Such laws are valid even if they are inconsistent with any provision relating to religion, citizenship or language (Article 150(5)(b)).

223. Article 150 is a very special provision because it confers very wide legislative powers on the executive. Under Article 150(2), the President may legislate only when the emergency is declared and Parliament is not sitting. Thereafter, the President is required to summon Parliament as soon as is practicable. He or she has powers to promulgate ordinances until Parliament is sitting. Under Article 150(3), a Proclamation of Emergency may be revoked, or may be annulled by a resolution of Parliament. A lot of delegated legislation is often passed during an emergency. While ordinary legislation inconsistent with the Constitution may be validated by Article 150(5)(b), this provision does not appear to protect delegated legislation.

§5. Some Singapore Innovations

224. In the last twenty years, several interesting developments have taken parliamentary democracy in Singapore further away from its original Westminster model. We consider three of the most significant ones: (1) GRCs and Town Councils; (2) Nominated MPs; and (3) creation of Community Development Councils (CDCs) and the Mayoral system.[107]

107. *See* generally, Hussin Mutalib, *Constitutional-Electoral Reforms and Politics in Singapore*, 27 Legis. Stud. 659–672 (2002).

I. The Town Councils and Team MPs

225. The Town Council idea was first mooted just before the 1988 general elections and came hand-in-hand with the proposal to create GRCs.[108] Town Councils were formed to give residents a say in the running of their estates. The stated objectives of the Councils were to: (a) transfer the management of housing estates from the HDB to a local council, thus allowing participation by residents; (b) allow residents to become involved in decision-making on local matters; and (c) allow the elected MP to decide what should be done for the electorate in the new town; and (d) to raise the level of social discipline and responsibility among residents.

226. Under the original proposal, each Town Council took charge of three adjoining constituencies grouped by proximity. The Chairman of each Council is an MP who is empowered to appoint any person to help in the management of the estate. He or she is given great flexibility in appointing town councillors who are usually residents and grassroots leaders.

227. The GRC concept was introduced because the Government observed that there was 'a voting trend which showed young voters preferring candidates who were best suited to their own needs without sufficiently aware of the need to return a racially balanced party slate of candidates'. Article 39 of the Constitution was amended to allow Parliament to provide for 'any constituency to be declared by the President ... as a group representation constituency to enable any election in that constituency to be held on the basis of a group of 3 candidates'. Furthermore, 'at least one of the three candidates in every group shall be a person belonging to the Malay' or 'Indian or other minority communities'.

228. The concept of the Town Council was thus inextricably entwined with the concept of the GRC system; each Town Council consists of three constituencies and, as the argument goes, to minimize wastage and administrative costs due to duplication of services, members of the Council should ideally come from the same political party. This prevents politicking at the Council level and therefore makes for efficient running of the estates.[109]

229. The first GRCs were created in time for the 1988 general elections and conflated two fundamentally different objectives: that of ensuring minority representation in Parliament, and that of efficiently managing Singapore's public housing

---

108. Report of the Select Committee on the Parliamentary Elections (Amendment) Bill and the Constitution of the Republic of Singapore (Amendment No. 2) Bill, Parl 3 of 1988, presented to Parliament on 5 May 1988.
109. For a critique of the GRC system, *see* Li-ann Thio, *Choosing Representatives: Singapore Does It Her Way*, in *The People's Representatives: Electoral Systems in the Asia-Pacific Region* 38–58 (Graham Hassell & Cheryl Saunders eds, Allen & Unwin 1997); Kevin Tan Yew Lee, *Parliament and the Making of Law in Singapore*, in *The Singapore Legal System* (Kevin Y.L. Tan ed., Sing. U. Press 2d ed. 1999); Kevin Y.L. Tan, *Constitutional Implications of the 1991 Singapore General Election*, 13 Sing LR 1 (1992); and Kevin Y.L. Tan, *Is Singapore's Electoral System in Need of Reform?*, 14 Commentary 109 (1997).

estates. This conflation is problematic to say the least, and begs the question: which objective has priority? Since 1988, the GRC scheme has been expanded twice, in 1991, just prior to the general elections, and again in late 1996, again in time for the general elections. In both instances, the number of GRCs was increased, and more significantly, the number of members within each GRC team was also increased. In 1991, the number was increased from three to four on the grounds that an expanded Town Council needed more MPs to man, and that expanded Town Councils would enjoy enhanced economies of scale. The same logic was cited in 1996 when the number was once again increased from four to six members.

230. During the 1988 general elections, there were thirteen GRCs with a total of thirty-nine seats up for grabs. In 1991, there were fifteen GRCs with sixty seats up for grabs, and in 1997, the total number of GRCs was kept at fifteen, but a total of seventy-four seats were contested through the system, while in 2001, there were fourteen GRCs comprising seventy-five seats in all. Between 1988 and 2011, the Government sought to increase the number of seats in GRCs to bring ever-larger segments of Singapore's voting population under GRCs. In the 1997 elections, eighty-three seats were contested, of which seventy-four were in GRCs, while only nine seats were contested as single-member seats. In 2001, seventy-five out of eighty-four seats in fourteen GRCs were contested, while only nine seats were contested as single-member wards. By this time, all GRCs consisted of either five or six members. There were no four-member GRC teams in the 2001 general elections. This trend was reversed somewhat after the 2011 general election when the PAP lost Aljunied GRC to the opposition Workers' Party. This was the first time the PAP had lost a GRC and this triggered a change in thinking with the number of six-member GRCs being reduced and the number of four-member GRCs increased. In the 2020 general election, there were no six-member GRCs, eleven five-member GRCs and six four-member GRCs.

231. At the same time, the *minimum* number of minority members in Parliament appears to have peaked at seventeen during the 2020 general elections. The argument that larger GRCs mean better 'economies of scale' seems flawed since it would be churlish to deny to the remaining SMCs the same economies of scale. More significantly, the combined effect of enlarging the GRCs and constant drawing and redrawing of electoral boundaries at short notice (just prior to each general election) is to give the incumbent political party immense advantages in any electoral contest.

232. On 27 May 2009, Prime Minister Lee Hsien Loong announced in Parliament that changes were afoot for the various schemes of parliamentary membership. Emphasizing the need to retain the single-plurality system of elections, Lee proposed three changes. First, he proposed the increase in the maximum number of NCMPs from the current six to nine so that at least one-tenth of the number of MPs is directly elected. This was effected by a constitutional amendment in 2010.[110] He further proposed to cap the number of NCMPs coming from any one GRC at two

110. Constitution of the Republic of Singapore (Amendment) Act, Act 9 of 2010.

to 'spread out the NCMPs more evenly and make them more representative of those voters who have voted for the Opposition nation-wide in a general election'.

233. Second, Lee proposed to alter the NMP scheme by broadening 'the representation of various interest groups' by expanding the number of groups the Special Select Committee typically invites nominees from. At present, nominations are invited from the following six groups: business and industry, the professions, the labour movement, social and community organizations, media, arts and sports and tertiary education institutions. Lee proposed that the Committee broadens its reach to invite nominations from the 'people sector'. A constitutional amendment in 2010 increased the number of NMPs from six to nine.[111]

234. Third, Lee proposed reducing the size of GRCs to have no more than an average of five members per GRC and increasing the total number of SMCs from the present nine to twelve. This was effected in the 2011 general election and subsequent elections.

II. The NMP Scheme

235. The NMP scheme was seen as a 'logical progression of the NCMP scheme' and was meant to fulfil the PAP's 1984 election promise to 'systematically create more opportunities for Singaporeans to participate actively in shaping their future'. Then First Deputy Prime Minister Goh Chok Tong argued, in moving the Bill, that opposition members did not 'adequately express significant alternative views held outside' Parliament. He lamented the fact that he was unable to attract talented individuals into politics, and pointed out that the new scheme would allow the appointment of individuals:

> who have rendered distinguished public service, or who have brought honour to the Republic, or who have distinguished themselves in the field of arts and letters, culture, the sciences, business, industry, the professions, social and community service or the labour movement.

236. The Bill was passed notwithstanding strong opposition from a number of PAP backbenchers. As a compromise, a 'sunset clause' was included in the legislation. Each new Parliament may decide whether or not any NMP would be appointed. This clause was removed by an amendment to Article 39 of the Constitution in 2010, and the NMP is now a permanent feature of Singapore's legislative landscape.[112] When the scheme was approved in 1989, Parliament had room for a maximum of six NMPs, but only two candidates were appointed for the first term.

111. *Ibid.* On these changes, *see*, Kevin YL Tan, *Legal and Constitutional Changes in Voting in Change: Politics of Singapore's 2011 General Election* 49–66 (Kevin YL Tan & Terence Lee eds, Ethos Books 2011).
112. Constitution of the Republic of Singapore (Amendment) Act, Act 9 of 2010.

Following the PAP's victory in the 1997 general elections, Prime Minister Goh Chok Tong stated that he wanted to 'build up' the NMP scheme in order to ensure a high quality of parliamentary debate in the House. Later that year, the Constitution was amended to provide that the total number of NMPs be increased from six to nine.

237. Under section 3(2) of the new Fourth Schedule of the Constitution, a Special Select Committee was given the responsibility of selecting nominees who:

> shall be persons who have rendered distinguished public service, or who have brought honour to the Republic, or who have distinguished themselves in the field of arts and letters, culture and sciences, business, industry, the professions, social or community service or the labour movement; and in making any nomination, the Special Select Committee shall have regard to the need for nominated members to reflect as wide a range of independent and non-partisan views as possible.

238. In 1990, even though a maximum of six NMPs were allowed under the new constitutional provisions, Parliament decided to nominate just two NMPs in the first round: businessman Leong Chee Whye and cardiologist Maurice Choo were appointed in December 1990 but did not have much time to contribute to parliamentary proceedings since Parliament dissolved within a year and a half of their appointment.

239. The number of NMPs was increased from six to nine in 1997. In 2002, the two-year term of the NMP was extended to two-and-a-half years to avoid the need to select NOPs three times within a particular Parliament's five-year life. The NMP scheme, which had been renewed at each Parliament, was made a permanent feature of the Constitution in 2010. Today, the NMP scheme is seen as a form of sectoral representation within Parliament with NMPs nominally representing higher education and academia, women's interests, arts and the community, labour and business.

III. The Community Development Councils

240. In his 1996 National Day Rally speech, the then Prime Minister Goh Chok Tong stated that to promote greater social cohesion and harmony in the community, CDCs would be introduced. The CDCs would help take care of the less fortunate members of any community and were to be linked to Town Councils. When the scheme was first announced, Goh gave a long list of schemes which would be managed by the CDCs, including improvement projects like HDB upgrading, more bursaries and scholarships for students who make above-average improvements, better kindergartens and better-trained teachers, before- and after-school care service centres and programmes to take care of the elderly. However, when the CDCs were eventually set up, three main government schemes in the areas of public welfare and assistance and medical welfare were assigned to them.

241. In August 1997, Home Affairs Minister Wong Kan Seng unveiled the CDC plan for Singapore. In all, nine CDCs would cover the whole of Singapore, with the two smallest CDCs covering the two opposition wards of Potong Pasir and Hougang. Two Mayors – Ow Chin Hock and Eugene Yap – were appointed Mayors of the two largest CDCs: Tanjong Pagar and Marine Parade, respectively. Legally speaking, these Mayors – Singapore's first since independence – are constitutional non-entities. The Prime Minister, as Chairman of the Peoples' Association, appoints the Mayors from among the MPs of the constituencies covered by the CDCs. In 2021, there are five Mayors: Desmond Choo (North East District); Denise Phua (Central Singapore District); Mohamad Fahmi Aliman (South East District); Alex Yam (North West District); and Low Yen Ling (South West District).

242. The Opposition denounced the CDC scheme as nothing more than a ploy to entrench the ruling party. Originally, there were no plans to establish CDCs in the opposition wards. Eventually, the Government decided to involve the opposition wards in the CDCs and because the Government expected 'residents and other volunteers, community leaders and other leaders working in various other organizations to come forward to support and serve in the CDCs'.

243. Today, CDCs function as the area's local administration, initiating, planning and managing community programmes to promote community bonding and social cohesion. They also provide various community and social assistance services delegated from the ministries. Each CDC is managed by the Mayor and a Council comprising between twelve and eighty members, appointed by the People's Association Chairman (who by law is the Prime Minister) or Deputy Chairman. The CDCs are governed by the CDC Rules 1997.

§6. Some Closing Thoughts

244. These innovations should be welcomed, if nothing else, for the interest it has stirred among Singaporeans. Whether or not they will strengthen democracy in Singapore remains to be seen. The PAP's hegemonic dominance of Parliament has put a great strain on Parliament as an institution. This is not only because laws and policies are so quickly and efficaciously passed but also because of its waning prestige and the erosion of its legitimacy. Constituents may no longer see the Assembly as representing them but as a mere 'rubber stamp' for governmental policies. This has not been helped by the way Government has grown in Singapore. The state pervades every facet of Singaporean life, and the absence of an effective opposition in Parliament compounds this growing problem.

245. If there exists an inverse relation between economic development and political development, then Singapore must be the ideal model. During the late

1960s and early 1970s, when Singapore was riding the crest of its economic development tide, there was a corresponding massive depoliticization of its people. The creation of an administrative state where elected politicians are overshadowed by economic specialists and bureaucrats further buttresses the process of depoliticization. Chan Heng Chee argued that politicians in such a system assume that first 'the masses have a high ceiling of tolerance' and that it is the outsider who stirs up discord, and second, 'human beings are malleable' and 'people can be taught to accept and adapt to anything'. This creates a sense of hopelessness and inevitability among constituents who expect their views to be sought and heeded, especially on unpopular policies.

246. The establishment of the GPCs gave Parliament a much-needed shot in the arm. Depending on the performance of the various Committees, legitimacy and confidence can to a large extent be restored to the elected representatives and Parliament as an institution. Critical self-examination and introspection, coupled with a willingness to consult and persuade, are possibly better means of gaining an electorate's confidence than the implantation of an artificial entity like the NCMP. It is thus important that dialogue between the GPCs and the Government benches be open, frank, and, above all, sincere. Unfortunately, whatever its merits, the GPCs are still informal *party* machinery and do not have the necessary bite teeth of a politically independent constitutional animal.

247. The same can be said of the NMP scheme. With the participation of NMPs, the quality of debate in Parliament has improved significantly. Pertinent issues continue to be raised and the executives are kept on their toes. But when push comes to shove, the NMP is still a toothless tiger. In the short term, I think that the NMP scheme has been useful, serving as a credible ersatz loyal opposition who do not oppose for the sake of opposition alone. In the longer term, they may prove detrimental to the development of a full-fledged bipartisan party system in Singapore.

248. As for the growth of the GRC concept, feelings are mixed. On the one hand, decentralization of political power and the willingness to allow the people to have a greater say in at least a facet of their daily living would go a long way towards the transformation of Singapore's political culture. On the other hand, critics and more sceptical electors will see the proposal as another ruse by the ruling party to first relieve the HDB of the unpleasant burden of maintenance of its estates and second to reinforce the PAP's already dominant position by snuffing out the Opposition by careful and strategic placing of so-called strong candidates during a general election. The developments in the last two general elections further reinforce this latter concern, for changes to electoral boundaries at short notice and increasing the number of GRC members benefit no one but the incumbents. In its quest for operational efficiency and economies of scale, the Government has lost sight of the original purpose of the GRC, which was to secure minority representation in Parliament.

§7. Representing the People: Elections in Singapore

249. Three things are necessary for the satisfactory working of representative government: (1) a truly representative assembly; (2) members of the Assembly who are able to discuss issues freely and frankly; and (3) the binding nature of that Assembly's decisions. For an assembly to be truly representative of the people, its members must be elected through a system that the general population regard as fair and legitimate.

250. The conduct of parliamentary elections in Singapore is governed by three main pieces of legislation: (1) the Constitution (Part VI); (2) the Parliamentary Elections Act (Cap 218); and (3) the Political Donations Regulations. Under Article 65(4) of the Constitution, Parliament 'unless sooner dissolved, shall continue for five years from the date of its first sitting and shall then stand dissolved'. This means that a general election must be held at least once in five years. Although a by-election may be called if one of the seats should become vacant, the Constitution does not compel the Government to hold such an election.

I. Constituencies and Constituents

251. In an election, most countries are divided into electoral divisions or constituencies. Under Article 39(1)(a) of the Singapore Constitution, the number of elected Members of Parliament must be equal to the number of constituencies. The total number of constituencies may be determined by the legislature. The main statute dealing with the electoral process is the Parliamentary Elections Act. Under section 8(1) of this Act, the Minister may 'from time to time, by notification in the *Gazette*, specify the names and boundaries of the electoral divisions of Singapore for the purposes of elections'.

252. Section 8(2) states that the number of constituencies will equal the electoral divisions as laid down under section 8(1). This means that the Minister need only specify the names and boundaries of the electoral divisions by notification in the Gazette to increase the number of constituencies without tabling an amendment via the Parliamentary Membership Act.

253. Singapore inherited what political theorists call the 'simple plurality system', known more popularly as the 'first-past-the-post system'. Under this system of voting, the candidate who secures the greatest number of votes is declared elected. This system was introduced by the British and continues to be used extensively in the Commonwealth even though it is not so popular elsewhere. One major problem with this electoral system works best when there are only two candidates. When three or more candidates contest a constituency or ward, the candidate with the most votes may not necessarily command the majority of votes. For example, a candidate may only get 40% of the vote and yet win the election if the other 60% is distributed evenly between the other two candidates. In such a case, the candidate elected cannot be said to be truly representative of the sentiments of the majority of the electorate who effectively cast 60% of their votes against him or her.

254. Unlike countries like India, Singapore does not have an independent Election Department. Singapore's Elections Department is part of the PMO and reports to the PMO's Permanent Secretary. The Election Department is responsible for the conduct of elections in Singapore, including the maintenance of the electoral registers. The Election Department is not, however, directly responsible for determining how electoral boundaries are drawn. This is the responsibility of the Electoral Boundaries Review Committee which is constituted periodically, just before an upcoming general election. This Committee has no constitutional standing, and there is no law that mandates its creation. Typically, the Prime Minister appoints the Committee just before a pending general election, to review the electoral division boundaries and recommend changes to him or her.[113] The Committee comprises a number of senior public servants as well as the Head of the Elections Department. They consider factors like population growth and population shifts arising from housing developments since the last boundary delineation exercise before issuing their report.

255. Under section 8 of the Parliamentary Elections Act, the Minister (in this case, the Prime Minister) may, 'from time to time, by notification in the *Gazette*, specify the names and boundaries of the electoral divisions of Singapore for purposes of elections'. This power to determine electoral boundaries gives the incumbent Prime Minister almost unbridled power to shift these boundaries for his or her party's best advantage. These problems are dealt with below.

II. Types of Membership

256. Under the Constitution, there are three categories of members (MPs) in the House. The first category consists of members who are elected directly by their constituencies; this category can be divided into those who are elected from the GRCs and those elected in the SMCs. The second category comprises NCMPs who are not directly elected in the sense that they did not poll the highest number of votes in the constituencies in which they contested but got the next highest votes in the overall results during a general election. The number of such members cannot exceed six, and their inclusion is 'to ensure the representation in Parliament of a minimum number of Members from a political party or parties not forming the Government'. The final category of members – the NMP – was created in 1989. The NMPs do not represent any political party; in fact, they do not even stand for elections. They were introduced into Parliament to provide alternative views 'held outside Parliament'.

113. On the shortcomings of this institution and difficulties in electoral boundary delineation, *see* Kevin Y.L. Tan *Delineation and Discretion: The Drawing of Electoral Boundaries in Singapore*, in *Voting in a Time of Change: Singapore's 2020 General Election* 87–120 (Kevin Y.L. Tan & Terence Lee eds, Singapore: Ethos Books 2021).

The Constitution currently provides for a maximum of nine NMPs in Parliament. For a more detailed discussion of these various types of MPs and their genesis, *see* Chapter 3.

III. Qualifying to Stand

257. The qualifications for candidates wishing to stand for parliamentary elections are set out under Article 44 of the Constitution. To qualify, a person must be: (a) a Singapore citizen; (b) over the age of 21; (c) resident in Singapore at the date of nomination; (d) able to take an active part in the proceedings in Parliament; and (e) unless blind, be able to read and write one of the official languages of Singapore. The potential candidate must also be a registered voter and not be disqualified under Article 45.

258. A person may be disqualified from standing in an election if he or she: (a) is of an unsound mind; (b) is an undischarged bankrupt; (c) holds an office of profit (i.e., being the whole time in public service); (d) fails to lodge 'any return of election expenses'; or (e) has voluntarily exercised or acquired citizenship in a foreign country. Other disqualifications include being convicted of an offence entailing a term of imprisonment of one year or more or a fine exceeding SGD 2,000 or conviction of an offence under any law relating to elections to Parliament. Such disqualifications may be removed by the President under Article 45(2) and, if not so removed, shall automatically cease to apply after five years. No person can at the same time be an MP of more than one constituency.

259. The seat of an MP becomes vacant upon the dissolution of Parliament. Nonetheless, a vacancy can also occur if a member ceases to be a citizen of Singapore, ceases to be a member or is expelled from his or her political party, resigns his or her seat or absents himself or herself for 'two consecutive months in each of which sittings of Parliament ... are held' without permission from the Speaker, or is expelled from Parliament.[114]

IV. Qualifying to Vote

260. The qualifications for voters are set out under section 5 of the Parliamentary Elections Act. Any citizen of Singapore who is above the age of 21 and who is ordinarily resident in Singapore is entitled to have his or her name entered or retained in a Register of Electors. Among other things, the Register of Electors contains the following:

(a) name of the constituency and its subdivision known as polling districts; and
(b) particulars of the electors: (i) serial number, (ii) name, (iii) address, and (iv) sex.

114. Article 46(2).

261. A register is prepared for each constituency. At the time of writing, there are twenty-seven constituencies (sixteen GRCs and thirteen SMCs) in Singapore, and as such twenty-nine registers are prepared. After the registers have been prepared, they have to be exhibited for people to submit claims or raise objections. After this is done, the registers will be certified and will be used for the election until a new one is prepared. Voters may now check on their standing on the electoral register through the web.

262. An otherwise qualified voter may be disqualified if he or she: (a) owes his or her allegiance to another state or foreign power; (b) is serving jail sentence 'for an offence punishable with imprisonment for a term exceeding twelve months'; (c) is under sentence of death; (d) is of unsound mind; (e) is serving in 'any naval, military or air force not maintained out of moneys provided by Parliament'; or (f) is registered as a voter in any country. A person may also be prevented from voting if he or she has been convicted of 'a corrupt or illegal practice' under the Act or if his or her name has been expunged from the register under section 6(g).

263. Voting is compulsory in Singapore, and each person is entitled to only one vote which must be exercised in the electoral division in which he or she has been registered. Secret ballots are used in the electoral process, and results are published in the *Gazette.*

264. Singapore citizens who are living overseas are also entitled to vote. Under section 13A of the Parliamentary Elections Act, the following categories of persons are entitled to exercise their right to vote even though they may be living overseas:

(a) Singapore citizens who are not resident in Singapore but who have lived in Singapore for an aggregate of two years over the last five years immediately preceding an election.
(b) Members of the Singapore Armed Forces on full-time training or service outside Singapore.
(c) Public officers or employees of any public authority employed in full-time service outside Singapore.
(d) Singapore citizens over the age of 21 on full-time training outside Singapore that is sponsored by the Government or any public authority.
(e) Singapore citizens employed outside Singapore by an international organization of which Singapore is a member or by any other body or organization designated by the President under Article 135(1)(c)(ii) of the Constitution of the Republic of Singapore.
(f) The spouse or a parent, child or dependent of any person referred to above.

265. While the law clearly provides for overseas voting, the mechanism enabling this right to manifest remains unclear. In the 2001 general election, much controversy was stirred when the Government announced that it was scrapping the plan to allow overseas voting for security reasons in the wake of the World Trade Centre bombings of 11 September. In a statement issued by the PMO, the Government pointed out that the increased security measures at Singapore's key overseas diplomatic missions 'have seriously circumscribed the facilities for overseas voting'. This temporary measure was effected through the Parliamentary Elections (Temporary Suspension of Overseas Voting) Act 2001.[115] Overseas voting was restored in time for the 2006 general election.

266. One upshot of this decision prompted a wide-ranging debate at home in Singapore as to whether voting was a right or privilege. Some commentators argued that voting was a right and that the failure by the Government to provide facilities for overseas voting was a clear breach of this right. The words of the Constitution do not make voting a clear right, at least not in the same way as those rights protected under Part III of the Constitution which safeguards our fundamental liberties. Voting is a right in that the scheme of the Constitution envisages a parliamentary system of government, and that government is to be democratically elected. Implicit in this scheme is the right to vote. How else can you have a democratically elected legislature? Can an overseas voter take out an action demanding that the Government provide facilities for voting? Arguably, this is possible even though it has never been done before.[116]

§8. Conduct of Elections

267. Before general elections can be called, the President must dissolve Parliament and issue a Writ of Election to the Returning Officer.[117] This writ will specify: (a) when the nomination of candidates will take place (not earlier than five days nor later than one month from the date of the writ); and (b) the place of nomination.[118] Once the President issues the writ of election, the Returning Officer will issue a notice stipulating: (i) the date, time and place for nomination of candidates; (ii) the nomination paper to be signed by any six or more electors (i.e., those qualified to vote); and (iii) the payment of deposit (a sum equal to fixed monthly payable to MPs in the month immediately before the date of dissolution of Parliament, rounded to the nearest SGD 500).[119]

I. Nomination Day

268. On Nomination Day, candidates must present their nomination papers, statutory declarations and certificate personally at the nomination centre. At the close of the nomination period, if there is only one candidate (in the case of an SMC), or one group of candidates (in the case of a GRC) for the ward, the Assistant Returning Officer will declare at the nomination centre that the candidate or the

115. Act No. 45 of 2001.
116. On the right to vote, *see* Thio Li-ann, *The Right to Political Participation in Singapore: Tailor-Making a Westminster-Modelled Constitution to Fit the Imperatives of 'Asian' Democracy*, 6 SJLS 181 (2002).
117. Section 24, Parliamentary Elections Act (Cap 218).
118. Schedule 1, Parliamentary Elections Act (Cap 218).
119. Section 28, Parliamentary Elections Act (Cap 218).

group of candidates have been returned as MP(s). However, where there is more than one candidate (SMC) or more than one group of candidates (GRC) nominated, the Returning Officer will adjourn to a date when a poll will be taken, that is Polling Day.

269. The Returning Officer will then issue the notice of contested elections giving:

(a) the date of the poll (not less than nine days nor more than eight weeks after publication of notice);
(b) the names of candidates, their symbols, proposers and seconders; and
(c) the names and locations of all polling stations.

II. Campaigning

270. Candidates can only start their election campaigns after nominations close. Electioneering can carry on right up to the eve of Polling Day. During that period, they can make house-to-house calls, distribute pamphlets, put up posters and banners and hold election rallies. Political parties will also be given airtime by the Singapore Broadcasting Authority. The length of airtime depends on the number of candidates each party is fielding.

271. To prevent 'money-politics' and expensive election campaigns, the Parliamentary Elections Act specifies that the maximum amount any candidate or his or her election agent can pay or incur is: (a) in the case of a GRC, an amount equal to SGD 4.00 for each elector divided by the number of candidates in the group; or (b) in the case of an SMC, an amount equal to SGD 4.00 for each elector.[120]

III. Polling Day

272. Every voter will receive a poll card informing him or her of Polling Day and where he or she may cast his or her vote in person. Polling takes place from 8.00 am to 8.00 pm. At the end of the day, the ballot boxes are sealed and witnessed by the candidates and/or their agents. The ballot boxes are then delivered to their respective counting centres where they will be opened in front of the candidates and/or their counting agents. The ballot papers are then sorted and counted.

273. After the count, the Assistant Returning Officer will inform the Group Assistant Returning Officer of the results of counting at the principal counting place. The Assistant Returning Officer will then collate the results and notify the representatives of the candidates (principal election agents, election agents or the candidates) of the results before transmitting them to the Returning Officer who will

120. Third Schedule, Parliamentary Elections Act (Cap 218).

make his or her announcement at the Announcement Centre for public consumption. The results will be officially published in the *Government Gazette*.

§9. Political Donations

274. The Political Donations Act and its Regulations came into operation on 15 February 2001. The Act seeks to prevent foreigners from interfering in Singapore's domestic politics by funding candidates and political associations or parties. Political associations and candidates may only accept donations from 'permissible donors' and may not accept more than SGD 5,000 of anonymous donations per annual reporting period.

§10. Is Singapore's Electoral System in Need of Reform?

275. Singapore's electoral system has been amended at least four times since 1984. More importantly, these amendments came just shortly before the general elections. The very short lead time between the constitutional changes and Nomination Day is a cause for some concern. While there is nothing in the Singapore Constitution requiring Parliament to treat all political parties with fairness, principles of natural justice require that sufficient notice of major changes be given to all parties contesting general elections. This timing problem is compounded by the fact that before any general election is held, the Electoral Boundaries Review Committee must first issue its report which lays out the constituencies to be contested. Boundaries of electoral divisions change from time to time because of shifting populations and expansion of wards.[121] They are also changed in accordance with changes made to the Constitution. Below are the dates of elections and the dates on which the Committee released its reports:

Date of Report	*Date of Elections*	*Lead Time*
28 June 1984	22 December 1984	6 months
14 June 1988	3 September 1988	<3 months
8 August 1991	31 August 1991	<4 weeks
6 November 1996	2 January 1997	<2 months
10 October 2001	25 October 2001	2 weeks
3 March 2006	6 May 2006	2 months
24 February 2011	7 May 2011	<3 months
24 July 2015	11 September 2015	<2 months

121. *See* Kevin Y.L. Tan, *Delineation and Discretion: The Drawing of Electoral Boundaries in Singapore*, in *Voting in a Time of Change: Singapore's 2020 General Election* 87–120 (Kevin YL Tan & Terence Lee eds, Ethos Books 2021).

Date of Report	*Date of Elections*	*Lead Time*
13 Mar 2020	10 Jul 2020	<4 months

276. This means that aspiring political candidates who have been 'working the ground' may sometimes find their 'ground' being swept up from under them. Constituency boundaries are redrawn just months before elections, and a candidate's 'ground' may either be cut up into several parts and merged with other constituencies, or being transformed into a GRC. Let us take the example of Sin Kek Tong, the SPP's candidate who announced very early on that he was contesting the Braddell Heights seat which has hitherto been an SMC. When the Committee's report was released on 6 November, he must have been shocked to find his intended ward merged with Marine Parade GRC.

277. The problems are thus obvious. How can political aspirants work the ground with confidence, cultivating the grassroots and seeking the people's mandate if he or she cannot be sure that the 'ground' on which he or she may spend years campaigning in is going to remain unscathed by the Committee's report? Worse still, what if it becomes a six-member GRC? Where is he or she going to get five other GRC members at such short notice?

278. The function of law is to give certainty and stability to social, economic and political life. No one can plan ahead if laws are constantly changed at the last moment. Teams can hardly be expected to compete fairly if the rules of the game are constantly being changed. Businesses would atrophy, and people will be kept in a state of great tension and mistrust. It would be much fairer and sensible if any change to the electoral system should take effect only in the following election and not the impending one? This will guarantee sufficient lead time for all parties in the contest and would go a long way in allaying the peoples' fears that the incumbent party will abuse its constitutional powers just to fix the opposition through gerrymandering.

279. The next problem is one concerning majority votes and representation. Ideally, elections should enable the voice of the people to be heard through their votes. The more votes a political party or a candidate wins, the more likely that party or candidate can be said to represent the voters. However, the combined effect of having GRCs and a first-past-the-post system in Singapore diminishes this majoritarian ideal. Let us look at some figures.

280. In 2001, a total of 1.83 million votes were allocated to the GRCs (seventy-five seats), while 205,420 votes were allocated to SMCs. Taking 51% of the total votes cast for GRCs, any party can win seventy-five seats or 89% of all parliamentary seats with just 933,300 votes or 51% of 1.83 million votes. The figure of 933,300 translates into only 45% of the total votes cast in 2001. In our hypothetical situation, only two parties are factored into the equation. If more parties contested in the GRCs, the figures would be even more telling.

281. While the mechanical flaws of the system are unlikely to be exposed through freak election results for the time being, it may be timely for us to consider alternatives to our system of voting. Perhaps we have evolved to a point where we should be looking at something akin to the German list system of elections where electors vote for parties and each party nominates candidates in accordance with the total number of votes cast. Or perhaps we should be moving towards a system of proportional representation where parties nominate members to Parliament based on the number of votes they received in an election. Whatever system we decide, an urgent re-examination is needed.

§11. Conclusion

282. The various amendments taken *in vacuo* may make for the better administration of Singapore's constituencies. The MPs will now see their roles enlarged, and this may bring them closer to the people on the ground. Indeed, as former Nominated MP Walter Woon pointed out, the changes could even work to the advantage of the opposition parties in the future. However, the timing of these changes invites constant challenges from the PAP's opponents. It also flouts the fundamental principles of natural justice in failing to give adequate warnings on major changes in the law. It is perhaps timely for Parliament to create an independent Elections Commission which will review the current system, propose changes thereto and to take over the delicate task of determining how electoral boundaries are drawn rather than leave it to the incumbent Prime Minister's discretion.

Chapter 5. The Executive

§1. Introduction

283. It is ironic that in the Westminster *parliamentary* system of government, the most powerful branch of the Government is the *executive*. In Singapore, the executive branch of government consists of the President, the Prime Minister and the Cabinet.

284. The *Cabinet* is a body of high-ranking members of government. In some countries, they may be referred to as the Council of Ministers. Under the parliamentary system of government, the Cabinet wields tremendous power and determines and directs state policy. In some other countries, such as the United States, the Cabinet functions largely as an advisory council to the President or Head of State. Interestingly, the functions and powers of the Cabinet in present-day America are far more similar to the traditional role of cabinets.

285. Historically, cabinets emerged in England during the reigns of Kings George I (1660–1727) and George II (1683–1760). Both monarchs came from Hanover in Germany and spoke very little English. As such, they relied heavily on a small group of advisors to help them decide state policy. The most important of these advisors was Sir Robert Walpole (1676–1745) who became, over a period of twenty-one years, England's first Prime Minister. The modern Cabinet system developed further and acquired greater and greater powers in nineteenth-century England under prime ministerships of Palmerston (1784–1865), Disraeli (1804–1881) and Gladstone (1809–1898). The title of Prime Minister was unofficial and unrecognized under British law until the passing of the Ministers of the Crown Act 1937.

286. In Singapore, the modern Cabinet emerged from the old Executive Councils established under the British. The first Executive Council (or 'Exco' for short) was established in 1877 to advise the Governor of the Straits Settlements. The Governor was expected to consult the Exco on all affairs of importance even though the Governor had tremendous veto powers over both the Exco and the LegCo. Singapore's first modern Cabinet emerged from the Rendel Constitution of 1954, and following the 1955 general elections. David Saul Marshall of the Labour Front became Singapore's first elected Chief Minister and led the first Cabinet or Council of Ministers comprising six elected members and three ex officio Official Members appointed by the Governor.

§2. Singapore's Cabinet Today

287. Article 24(1) of the Constitution provides that there shall be 'a Cabinet which shall consist of the Prime Minister and such other Ministers as may be appointed in accordance with Article 25'. Nothing is said about the size of the Cabinet or how many ministries there can be. It is up to the Government of the day to decide. In 2010, Singapore's Cabinet comprises twenty elected Members of Parliament, each heading a government department, known as a 'ministry', such as education or defence. Each of them is known as a 'minister', and their leader is the Prime Minister who is appointed by the President. The Prime Minister is selected from among the elected Members of Parliament as the leader who commands the confidence of the majority of members. The ministers are also appointed by the President upon the Prime Minister's advice and collectively, they comprise the Cabinet.

288. In normal conversation, we often refer to the Cabinet as 'the Government' (with a capital 'G'). The Cabinet is responsible for state policies and the day-to-day administration of the country. Constitutionally, the Cabinet is collectively responsible to Parliament. At the time of writing, the Cabinet comprises the Prime Minister, the Deputy Prime Minister, two Senior Ministers, and the Ministers in charge of the ministries of Communications and Information, Culture, Community, and Youth; Defence; Education; Foreign Affairs; Health; Home Affairs; Law; Manpower; National Development; Social and Family Development; Sustainability and the Environment; Trade and Industry; Transport; and the PMO.

§3. Singapore's Prime Minister

289. Under Article 25(1) of the Constitution, the President must appoint as Prime Minister the person who 'in his judgment is likely to command the confidence of the majority of the Members of Parliament'. How does the President determine this 'confidence'? Typically, the President will see which political party controls Parliament. The leader of that party will almost certainly become the Prime Minister.

290. Singapore has only seen two Chief Ministers and three Prime Ministers since 1955. David Saul Marshall (1908–1995) and Lim Yew Hock (1914–1984) were both leaders of the Labour Front, while Lee Kuan Yew (1923–2015), Goh Chok Tong (b 1941) and Lee Hsien Loong (b 1952) were all leaders of the PAP. Since 1959, the PAP has dominated Parliament and consequently, Singapore politics and transitions between the Prime Ministers have been carefully stage-managed affairs. The PAP's leader, just like that of most other political parties in Singapore, is the party's secretary general and not its Chairman. This does not mean that the secretary general automatically becomes the Prime Minister. When Lee Kuan Yew stepped down as Prime Minister in 1990, he continued as the PAP's secretary general till 1992. Lee Hsien Loong succeeded Goh Chok Tong as Prime Minister on 12 August 2004, but Goh remained secretary general of the party till December 2004.

291. The Prime Minister is the most powerful member of the Cabinet. This is not only because of his or her appointment but because of his or her control over his or her party which commands the majority of Parliament's seats. In Singapore, political parties observe very strict *party discipline*. This means that members of a particular political party will loyally vote according to that party's dictates. No member of a political party will vote against his or her own party's policies, legislation or proposals. If he or she does so, he or she will be taken to task by the party's disciplinarian, the *Whip*. He or she might even lose his or her party membership, and thus lose his or her seat in Parliament. Occasionally, the Whip will be lifted and all parliamentarians be allowed to vote according to conscience rather than along party lines. The Whip can be lifted at the special request of party members or where the Bill is particularly controversial, such as the Parent's Maintenance Bill (1991) and the amendments to the Organ Transplant Act (2003).

§4. Ministers and Ministries

292. In Singapore, there are nineteen key Ministers who form the Cabinet. Other junior ministers or ministers of state are not members of the Cabinet but assist in running the various government ministries. Ministers are drawn from the ranks of elected parliamentarians. In Singapore's case, all the ministers have been drawn from ranks of PAP MPs since 1963. This is because the PAP has such an overwhelming majority in Parliament that it is not necessary for the party to accommodate any opposition members in the Cabinet line-up. In some countries, where the majority of the leading party is much less clear or where the ruling party does not command a majority of seats in the legislature, opposition members may be included in a coalition government and in the Cabinet as well. He or she will then recommend to the President that they be appointed. The appointment will take place at an official ceremony where the Minister-to-be will take an oath of allegiance before the President and is handed his or her letter of appointment. The appointment will then be published in the *Government Gazette*.

293. The Prime Minister is responsible for selecting and emplacing his or her ministers. Under Article 30 of the Constitution, the Prime Minister is empowered to 'charge any Minister with responsibility for any department or subject' as well as to 'revoke or vary any directions given'. The Prime Minister may also 'retain in his charge any department or subject'. This means that the Prime Minister can hold additional posts, such as Finance Minister or Defence Minister. For example, when Lee Hsien Loong took over as Prime Minister, he retained his post as Finance Minister.

294. From time to time, the Prime Minister may move his or her ministers around. This is often known as a Cabinet reshuffle and is carried out to test ministers in different capacities or promote or retire ministers. In Singapore, Cabinet reshuffles often draw much speculation from the public but are fairly low-key affairs. This is in marked contrast to the situation in some other countries. In 1962, Britain's Prime Minister Harold MacMillan abruptly sacked six of his ministers in an episode now known as the 'Night of the Long Knives'.

295. Although the structure of Singapore's Cabinet follows closely that of the United Kingdom, it has some unique features. Since 1980, the Cabinet included a Minister Without Portfolio who was also secretary general of the National Trades

Union Congress. The first holder of this post was Lim Chee Onn who left the Cabinet abruptly in 1983 and was succeeded by Ong Teng Cheong who later became Deputy Prime Minister and then President. Following the defeat of NTUC Secretary General Ng Chee Meng in the 2020 general election, there is at present no Minister Without Portfolio. Another oddity in the Cabinet since 1988 has been the post of Senior Minister in the PMO. This post was occupied by S Rajaratnam (b 1915) from 1988 to 1991; Lee Kuan Yew from 1991 to 2004; and Goh Chok Tong from 2004. When he became Singapore's third Prime Minister, Lee Hsien Loong created the unique Cabinet post of Minister Mentor for Lee Kuan Yew who held the post till 2011 when he stepped down from Cabinet.

296. The Cabinet line-up also includes junior ministers, called 'Ministers of State', but none of these offices are specifically provided for in the Constitution. The Constitution does, however, provide specifically for the appointment of parliamentary secretaries and Permanent Secretaries. Under Article 31(1), the President, acting on the Prime Minister's advice, may appoint 'Parliamentary Secretaries from among the Members of Parliament to assist Ministers in the discharge of their duties and functions'.

297. Article 34(1) mandates that there shall be one or more Permanent Secretaries for each ministry. These Permanent Secretaries are senior civil servants whose job is to 'exercise supervision over the department or departments to which he is allocated' under the Minister's general direction and control. Like all other key appointments, Permanent Secretaries are appointed by the President acting on the Prime Minister's advice. However, the choice of candidates is limited to a list of names submitted by the Public Service Commission. Unlike junior ministers and parliamentary secretaries, the Permanent Secretary is not a political appointee. This senior official remains in office regardless of the change in his or her political masters, hence the term 'permanent'. However, the Prime Minister is vested with the power to determine where each Permanent Secretary is allocated.

§5. Policy Formulation, Decision-Making and Collective Responsibility

298. Cabinets make decisions affecting all aspects of our lives. So long as the ruling party maintains its majority in Parliament, the Cabinet can practically do anything it wants – declare war, make treaties, raise taxes, make laws, and so on. Walter Bagehot noted in his classic book *The English Constitution* (1867) that the efficiency of British government lies in the 'close union and nearly complete fusion of the executive and legislative powers'.

299. Under Article 28(1), the Cabinet can only be summoned by the Prime Minister, and the Prime Minister must, as far as possible, 'attend and preside at meetings of the Cabinet'. If the Prime Minister is indisposed or is overseas, he or she may appoint another Minister to preside in his or her place. All proceedings of the

Cabinet are confidential and are valid even if some unauthorized person took part in its proceedings or voted at the meeting (Article 29).

300. Before decisions are taken at the Cabinet level, a process of policy formulation is set in motion. Typically, key decision-makers identify issues and problems, analyse their causes and formulate solutions for an effective response. In Singapore, most public policies are formulated by the Cabinet. Article 24 of the Constitution provides that 'Cabinet shall have the general direction and control of the Government.' This means that each Minister has control over and direction of the civil servants and staff in his or her ministry. Oftentimes, the ministry staff initiate the policymaking process by highlighting issues and problems to the Minister in charge.

301. These issues and problems are then discussed and ironed out at Cabinet meetings. In 1975, scholar Kawin Wilairat identified four members of Lee Kuan Yew's Cabinet – namely Lee himself, Goh Keng Swee, Toh Chin Chye and S Rajaratnam – as members of an 'inner circle' of the Cabinet and of the PAP who set the pace of discussions and decision-making. Naturally, this inner circle changes over time with the retirement of old ministers and the induction of new ones. This inner circle is an informal and dynamic political arrangement and finds no expression in the Constitution. Much depends on the personality of the key players. For the longest time, Lee Kuan Yew was the most important policymaker in this circle, and his influence did not diminish until his retirement from politics in 2011.

302. Outside the Cabinet, policies may also be formulated by civil servants, but this is rare. Cabinet ministers typically meet weekly. Prior to their full Cabinet meetings, they attend pre-Cabinet meetings which are informal lunchtime sessions preceding full Cabinet meetings. It appears that it is at the pre-Cabinet meetings that some kind of consensus building takes place among the inner circle and key decision-makers. Recently, it was publicly acknowledged that when Goh Chok Tong was Prime Minister, he kept Lee Kuan Yew out of the pre-Cabinet meetings.

303. Whatever decisions are taken at the Cabinet, all ministers are collectively responsible to Parliament (Article 24(2)). This means that once the Cabinet makes a decision, every member of that Cabinet is bound by it and held personally responsible for it. He or she must also support and defend it in public even if he or she disagrees personally with it. Thus, if a policy proves unsuccessful or highly unpopular with Parliament, the entire Cabinet must resign. While this principle of collective responsibility is mandated under the Constitution, there has never been an occasion of it being put to the test. This is possibly due to two reasons. The first is the fact that a single-party – in this case, the PAP – controls almost all seats in Parliament. Since the Cabinet is made up of the most senior and important members of the party, the MPs are not likely to want to have them removed. Second, the strict party discipline imposed by the Party Whip ensures that no one votes against the Government line anyway.

§6. Choosing the Prime Minister and Cabinet

304. The task of appointing the Prime Minister falls on the President. Under Article 25, the President must select as Prime Minister:

> a Member of Parliament who in his judgment is likely to command the confidence of the majority of the Members of Parliament and shall, acting in accordance with the advice of the Prime Minister, appoint other Ministers from among the Members of Parliament.

305. Once appointed, the Prime Minister has a free hand to decide who he or she would like to have in his or her Cabinet. In the case where Parliament has more than one party and the Prime Minister is trying to forge an alliance or coalition government, he or she may pick members from other parties to join his or her Cabinet.

306. So long as the member is qualified to be an MP, he or she is eligible to serve as a cabinet minister. As we saw in Chapter 3, there are three types of MPs in Singapore: regular MPs, non-constituency MPs and nominated MPs. Theoretically, they are all eligible to serve as cabinet ministers and can be appointed as such, provided the Prime Minister chooses them. In reality, the Prime Minister of a party which has hegemonic control of Parliament has no incentive to do this. Indeed, other than from 1955 to 1958, Singapore's Cabinet has always been made up of ministers from the same party.

307. Once appointed, the Prime Minister and his or her Cabinet remain in office for the duration of that government. This period lasts a maximum of five years, from the time they are elected at a general election to the time Parliament is dissolved for the next general election. There is no minimum period for a Cabinet appointment since it is theoretically possible for a Prime Minister to call a snap election even just six months after being elected.

308. The President will declare the office of Prime Minister vacant in two instances: (1) when the Prime Minister resigns by writing to the President and (2) if the President, 'acting in his discretion is satisfied that the Prime Minister has ceased to command the majority of a majority of the Members of Parliament' (Article 26). In the second instance, the President must first inform the Prime Minister that he or she is satisfied that the Prime Minister has lost the confidence of the House, and if the Prime Minister requests, the President must dissolve Parliament to pave the way for elections instead of making such a declaration.

309. A cabinet minister may vacate his or her office if: (a) the President, acting on the Prime Minister's advice, revokes that Minister's appointment; or (b) the Minister resigns by writing to the President (Article 26). Just because a Minister has resigned does not preclude him or her from being appointed as a cabinet minister at a subsequent time.

310. If the Prime Minister is ill or has to be absent from Singapore or has been granted leave of absence from his or her duties, his or her duties and functions shall be exercisable by any other Minister authorized by the President. Naturally, the President may also revoke his or her appointment of any Minister acting as Prime Minister. Can the President appoint anyone he or she likes to act as Prime Minister? Under Article 26(4)(c), the President must act under the advice of the Prime Minister in this appointment. However, if the President may act 'in his discretion, if in his opinion it is impracticable to obtain the advice of the Prime Minister owing to the Prime Minister's illness or absence'.

311. Article 33 of the Constitution prohibits any member of the Cabinet or parliamentary secretary from holding 'any office of profit' and from 'actively engaging in any commercial enterprise'. Article 2 of the Constitution defines 'office of profit' as 'any whole time office in the public service'. This does not prohibit such a person from receiving:

> any remuneration or allowances (including a pension or other like allowance) in respect of his or her tenure of the office of President, Prime Minister, Chief Justice, Speaker, Deputy Speaker, Minister, Parliamentary Secretary, Political Secretary, Member of Parliament, Ambassador, High Commissioner or such other office as the President may, from time to time, by order, prescribe.

§7. The Executive: An Elected Dictatorship?

312. With so much power centred on the Prime Minister and Cabinet, what is there to prevent them from abusing it? The theory of the separation of powers which we discussed in Chapter 2 requires that as far as possible, legislative and executive power should repose in two different and distinct bodies. In the Westminster parliamentary system of government, the distinction between the legislative and executive branches of government is blurred by the combination of two factors: (1) Prime Minister and Cabinet being drawn from members of Parliament; and (2) strict party discipline which requires members of the same political party to vote according to party lines.

313. This situation is exacerbated by the fact that since 1968, there has never been any real opposition in the Singapore Parliament. From 1968 to 1981, the PAP held every single seat in Parliament. Since 1981, there have at most been only four elected opposition politicians at any one time. In a Parliament of eighty members, this makes hardly a dent on the ruling party's majority in the House. As such, the idea that the Prime Minister and Cabinet are answerable to Parliament is tenuous at best since Parliament has little real power to shape or change a decision already made by the Cabinet.

314. In other countries, where there is a substantial opposition, it will be much more difficult for the Cabinet to secure the majority it needs in Parliament to push its political agenda forward. Outside these constitutionally prescribed control mechanisms, cabinets in other countries, such as Great Britain, are subject to checks and balances through the actions of pressure or special interest groups as well as a critical press. These external checks are practically absent in Singapore, and there is really little to check the executive's power on a daily basis. The only way the Cabinet and government can be controlled is through the ballot box, but even that will only work if there is a chance the incumbent party may be displaced.

Chapter 6. The Judiciary

§1. Introduction

315. In this chapter, we examine the third branch of government under Montesquieu's classification – the judiciary. Ironically, while the judiciary has often been considered a branch of government, it defines itself and its powers by its very independence from the other branches. Alexander Hamilton considered the judiciary to be the least dangerous branch and was concerned with the preservation of its independence.

316. The judiciary's role in maintaining law and order according to the Constitution is crucial if the democratic system of government is to function properly. It is the judiciary who is empowered under the Constitution to check on the arbitrary use of power and administrative abuse through the exercise of its judicial power.

§2. Judicial Power: Meaning, Nature, Content and Scope

317. The classic definition of 'judicial power' was given in the Australian case of *Huddart Parker Pty Ltd v. Moorehead*,[122] which held that it is 'the power which every sovereign authority must of necessity have to decide controversies between its subjects or between itself and its subjects, whether the rights relate to life, liberty or property'. This definition was adopted and applied to the condition of a constitutional supremacy by the Singapore Court of Appeal (SGCA) in the case of *Yong Vui Kong v. Attorney-General* when it held that:

> by virtue of the judicial power vested in the Supreme Court … [it] has jurisdiction to adjudicate on every legal dispute on a subject matter in respect of which Parliament has conferred jurisdiction on it, including any constitutional dispute between the State and an individual.[123]

318. In any Constitution that purports to operate under a separation of powers, the judicial branch assumes this power. Sometimes, the Constitution explicitly vests the judicial power in the superior courts. For example, Article 93 of Singapore's Constitution provides that:

> 93. The judicial power shall be vested in a Supreme Court and such subordinate courts as may be provided by any written law for the time being in force.

319. This does not mean that judicial power must be explicitly vested in the courts by the Constitution for the courts to possess such powers. Indeed, this issue

122. (1908–1909) 8 CLR 330.
123. [2011] 2 SLR 1189, at 1213.

was discussed in great depth by the Privy Council in two remarkable cases: *Liyanage v. The Queen*[124] (from Ceylon) and *Moses Hinds v. The Queen*[125] (from Jamaica), as well as by the local case of *Mohammad Faizal bin Sabtu v. Public Prosecutor*.[126]

320. The only time the question of what constitutes 'judicial power' was considered locally was in the High Court case of *Mohammad Faizal bin Sabtu v. Public Prosecutor*.[127] In this case, the petitioner was charged with one count of consuming morphine, a prohibited drug under the Misuse of Drugs Act. He had, on two previously occasions, been apprehended and committed to drug rehabilitation centre for treatment. At the time of the petitioner's conviction, he was to be sentenced under section 33A(1)(a) of the Misuse of Drugs Act which provided for mandatory minimum punishment for repeat offenders. The question before the court was whether the provisions of section 33A(1)(a) violated the principle of the separation of powers in that it required the court to impose a mandatory *minimum* sentence on him.

321. In the High Court, Chief Justice Chan Sek Keong held that while the Constitution does not define 'judicial power', certain hallmarks distinguish it from legislative and executive powers:

> It can be seen … that despite the definitional difficulties apropos the term 'judicial power', a reasonably clear judicial consensus as to the nature of the judicial function has emerged from case law. In essence, the judicial function is premised on the existence of a controversy either between a State and one or more of its subjects, or between two or more subjects of the State. The judicial function entails the courts making a finding on the facts as they stand, applying the relevant law to those facts and determining the rights and obligation of the parties concerned for the purposes of governing their relationship for the future.

322. Applying these principles to the fact, the court went on to hold that historically, the sentencing power (i.e., the discretion to determine the measure of punishment to impose on an offender) was neither inherent nor integral to the judicial function. The power to enact offences and prescribe the punishment for their commission was a legislative, and not judicial, power.

323. The judgment of Chan CJ was endorsed by the Court of Appeal in *Yong Vui Kong v. Public Prosecutor* (2015).[128]

---

124. [1967] AC 259.
125. [1977] AC 632.
126. [2011] 4 SLR 947.
127. *Ibid.*
128. [2015] 2 SLR 1129.

§3. JURISDICTION OF THE COURTS

I. General

324. Singapore courts may exercise their judicial power only after they are seized of jurisdiction. This means that the court must first take control of the case before exercising its judicial power, not before. Jurisdiction is generally limited by geography. A Singapore court cannot hear a case with no connections to Singapore and whose facts occurred solely in say England or Malaysia. This is especially true when the court is asked to invoke its jurisdiction for the first time (i.e., when it hears a case for the first time). Most of the conditions limiting a court's jurisdiction are spelt out in various statutes such as the Supreme Court of Judicature Act and the State Court Act.

II. Original and Appellate Jurisdictions

325. Generally speaking, a court's jurisdiction can be divided into: (i) criminal and civil jurisdictions; and (ii) original and appellate jurisdictions. The first distinction is not so important in Singapore since most courts possess both criminal and civil jurisdictions. This means that they have power to hear both civil and criminal cases. A few courts, such as the Family Court, or the Small Claims Tribunal has only civil jurisdiction. Original jurisdiction is the power to hear the case for the first time.

326. In most cases, monetary limits (in the case of civil cases) or the power to inflict punishment (in criminal cases) limit a court's jurisdiction. Obviously, the higher up the court is in the judicial hierarchy, the greater its jurisdiction. For example, the High Court has an unlimited jurisdiction in that it can hear any type of case, regardless of how trivial or important it may be. This does not mean that the court will hear very small claims. The jurisdictional threshold for the High Court in Singapore for civil actions is SGD 250,000. Claims less than that are heard in the State Courts. The High Court's jurisdiction is unlimited as to the amount or punishment involved. However, jurisdiction may still be limited by statute. Under section 16 of the Supreme Court of Judicature Act, for example, the High Court does not possess extraterritorial jurisdiction in civil cases. In other words, this jurisdiction extends only to cases that can be linked in some way to Singapore.

327. In addition to these general classifications, the jurisdiction of the High Court can be further divided as follows.

III. Inherent Jurisdiction[129]

129. *See* generally, Jeffrey Pinsler, *Inherent Jurisdiction Re-Visited: An Expanding Doctrine*, 14 SALJ 1 (2002); and Goh Yihan, *The Inherent Jurisdiction and Inherent Powers of the Singapore Courts: Rethinking the Limits of their Exercise,* SJLS 178 (2011).

328. This refers to a superior court's power to hear and determine cases. It is a necessary corollary of the judicial power, and it is a jurisdiction asserted and claimed by the highest common law courts. The court's inherent jurisdiction is part of its general jurisdiction as a superior court of record and is unlimited in scope except where explicitly taken away by legislation. As Lord Morris said in the English case of *Connelly v. DPP*:[130]

> There can be no doubt that a court which is endowed with a particular jurisdiction has powers which are necessary to enable it to act effectively within such jurisdiction. I would regard them as powers which are inherent in its jurisdiction. A court must enjoy such powers in order to enforce its rules of practice and to suppress any abuses of its process and to defeat any attempted thwarting of its process.

329. Historically, the High Court's inherent jurisdiction consisted mainly of the power to punish for contempt of court and regulate the practice of the court to prevent an abuse of its processes. In *Li Sheng Wu v. Attorney-General*,[131] the Court of Appeal held that both the High Court and the Court of Appeal 'possess an inherent jurisdiction – and not only inherent powers – to hear and punish cases of contempt'.[132] In *Chee Siok Chin v. Minister for Home Affairs*,[133] V.K. Rajah J held that the court 'retains a residual and inherent jursidction to strike out an action and/or pleadings on the basis that the proceedings are frivolous, vexatious or an abuse of the process of the court' and that this jurisdiction is statutorily acknowledged under Order 92 Rule 4 of the Rules of Court. Rajah J then cited with approval the definition of 'inherent jurisdiction of the court' in the article 'The Inherent Jurisdiction of the Court' by Sir Jack Jacob,[134] as referring to the:

> … residual source of powers, which the court may draw upon as necessary whenever it is just or equitable to do so, and in particular to ensure the observance of the due process of law, to prevent improper vexation or oppression, to do justice between the parties and to secure a fair trial between them.[135]

330. Save for the law of contempt, Jacob classified cases into three categories: (1) control over process; (2) control over persons; and (3) control over powers of inferior courts and tribunals. With respect to the category of the court's power to 'control over process', Rajah J held that this could further be subdivided into: (i) regulating process and proceedings; (ii) addressing abuse of process; and (iii) compelling observance of process.

---

130. [1964] AC 1254.
131. [2019] 1 SLR 1081 (Court of Appeal, Singapore).
132. *Ibid.*, at [104].
133. [2006] 1 SLR(R) 582 (High Court, Singapore).
134. Jack I.H. Jacob, *The Inherent Jurisdiction of the Court* Current Legal Problems 23 (1970).
135. [2006] 1 SLR(R) 582, at [30].

IV. Review Jurisdiction

331. This refers to the High Court's power to reconsider its own previous decision. It should not be confused with its judicial review jurisdiction discussed below. Traditionally, the Lord Chancellor (England's highest judicial officer) possessed the right to rehear his or her own decisions or those of the previous Lord Chancellor. In Singapore, the court's review jurisdiction in criminal matters is found in section 301 of the Criminal Procedure Code which provides that:

> 301(1) Where a court has delivered its judgment, it may rectify a clerical error at any time, and any other error, including an error in the exercise of its sentencing powers, may be rectified by the court by the next working day after the delivery of the judgment.
> (2) For the avoidance of doubt, any error resulting from a sentence imposed by a court which it subsequently views as being too harsh or too lenient is not such error within the meaning in subsection (1).

332. Under the doctrine of res judicata, once a case is heard and judgment pronounced, it cannot be reheard, unless there are provisions for its appeal. Thus, if new evidence is discovered that would alter the court's decision, it would be imprudent of the court to refuse to review its previous decision as the error would be allowed to stand and perpetuate itself.

333. In *Management Corporation Strata Title Plan No 301 v. Lee Tat Development Pte Ltd*,[136] the Court of Appeal asserted its inherent right to review previous cases, but only in exceptional circumstances, such as where a decision was made in breach of the rules of natural justice.[137] In *Kho Jabing v. Public Prosecutor*,[138] the Court of Appeal further explicated this inherent jurisdiction as follows:

(a) The Court of Appeal, as the final appellate court in Singapore, has the inherent power to reopen a concluded criminal appeal in order to prevent a miscarriage of justice. This power is a facet of the judicial power which is vested in the Court of Appeal by virtue of Article 93 of the Constitution. When the court exercises this power of review, it is acting within the scope of its statutorily conferred appellate jurisdiction, which is not completely exhausted merely by the rendering of a decision on the merits of the appeal.
(b) A review of a concluded criminal appeal is not to be confused with an appeal. In reviewing a case, the Court of Appeal is primarily concerned not with the correctness of the decision under review, but with the question of whether there has been a miscarriage of justice. To justify the exercise of the court's inherent power of review, the applicant must satisfy the court that there is sufficient material on which it may conclude that there has been a miscarriage of justice.

136. [2011] 1 SLR 998 (Court of Appeal, Singapore).
137. *Ibid.*, at [103].
138. [2016] 3 SLR 135 (Court of Appeal, Singapore).

In this regard, the mere fact that the material relied on by the applicant consists of new legal arguments involving constitutional points does *not*, without more, suffice.

(c) In deciding whether to exercise its inherent power of review, the Court of Appeal will consider the following two matters (as set out in sub-paras (d) and (e) below).

(d) The first is whether the applicant has discharged his burden of producing 'sufficient material' to warrant the court exercising its inherent power of review. The material put forward must possess two signal features in order to be considered 'sufficient': (i) it must be 'new' – i.e., it must not previously have been canvassed at any stage of the proceedings prior to the filing of the application for review, and it must be something which could not, even with reasonable diligence, have been adduced in court earlier; and (ii) it must be 'compelling' – i.e., it must be reliable, substantial, powerfully probative, and therefore, capable of showing almost conclusively that there has been a miscarriage of justice.

(e) The second condition is whether the applicant has discharged his burden of proving that there has been a 'miscarriage of justice'. Generally, the court will only find that there has been a 'miscarriage of justice' in one of the following two situations:

   (i) The first is where a decision of the court on conviction or sentence is shown to be 'demonstrably wrong'. In relation to a decision on conviction, it is not sufficient for the applicant to show that there is a real possibility that the decision concerned is wrong; instead, it must be apparent, based on the evidence tendered in support of the application alone and without the need for further enquiry, that there is a powerful probability that the decision is wrong. In relation to a decision on sentence, it must be shown that the decision under challenge was based on some fundamental misapprehension of the law or the facts, thereby resulting in a decision that is blatantly wrong on the face of the record. An application for a review on the ground that a decision (whether on conviction or sentence) is 'demonstrably wrong' is usually available only to the accused.

   (ii) The second scenario is where the decision under challenge is tainted by fraud or a breach of natural justice, such that the integrity of the judicial process is compromised. An application for a review on the ground of fraud or breach of natural justice is available to both the accused and the prosecution.

V. Judicial Review Jurisdiction

334. This refers to the court's power to pronounce on the constitutionality of a statute. While the Constitution vests judicial power in the judiciary, it explicitly gives the courts authority to pronounce on the constitutionality of statutes passed by the legislature. Even so, this authority is part of the court's inherent power and is asserted by the court. Furthermore, Article 4 of the Constitution provides that:

> This Constitution is the supreme law of the Republic of Singapore and any law enacted by the Legislature after the commencement of this Constitution which is inconsistent with this Constitution shall, to the extent of the inconsistency, be void.

335. The power to decide whether a law is inconsistent with the Constitution falls on the court as does the power to pronounce on its constitutionality. As observed by Yong Pung How CJ in the Court of Appeal decision of *Chan Hiang Leng Colin v. PP:*

> The court has the power and duty to ensure that the provisions of the Constitution are observed. The court also has a duty to declare invalid any exercise of power, legislative and executive, which exceeds the limits of the power conferred by the Constitution, or which contravenes any prohibition which the Constitution provides.[139]

336. This statement of principle was affirmed by the Court of Appeal in *Nguyen Tuong Van v. Public Prosecutor.*[140]

VI. Supervisory Jurisdiction

337. This refers to the High Court's power to control the actions of subordinate courts or tribunals. This is discussed in greater depth in Chapter 8. General supervisory jurisdiction of the High Court is provided under section 27 of the Supreme Court of Judicature Act. The supervisory jurisdiction of the High Court is not to be confused with its appellate jurisdiction. In the words of Justice Lai Kew Chai in *Re Mohamed Saleem Ismail:*[141]

> in the exercise of the High Court's supervisory jurisdiction over inferior tribunals including administrative officers exercising judicial or quasi-judicial functions under a statute or subsidiary legislation the High Court is supervising and not reviewing; the High Court in its supervisory capacity cannot substitute its own views for those of the tribunal or officer which or who had been statutorily entrusted to make the decision.

338. The supervisory jurisdiction of the High Court depends entirely upon the use of its prerogative writs such as certiorari and mandamus. Traditionally, English

139. [1994] 3 SLR(R) 209, at [50] (Court of Appeal, Singapore).
140. [2005] 1 SLR(R) 103 (Court of Appeal, Singapore).
141. [1987] 2 MLJ 582.

courts could intervene in certain circumstances by the issue of prerogative writs. The main writs are certiorari, mandamus, *prohibition*, quo warranto and habeas corpus.

VII. Revision Jurisdiction[142]

339. This is the High Court's power to call for the records of a subordinate court for review. The general revisionary power is found in section 27 of the Supreme Court of Judicature Act under which the High Court may 'exercise powers of revision in respect of criminal proceedings and matters in subordinate courts' and to 'call for and examine the record of any civil proceedings before any subordinate court for the purpose of satisfying itself as to the correctness, legality or propriety of any decision recorded or passed, and as to the regularity of any proceedings of any such subordinate court'. The powers of revision cannot be exercised if an appeal lies from the decision of the subordinate court. This power may be invoked when 'it appears desirable in the interests of justice' either of the court's own motion or at the instance of an interested party.

§4. Establishing Jurisdiction and *Locus Standi*

340. While the courts are vested with extensive powers of judicial review, there are instances where judicial review is not permitted. Generally, courts will only pronounce on or decide cases brought by litigants before them. For example, in the Malaysian case of *Karpal Singh v. Sultan of Selangor*,[143] the lawyer politician Karpal Singh wanted the court to declare that the Sultan of Selangor's statement – that he will not pardon any person convicted of a drug offence – violated the Federal Constitution. The High Court of Malaysia rejected his application on the ground that the case was merely hypothetical. In the course of his judgment, Abdul Hamid, Chief Justice of Malaya, quoting Lord Dunedin in *The Russian Commercial & Industrial Bank v. British Bank for Foreign Trade* (1921) held:

> The question must be a real and not a theoretical question; the person raising it must have a real interest to raise it; he must be able to secure a proper contradictor, that is to say, someone presently existing who has a true interest to oppose the declaration sought.

341. In the Court of Appeal decision in *Tan Eng Hong v. Attorney-General*, the Court of Appeal had occasion to reinforce this threshold requirement. V.K. Rajah JA held:

142. *See* generally, Goh Yihan, *The Jurisdiction to Reopen Criminal Cases: A Consideration of the (Criminal) Statutory and Inherent Jurisdiction of the Singapore Court of Appeal*, SJLS 395 (2008).
143. [1988] 1 MLJ 64.

The need for the existence of a real controversy between the parties to an action stems from the function of the courts to adjudicate on and determine disputes between parties. Without a *lis*, the courts may find themselves being called on to give advisory opinions on abstract, hypothetical and/or academic questions instead of deciding on real disputes. In *Salijah bte Ab Latef v Mohd Irwan bin Abdullah Teo* [1996] 2 SLR(R) 80 ('*Salijah*') at [57], the court explained the rationale underlying the 'real controversy' requirement as follows (citing *Russian Commercial and Industrial Bank v British Bank for Foreign Trade, Limited* [1921] 2 AC 438 at 448):

> The question must be a real and not a theoretical question; the person raising it must have a real interest to raise it; he must be able to secure a proper contradictor, that is to say, some one presently existing who has a true interest to oppose the declaration sought.

342. The court also quoted with approval the editors of Woolf & Woolf, *The Declaratory Judgment* (2nd) (Sweet & Maxwell, 1993) who argued that if courts were to deal with theoretical issues, it would distract them from 'deciding real, subsisting problems'. In addition, if there was in fact no real subsisting issue, that matter would not be res judicata and this would allow litigants to reopen the issue 'again and again'.

343. As such, before a court will adjudicate on a case, three key conditions must be met: (1) the case must be 'ripe' for decision; (2) it must not be a 'collusive' case; and (3) the person bringing the case must have *locus standi* or standing to bring the case. Under the doctrine of ripeness, the court is prohibited from giving advisory opinions. The court does not act as a roving commission to investigate into every single wrongdoing, nor does it institute its own proceedings. Whether a matter is justiciable is up to the court to decide.

344. A *collusive* case is one that is brought before the court through a secret pact between the two parties. A real dispute must exist before the court makes a determination. The court does not exist to render advisory opinions on theoretical or hypothetical questions of law. For example, in the American case of *United States v. Johnson*,[144] the plaintiff brought the suit under a fictitious name at the defendant's request. The plaintiff's lawyer had in fact never seen the plaintiff (quite naturally, since he did not exist), and was assured by the defendant that he would incur no expense in connection with the suit. The case was dismissed as being collusive.

345. To invoke the court's jurisdiction, the applicant must have a standing (right of appearance before the court) or *locus standi*. He or she must have an interest to protect and not merely be an interested person. Where constitutionally guaranteed

144. 319 US 302.

liberties are at stake, a citizen's *locus standi* is prima facie established when a constitutional right has been violated.[145] In *Tan Eng Hong v. Public Prosecutor*, the Court of Appeal explained what M. Karthigesu JA meant when he stated in *Chan Hiang Leng Colin & Ors v. Minister for Information and the Arts*:[146]

> If a constitutional guarantee is to mean anything, it must mean that any citizen can complain to the courts if there is a violation of it. The fact that the violation would also affect every other citizen should not detract from a citizen's interest in seeing that his constitutional rights are not violated. A citizen should not have to wait until he is prosecuted before he may assert his constitutional rights.

346. According to the Court of Appeal, this did not mean that the mere fact of citizenship vested would be a petitioner with *locus standi*:

> the mere fact of citizenship in itself does not satisfy the standing requirement for constitutional challenges. We agree with the holding in *Colin Chan* that an applicant must demonstrate *a violation of his* constitutional rights before *locus standi* can be granted. This will prevent 'mere busybodies' whose rights are not affected from being granted standing to launch unmeritorious constitutional challenges. It is only where a person's rights have been or are threatened to be violated that that person ceases to be a 'mere busybody'. ... Sufficiency of interest still needs to be shown, but this is *prima facie* made out once there is a violation of a constitutional right (emphasis added).[147]

347. In *Tan Eng Hong v. Attorney-General*,[148] the Court of Appeal had to consider the test to be applied for *locus standi* in constitutional challenges and held that the test set out in *Karaha Bodas Co LLC v. Pertamina Energy Trading Ltd*[149] laid down three elements which must be satisfied: (1) a real interest in bringing the action; (2) a real controversy between the parties concerned; and (3) a violation of a personal right. The sufficiency of interest would prima facie be made out once there is a violation of a constitutional right since every constitutional right is a personal right. A 'violation of a constitutional right may also be brought about by the existence of an allegedly unconstitutional law in the statute books and/or by a real and credible threat of prosecution under an allegedly unconstitutional law'.[150]

348. In the case of *Jeyaretnam Kenneth Andrew v. Attorney-General*,[151] the Court of Appeal had to consider whether a civic-minded member of the public had

145. *Tan Eng Hong v. Public Prosecutor* [2012] 4 SLR 476.
146. [1996] 1 SLR 609.
147. *Ibid.*, at 514–515.
148. [2012] 4 SLR 476 (Court of Appeal, Singapore).
149. [2006] 1 SLR(R) 112 (Court of Appeal, Singapore).
150. *Ibid.*, at [115].
151. [2014] 1 SLR 345 (Court of Appeal, Singapore).

standing to apply for one of the prerogative writs, as well as a declaration against the Singapore Government when the applicant suffered no special damage nor loss by the Government's actions. In this case, the applicant sought to challenge the Singapore Government's decision to grant a contingent USD 4 billion loan to the International Monetary Fund on the ground that it was unconstitutional as it had not been given with the President's concurrence under Article 144 of the Constitution. As a preliminary issue, the court had to consider whether the applicant, who was Secretary General of the Reform Party, one of Singapore's political parties, had *locus standi* to make the application.

349. After an exhaustive examination of the local authorities, Chao Hick Tin JA held that the law on *locus standi* in Singapore stands as follows:

> there must firstly be a public duty which has been breached; without such a breach, there can be no question of whether an applicant has standing or not. Where this public duty generates correlative private rights … or public rights … the applicant would have *locus standi*. However, in the rare case where a non-correlative rights generating public duty is breached, and the breach is of sufficient gravity such that it would be in the public interest for the courts to hear the case, an applicant *sans* rights may be accorded *locus standi* as well, at the discretion of the courts.[152]

350. The court went on to hold that none of these categories had been made out and the appellant thus had no *locus standi*.

§5. Limits on Judicial Review

351. As a matter of general principle, the courts treat most issues as justiciable. As Chan Sek Keong CJ opined in *Yong Vui Kong v. Attorney-General*,[153] 'by virtue of the judicial power vested in the Supreme Court under Art 93 of the Singapore, Constitution, the Supreme Court has jurisdiction to adjudicate on every legal dispute on a subject matter in respect of which Parliament has conferred jurisdiction on it, including any constitutional dispute between the State and an individual'. The learned Chief Justice added that '[i]n any modern State, whose fundamental law is a written Constitution based on the doctrine of separation of power (ie where the judicial power is vested in an independent judiciary), there will (or should) be few, if any, legal disputes between the State and the people from which the judicial power is excluded'. That said, Chan CJ explained that there are matters which are 'intrinsically incapable' of adjudication, such as where a matter involves 'an infinity of considerations, military and diplomatic, technical, psychological and moral' which are 'not within the province of the courts to assess'. Thus, even after a court

152. *Ibid.*, at [64].
153. [2011] 2 SLR 1189 (Court of Appeal, Singapore).

has established its jurisdiction to hear a case, it may still decline to hear it for a number of reasons. These may broadly be divided as follows: (a) political questions, (b) legislative prohibition, (c) laches, (d) res judicata, (e) executive prerogative powers and (f) judgments of superior court.

I. Political Questions

352. Generally, a court will decline jurisdiction in cases where political questions are involved. This is because questions that are political in nature are best resolved through the political rather than judicial means. Any attempt by the judicial branch to decide purely political questions is tantamount to a breach of the separation of powers doctrine and a usurpation of the executive and legislative powers.

353. The political question doctrine has not been argued in the local courts, and there are no cases discussing it. Nevertheless, the approach taken in some decided cases suggests that so long as the issues are not wholly political, the jurisdiction of the court will not be ousted. If the issues are partially political or 'smack of political flavour', that alone does not oust the jurisdiction of the courts.

354. In *Lee Hsien Loong v. Review Publication Co Ltd*,[154] Sundaresh Menon JC (as he then was) had occasion to consider the question as to what a court might consider to be non-justiciable, the principles of which he summarized as follows:

(a) Justiciability depends not on the source of the decision-making power but on the subject matter that is in question. Where it is the executive that has access to the best materials available to resolve the issue, its views should be regarded as highly persuasive, if not decisive.
(b) Where the decision involves matters of government policy and requires the intricate balancing of various competing policy considerations that judges are ill-equipped to adjudicate because of their limited training, experience and access to materials, the courts should shy away from reviewing its merits.
(c) Where a judicial pronouncement could embarrass some other branch of government or tie its hands in the conduct of affairs traditionally regarded as falling within its purview, the courts should abstain.
(d) In all cases of judicial review, the court should exercise restraint and take cognizance of the fact that our system of government operates within the framework of three coequal branches. Even though all exercise of power must be within constitutional and legal bounds, there are areas of prerogative power that the democratically elected Executive and Legislature are entrusted to take charge of, and, in this regard, it is to the electorate, and not the judiciary, that the Executive and Legislature are ultimately accountable.[155]

---

154. [2007] 2 SLR(R) 453 (High Court, Singapore).
155. *Ibid.*, at [98].

II. Legislative Prohibition

355. Statutes relating to administrative matters may sometimes establish tribunals or boards of hearing. In many of such statutes, there is usually an ouster clause which prohibits the court from reviewing the case in any manner whatsoever. In particular, these statutes aim at ousting the supervisory jurisdiction of the High Court.

III. Laches

356. Laches refers to an unreasonable delay or negligence in pursuing a right or claim, especially if it is an equitable one. Laches can occur when the aggrieved party is statutorily barred by being out of time, or where they have waited far too long to bring their case before the courts. Since laches proceeds on the equitable maxim *vigilantibus non dormientibus jura subveniunt*, meaning 'the laws aid those who are vigilant, and not those who sleep upon their rights', in cases where the position of the parties have changed substantially, it would be inequitable for the court to have jurisdiction to entertain the suit.

IV. Prerogative Powers

357. Under the Constitution, the President is given certain prerogative powers, such as the power to dissolve Parliament and the power of pardon. These are not subject to judicial review.

V. Judgments of Superior Courts

358. In the exercise of its supervisory jurisdiction (not to be confused with its appellate jurisdiction, *see* below), the High Court pronounces on the validity of decisions of inferior or subordinate tribunals. It has no power to exercise supervisory jurisdiction over a superior court or one of coordinate or equal jurisdiction, such as the Court of Appeal or a differently constituted High Court bench.[156]

VI. Res Judicata

359. Where a court has given a final decision in a case, it cannot be reopened, and the decision cannot be challenged on the matter decided. This principle applies only where the parties are the same, the issue is the same, and the method of raising the question before the court has previously been considered. The idea is that once a case has been authoritatively decided, it would be unfair and unjust to reopen it, since this could lead to endless litigation. There would also be great uncertainty in the law if cases could be heard and reheard over and over again.

156. *See Marplan Pte Ltd v. Attorney-General* [2013] 3 SLR 201 (High Court, Singapore).

§6. Public Law Remedies

360. Under section 18(2) of the Singapore Supreme Court of Judicature Act, the High Court has the power to issue 'to any person or authority directions, orders or writs, including writs of the nature of habeas corpus, mandamus, prohibition, *quo warranto* and certiorari, or any others, for the enforcement of the rights conferred under Part II of the Constitution, or any of them, or for any purpose'. It is under these express prerogative writs that the courts grant constitutional remedies. In addition to these prescribed remedies, injunctions and declarations are also used by the courts.

§7. Doctrine of Prospective Overruling

361. If a statute (or part of it) is declared unconstitutional, that portion of the legislation becomes void (*see* Article 5 of the Constitution). When a statute is declared void, it is void *ab initio* and the effect is as if this statute had never existed in the first place. This presents a problem. Certain statutes may have stood for many years before being declared unconstitutional. Many individuals, lawmakers and administrators would have relied on the impugned provisions and ordered their activities accordingly. To circumvent the problem of retrospectively reversing a whole series of legislation and decisions, the doctrine of prospective overruling was developed by the United States Supreme Court in *Linkletter v. Walker*[157] and accepted in Singapore in the Court of Appeal case of *PP v. Manogaran s/o R Ramu*[158] where Chief Justice Yong Pung How held:

> By judicial overruling of a previous decision, new law may be pronounced for the first time. The rule of law requires adherence to the maxim *ignorantia juris neminem excusat*: ignorance of the law excuses no one. However, if a person organizes his affairs in accordance with an existing judicial pronouncement about the state of the law, his actions should not be impugned retrospectively by a subsequent judicial pronouncement which changes the state of the law, without his having been afforded an opportunity to reorganize his affairs. This seeks to protect his reasonable and legitimate expectations that he did not act in contravention of the law.

§8. Constitution of Singapore's Judiciary

362. Singapore's judiciary may be divided into the Supreme Court and the State Courts. The Supreme Court comprises the Court of Appeal (as Singapore's highest court) and the High Court, while the State Courts comprise a number of courts, including the Magistrates' Court, District Court and even the Small Claims Tribunal.

---

157. (1965) 381 US 618.
158. [1997] 1 SLR 22.

I. The Court of Appeal

363. The Court of Appeal consists of the following judges: (a) the Chief Justice as President of the court; (b) Vice Presidents of the Court of Appeal; (c) Judges of Appeal (other than Vice Presidents); and (d) other puisne judges of the High Court who may be appointed from time to time. As its name suggests, the Court of Appeal has only appellate jurisdiction over all civil and criminal matters. It sits as a bench of at least three judges, but may sit as a bench of five or even seven. At present, there are only four judges appointed to this Court – the Chief Justice and three Judges of Appeal, with one of them serving as Vice President of the court.

364. Under the Supreme Court of Judicature Act, a Judge of Appeal may also preside in the High Court when he or she is otherwise unoccupied in the Court of Appeal. This means that the Chief Justice and the Judges of Appeal can sit in the High Court exercising original or appellate jurisdiction. At the same time, if help is needed up in the Court of Appeal, the Chief Justice is empowered to appoint a puisne judge to sit in the Court of Appeal. These provisions enhance the efficiency of the courts. However, this has been rare since 2006.

365. An appellate court such as the Court of Appeal only hears appeals on questions of law and not questions of fact. In other words, the Court of Appeal will not re-examine witnesses, documents and other materials tendered in the trial court. It will only consider points of law and their application to the particular case. The decision of the Court of Appeal on any matter is final and cannot be reopened or reheard in any other court. The Court of Appeal's decision is also binding on all other courts in the judicial hierarchy except itself. To qualify for appointment to the Court of Appeal, a person must have the same qualifications required for that of puisne judge (*see* below).

II. The High Court

366. The High Court consists of puisne judges and Judicial Commissioners. They are addressed as 'Your Honour', as are all judges in the Supreme Court. To qualify to be a Supreme Court judge, a candidate has to be a 'qualified person' within the meaning of the Legal Professions Act of at least ten years' standing.

367. The High Court has both original and appellate jurisdictions. Traditionally, the High Court only heard appeals from the State Courts, especially appeals from the Magistrates' Courts. However, in 2021, the Supreme Court of Judicature Act was amended to create an Appellate Division within the High Court to ease the workload of the Court of Appeal. Under the new rules, only cases specified in Schedule 6 of the Supreme Court of Judicature Act can be appealed directly to the Court of Appeal. These are cases involving: (a) constitutional or administrative law; (b) criminal law and contempt of court proceedings; (c) the Parliament Elections Act and the Presidential Elections Act; (d) insolvency; (e) corporate restructuring or dissolution; (f) patents; (g) arbitration law; (h) decisions of the International Commercial Court; (i) Mediation Act and the Singapore Convention on Mediation Act; (j) appeals provided under various specific laws for direct appeals to the Court of Appeal.

368. All other civil cases will be appealed from the High Court to the High Court's Appellate Division. Appeals from the High Court's Appellate Division may still lie to the Court of Appeal although there will be no further appeal in the following types of cases: (a) cases where the Court of Appeal does not grant leave; (b) incidental directions; (c) interim orders; (d) where the law specifies the High Court Appellate Division to be the final Court of Appeal.

369. The Appellate Division will normally sit in a *coram* of three judges although some appeals may be heard by two judges.

370. In its original jurisdiction, the High Court hears cases which are beyond the jurisdiction of the State Courts. Certain types of cases, for example, the offence of murder, can only be tried at the High Court. Likewise, cases where the damages involved amount to more than SGD 250,000 must be heard in the High Court and nowhere else.

371. In addition to its original and appellate jurisdictions, the High Court also has supervisory and revisionary jurisdictions.[159] In the case of its supervisory jurisdiction, the High Court ensures that all inferior courts and tribunals act within their allotted jurisdictional limits. The revisionary jurisdiction of the High Court empowers it to call for and examine proceedings of subordinate courts to satisfy itself of the correctness and legality of these decisions. This can mean looking at the finding of a case, or even the punishment meted out.

372. The High Court does not have jurisdiction over certain family matters under Muslim law, such as marriage and divorce. However, it does have concurrent jurisdiction with the Shariah Court over civil proceedings relating to maintenance of wife and child, custody and disposition and division of property on divorce in the case of Muslim marriages.

373. Specialist courts within the Supreme Court, such as the Admiralty Court and Intellectual Property Court (both created in 2002), have been established. In 2015, an International Commercial Court (ICC) division was created in the High Court to handle transnational commercial disputes. These courts function like the High Court in all respects except that the judges who preside over them have specialist knowledge in these areas of law. In the case of the ICC, judges are selected from a panel of local and international judges.

---

159. For a description and discussion of the Singapore High Court's appellate, supervisory and revisionary jurisdiction, *see* Yeo Tiong Min, *Jurisdiction of the Singapore Courts*, in *The Singapore Legal System* (Kevin Y.L. Tan ed., Sing. U. Press 2d ed. 1999).

374. One 'specialist' court that is constituted on an ad hoc basis is the Constitutional Tribunal which hears questions referred to it by the President on the effect of constitutional provisions. There is no appeal from the decisions of this court.

III. Family Justice Courts

375. The Family Justice Courts is a collective name for the body of courts comprising the Family Courts, the Youth Courts and the Family Division of the High Court. These courts are overseen by the Presiding Judge of the Family Justice Courts.

376. The Family Courts hear all family proceedings except those falling under the Children and Young Persons Act. These courts adopt a holistic and reconciliatory approach to resolving family disputes.

377. The Youth Courts deal with children and young persons who commit offences and other youth matters which fall under the ambit of the Children and Young Persons Act (CYPA). The Youth Courts' approach is restorative and aims to not only hold youths accountable for their offending behaviour but also reintegrate them into their families and communities. They are used to deal with youthful offenders, that is anyone below the age of 16 years. The rationale for setting up a separate court for these juveniles is the difference in approach towards these offenders. Instead of seeking to punish them, the Juvenile Courts treat them as children in trouble and try to help them out through appropriate treatment, rather than punishment. The Juvenile Court is presided over by a Magistrate, and he or she is assisted by two advisers (who come from a panel of advisers nominated by the President of Singapore). Among the things a Juvenile Court may do to an offender is to commit him or her to the care of a relative or other fit person, or make a probation order. The court can even commit the offender to the Young Offenders section in prison.

378. The Family Division of the High Court hears appeals from decisions of the Family Courts; appeals may be heard before one or three judges. Parties may apply for their case to be heard at first instance by the High Court (Family Division) where the case is complex, involves an important question of law, or for other satisfactory reasons.

IV. The State Courts

379. Up until January 2014, the lower courts in Singapore were collectively known as the subordinate courts and were constituted and regulated by the Subordinate Courts Act. In January 2014, Parliament passed the Subordinate Courts (Amendment) Act which renamed the subordinate courts as 'State Courts'. This amendment was motivated by the desire to reflect the importance of the lower courts in the administration of justice in Singapore. Under the State Courts Act, the following courts are State Courts: (a) District Courts, (b) Magistrates' Courts, (c) Coroner's Court, (d) Juvenile Court, (e) Family Court, and (f) Small Claims Tribunal.

380. The State Court is headed by the Presiding Judge of the State Courts who is a judge or Judicial Commissioner of the Supreme Court. The Presiding Judge is overall responsible for leading and managing the State Courts and is assisted by the Deputy Presiding Judge, Principal District Judges, the Registrar of the State Courts and other senior court administrators. There are three divisions within the State Courts: (1) Justice Division; (2) Judicial Administration Division; and (3) the Presiding Judge's Office.

381. The District Court is presided over by the District Judge who is appointed by the President on the advice of the Chief Justice. There are a number of District Judges in Singapore, and one Presiding Judge of State Courts of a rank equal to that of a Judicial Commissioner of the Supreme Court. To qualify as a District Judge, a person must be a qualified person of at least five years' standing. Unlike Supreme Court judges, judges of the State Courts do not have security of tenure.

382. The civil jurisdiction of the District Court for all matters founded in tort or contract is SGD 250,000. In equity matters, such as probate, the limit is SGD 3 million. Under the Criminal Procedure Code, the District Court is empowered to mete out the following sentences in the exercise of its criminal jurisdiction:

(a) imprisonment for a term not exceeding seven years;
(b) impose a fine not exceeding SGD 10,000;
(c) order caning of up to twelve strokes;
(d) any other lawful sentence combining any of the sentences which it is authorized by law to pass;
(e) any other lawful sentence combining any of the sentences which it is authorized by law to pass.

383. Some statutes such as the Misuse of Drugs Act give the District Court even higher jurisdictional limits. For example, it can impose a punishment of up to thirty years imprisonment and caning up to fifteen strokes under the Act.

384. The Magistrates' Courts are presided over by Magistrates who are appointed by the President on the recommendation of the Chief Justice. Under the State Courts Act, the President may appoint any 'fit and proper person' to be a Magistrate. In the old days, many Magistrates were laymen or community leaders, but in recent years, most Magistrates have been appointed from members of the Legal Service who are all law graduates. To be a Magistrate, a candidate must now be a qualified person of at least one year's standing.

385. The civil jurisdiction of the Magistrates' Courts for all civil matters is SGD 60,000. Its criminal jurisdiction is also established under the Criminal Procedure Code, and Magistrates are empowered to mete out the following:

(a) imprisonment for a term not exceeding two years;
(b) impose a fine not exceeding SGD 2,000;
(c) order caning of up to six strokes;
(d) any other lawful sentence combining any of the sentences which it is authorized by law to give.

386. Like the District Courts, certain Acts extend the Magistrates' Courts' jurisdiction beyond that prescribed by the Criminal Procedure Code. Again, the Misuse of Drugs Act is a case in point.

V. Coroner's Courts

387. Coroner's Courts are established to investigate enquiries into cases of unnatural death. The Coroner's qualification is the same as that of the Magistrate, and indeed, Coroners are usually drawn from the pool of Magistrates in the Legal Service. Where cases of unnatural death are reported, the Coroner may examine the body and determine whether or not an Inquest is necessary. If it is, a post-mortem of the body is usually carried out to establish the cause of death.

VI. The Small Claims Tribunal

388. The Small Claims Tribunal was established in 1984 under the Small Claims Tribunal Act to provide a quick method of dispute resolution for claims arising out of contracts for goods and services not exceeding SGD 10,000 in value or SGD 20,000 if both parties consent in writing. It does not function as a real court as such since lawyers are not permitted and claimants conduct their own cases. It is presided over by a Referee who must be a qualified person.

389. Claims must be brought before the tribunal within one year from the date the cause of action arises. A right of appeal from the tribunal lies to the High Court in questions of law.

§9. THE SHARIAH COURT AND MAJLIS UGAMA ISLAM SINGAPURA

390. The Administration of Muslim Law Act establishes the Shariah Court whose jurisdiction is to hear cases involving Muslim law relating to: (a) marriage; (b) divorce; (c) betrothal, nullity of marriage or separation; (d) disposition or disposal of property on divorce; or (e) payment of *maskahwin*, maintenance and consolatory gifts or *matta'ah.*

391. The Shariah Court is presided over by a President who is appointed by the President of Singapore. Cases from the Shariah Court are appealable to the Appeal

Board or the Majlis Ugama Islam Singapura, Singapura or Council of Muslim Religion, Singapore (Majlis, for short). The President of Majlis is also appointed by the President of Singapore and the decision of Majlis is final.

§10. Judicial Independence

392. So far, we have seen the importance of the court's role in determining the constitutionality of statutes and administrative actions. To perform this role effectively, courts must be independent from the other two branches of government. There are many ways to ensure this, but two main methods are institutionalized within the Constitution: (1) security of tenure and (2) security of remuneration.

I. Appointment and Tenure of Judges

393. In Singapore, all judges (including Magistrates) are appointed by the President. In appointing the Chief Justice, the Judges of Appeal and the Judges of the High Court, the President acts in his or her discretion and must concur with the Prime Minister's advice. In the appointment of State Court judges (i.e., District Judges and Magistrates), the President acts on the Chief Justice's advice.

394. Article 98(1) provides that:

> a judge of the Supreme Court shall hold office until he attains the age of 65 years or such later time, not being later than 6 months after he attains that age, as the President may approve.

II. Security of Remuneration

395. Article 98(6) of the Constitution provides that 'Parliament shall by law provide for the remuneration of the judges of the Supreme Court, and the remuneration shall be charged on the Consolidated Fund.' Furthermore, the Supreme Court judge's remuneration and terms of office including pension rights 'shall not be altered to his disadvantage after his appointment' (*see* Article 98(8)). This ensures that judges cannot be threatened with pay cuts.

III. Judicial Commissioners and Senior Judges

396. In 1971, the shortage of High Court judges led to an amendment to Article 94 of the Constitution to permit the appointment of 'supernumerary' or 'contract' judges. This allowed Judges of the Supreme Court who were compelled by the Constitution to retire at the age of 65 to stay on as judges on a contractual basis, usually for terms of between one and three years.

397. Difficulties in getting senior legal practitioners to accept appointments to the bench led to an amendment to the Constitution in 1979 to create the post of Judicial Commissioner (JC). Judicial Commissioners can be appointed on a temporary basis, and this allowed practitioners who take up such appointments to return to private practice when their terms are up. The terms of appointments for Judicial Commissioners, like those of supernumerary judges, are between six months and three years and are often viewed as a prelude to a full judgeship. In 1993, then Chief Justice Yong Pung How announced that he would appoint Judicial Commissioners for very short terms and to hear long cases that would otherwise disrupt normal court hearing schedules. So far, no Judicial Commissioners have been appointed to hear specific cases on a 'one-off' basis even though Article 94(5) does not preclude such an appointment.

398. In 2014, the Constitution was amended to make provision for the continued appointment of supernumerary judges who would henceforth be known as 'Senior Judges'. The continued employment of judges who are past retirement age was justified on the basis of a need for them to help clear the backlog of cases in the courts. The first five senior judges were: Chan Sek Keong (former Chief Justice); Kan Ting Chiu, Lai Siu Chiu, Tan Lee Meng and Andrew Ang (all former High Court judges). At the same time, amendments were also made to establish the Singapore International Commercial Court (SICC) as a division of the High Court of Singapore and the appointment of SICC judges, most of whom are foreign judges who do not reside permanently in Singapore. The panel of judges – which draws on distinguished jurists around the world – does not enjoy the security of tenure or remuneration. The SICC heard its first case – a contractual dispute between Australian and Indonesian firms – in November 2015. The coram comprised Justices Quentin Loh (Singapore), Vivian Ramsey (UK) and Anselmo Reyes (Hong Kong).

399. In September 1994, a new Article 100 was inserted into the Constitution. It established a *Special Tribunal* consisting of not less than three Judges of the Supreme Court. The President of Singapore may refer to this tribunal 'for its opinion any question as to the effect of any provision' of the Constitution. The tribunal is under a duty to 'consider and answer the question so referred as soon as may be and in any case not more than sixty days after the date of such reference'. Any dissenting opinions of any judge must accordingly be reflected in the opinion rendered to the President although the majority decision shall be considered the opinion of the tribunal and shall be pronounced in open court. The opinion is not subject to question in any court.

IV. Contempt of Court

400. In addition, the court has certain powers to ensure its independence. This is by way of contempt proceedings which may be initiated by the AG. There are four aspects of contempt of court. First, deliberately interfering with court proceedings and their outcomes, such as intimidating witnesses or bribing judges; second, *contempt in the fact of the court* in which a person uses abusive or threatening language in court;[160] third, *scandalizing the court*, where a person attacks the integrity or independence of the court; and finally, interfering with the administration of justice such as when a court order is disobeyed or if undertakings to the court are breached.[161]

401. The most detailed consideration of the principles behind the power of the court to punish for contempt is found in the Court of Appeal decision in *Pertamina Energy Trading Ltd v. Karaha Bodas Co. LLC and Others*[162] which restated and reiterated principles found in the English courts. An important point to note is that contempt of court proceedings is deemed necessary to protect the impartiality of the courts and are not a punitive means to safeguard the personal dignity of the judges.

402. The most significant aspect of the power to punish for contempt in which the Singapore courts have established a significant conservative jurisprudence is in the area of scandalizing the court. This was an offence created by the courts on the basis of common law and had no statutory basis. Furthermore, there were no limits on the punishment the courts could mete out on a person guilty of contempt. The basis for contempt by scandalizing the court was offered by Lord Diplock in *Attorney-General v. Times Newspapers*[163] where he stated:

> The due administration of justice requires first that all citizens should have unhindered access to the constitutionally established courts of criminal or civil jurisdiction for the determination of disputes as to their legal rights and liabilities; secondly, that they should be able to rely upon obtaining in the courts the arbitrament of a tribunal which is free from bias against any party and whose decision will be based upon those facts only that have been proved in evidence adduced before it in accordance with the procedure adopted in courts of law; and thirdly, that, once the dispute has been submitted to a court of law, they should be able to rely upon there being no usurpation by any other person of the function of that court to decide it according to law. Conduct which is calculated to prejudice any of these three requirements or to undermine the public confidence that they will be observed is contempt of court.
> Contempt of court is punishable because it undermines the confidence not only of the parties to the particular litigation but also of the public as potential suitors, in the due administration of justice by the established courts of law.

403. For many years, it was uncertain whether the courts should apply the 'inherent tendency' or the 'real likelihood' test. This uncertainty was brought to an

160. *See*, for example, *Chee Siok Chin v. AG* [2006] 4 SLR 541.
161. *See*, for example, *Pertamina Energy Trading Ltd v. Karaha Bodas Co. LLC and Others* [2007] 2 SLR 518; [2007] SGCA 10.
162. [2007] 2 SLR 518; [2007] SGCA 10, at 529–538.
163. [1974] AC 273.

end when the Court of Appeal ruled in favour of the 'real likelihood' test in *Shadrake Alan v. Attorney-General.*[164] Even as the *Shadrake* case was being heard, calls were made to put the law of contempt on a statutory footing. In September 2016, Parliament passed the Administration of Justice (Protection) Act. Under section 3 of the Act, a person commits the offence of scandalizing the court if he or she 'imputes improper motives to or impugns the integrity, propriety or impartiality of any court' and 'poses a risk that public confidence in the administration of justice would be undermined'. The test 'risk' simpliciter, as opposed to 'real risk', represents a clawback by Parliament. The rationale, explained by Law Minister K Shanmugam was as follows:

> If you allow constant attacks – attacks say of bias and corruption – over time, the public perception of the judiciary will be affected. This, I think, is self-evident ... if you allow baseless attacks on the Judiciary, you get erosion of trust in the Judiciary ... I want to make sure that the integrity of the Judiciary is pristine. This will give us a strong anchoring in the rule of law which, in itself, is of basic fundamental importance for our people.[165]

§11. Conclusion

404. The judiciary is the only branch of government that is not elected. Yet, they play a crucial part in interpreting the law and controlling the other two branches. This irony is often referred to as the 'counter-majoritarian' difficulty: a non-elected body putting the brakes on the actions of those who have the general support of the population. Can this be right?

405. Majoritarianism is a desirable but sometimes dangerous thing for the rights of the minority can be imperilled by the actions of the masses. It is the judiciary, through their interpretation of the law, that ensures that this does not happen. It is a very delicate and difficult business. Courts that are seen as being overly political or activist have been taken to task by the Government. This was what happened to the Malaysian judiciary in the late 1980s when several of the country's most senior judges, including the Lord President Salleh Abas, were removed for alleged misconduct.[166]

---

164. [2011] 3 SLR 778.
165. K. Shanmugam, *Speech at the Second Reading of the Administration of Justice (Protection) Bill*, 94 Singapore Parliamentary Debates Official Reports (15 Aug. 2016).
166. The literature on this unfortunate saga is voluminous. *See* H.P. Lee, *The Judiciary Under Seige*, in *Constitutional Conflicts in Contemporary Malaysia* (Oxford U. Press 1995); F.A. Trindade, *The Removal of the Malaysian Judges*, 106 L. Q. Rev. 51–86 (1990); Andrew Harding, *The 1988 Constitutional Crisis in Malaysia*, 39 ICLQ 57–81 (1990); R.H. Hickling, *The Malaysian Judiciary in Crisis*, Pub. L. 20–37 (1989); and Visu Sinnadurai, *The 1988 Judiciary Crisis and Its Aftermath*, in *Constitutional Landmarks in Malaysia: The First 50 Years 1957–2007* 173–196 (Andrew Harding & H.P. Lee eds, LexisNexis 2008).

406. To ensure the courts can do their work properly, constitutional protection is given to them to maintain their independence. However, in Singapore, two positions in our judiciary – Judicial Commissioners and supernumerary or contract judges – stand out as stark exceptions to these measures to maintain judicial independence. Singapore has the most efficient and highest-paid judiciary in the world. Surely it is possible to now do away with these two provisions that were introduced to cope with the shortage of top practitioners accepting appointments to the bench. Keeping judges beyond retirement age is not healthy. At 65 years, the current retirement age for judges is early, by international standards. For example, there is no retirement age for judges in America, and in England, judges retire at the age of 75. Perhaps it is also time to raise the retirement age of judges from 65 years to either 70 or 75 years.

Chapter 7. Independent Non-political Bodies in the Legislative or Executive Branch with an Advisory or Supervisory Task

§1. PRESIDENTIAL ELECTIONS COMMITTEE

407. The PEC is established under Article 18 of the Constitution. Its function is to ensure that candidates for the office of President have the requisite qualifications referred to under Article 19. The Committee consists of the Chairman of the Public Service Commission (who acts as Chairman); the Chairman of the Accounting and Corporate Regulatory Authority; and a member of the Presidential Council for Minority Rights nominated by the Chairman of the Council; a member or former member of the Council of Presidential Advisers; a person qualified to be or has been a Judge of the Supreme Court appointed by the Chief Justice; and a person 'who in the opinion of the Prime Minister has expertise and experience acquired in the private sector that is relevant to functions of the Committee'. The Committee regulates its own procedure and fixes the quorum for its meetings.

408. Any decision on a candidate's suitability made by the PEC is final and is not subject to appeal or review in any court.[167] If a candidate is found suitable, the Committee will issue the candidate with a Certificate of Eligibility before Nomination Day.

§2. COUNCIL OF PRESIDENTIAL ADVISERS

409. Part VA of the Constitution establishes the Council of Presidential Advisers to 'advise and make recommendations to the President on any matter referred to the Council by the President' under Article 21(3) and Article 21(4) of the Constitution.[168] This is in respect of the President's discretion in withholding his or her assent for Supply Bills that draw on Singapore's reserves as well as loans and guarantees given by the state.

410. The Council consists of eight members. Of these, three members are appointed by the President, acting in his or her discretion; three members are appointed by the President on the advice of the Prime Minister; one member is appointed by the President on the advice of the Chief Justice; and one member is appointed by the President on the advice of the Chairman of the Public Service Commission.[169] The Chairman is appointed by the President acting in his or her discretion. Each member of the Council is appointed for six years in the first instance and may be eligible for reappointment. Alternate members may be appointed by the President in place any member who 'is temporarily unable, whether by illness, absence or any other reason, to take part in any proceedings of the Council'.[170]

---

167. Article 18(12).
168. Article 37I.
169. Article 37B.
170. Article 37C(1).

411. To qualify as a member of the Presidential Council of Advisers, a person must be a citizen of Singapore aged 35 years and above; is a resident of Singapore; and not liable to any disqualification under Article 37E[171] (not being of unsound mind; is insolvent or an undischarged bankrupt; or has convicted of an offence by a court of law in Singapore or a foreign country and sentenced to a term of imprisonment not less than one year or a fine of not less than SGD 2,000).

412. All proceedings of the Council are in private, and the Council has the power to require 'any public officer or any officer of any statutory board or Government company to appear before the Council and give such information in relation to any matter referred' to the Council.[172] In making its recommendations to the President, the Council must state whether its advice or recommendation is unanimous or if not, how many votes were cast in favour of or against the recommendation.

413. The Council is required, 'as soon as practicable after advising or making any recommendation to the President', to send a copy to the Prime Minister and the Speaker of Parliament who 'shall cause the copy to be presented to Parliament as soon as possible'.[173] The Council of Presidential Affairs is paid 'such fees as may be determined by the President', such sums being charged on and paid out of the Consolidated Fund.[174]

414. The Chairman of the Council of Presidential Advisers acts as President of the country when the President is out of the country or is indisposed.

§3. Presidential Council for Minority Rights

415. The Presidential Council for Minority Rights is established under Part VII of the Constitution. It comprises a Chairman (appointed for three years), not more than ten members appointed for life and not more than ten members appointed for three years appointed by the President on the Cabinet's advice. To qualify for membership, a person must be a Singapore citizen, resident in Singapore and at least 35 years old. He or she must not be of unsound mind, an undischarged bankrupt or have been convicted of an offence carrying a term of imprisonment lasting one year or more or a fine of SGD 2,000 or more.

416. The Council has a general and a particular function. Under Article 76 of the Constitution, the Council's general function is to 'consider and report on such matters affecting persons of any racial or religious community in Singapore as may

171. Article 37D.
172. Article 37J.
173. Article 37K.
174. Article 37L.

be referred to the Council by Parliament or the Government'. Such a reference may be made by Parliament through the Speaker, or by the Government through a Minister.

417. The Council's particular function is 'to draw attention to any Bill or to any subsidiary legislation if that Bill or subsidiary legislation is, in the opinion of the Council, a differentiating measure'. Under Article 68, a 'differentiating measure' is one:

> which is, or is likely in its practical application to be, disadvantageous to persons of any racial or religious community and not equally disadvantageous to persons of other such communities, either directly by prejudicing persons of that community or indirectly by giving advantage to persons of another community.

418. Three types of Bills are exempted from the Council's scrutiny: 'Money Bills', Bills on a Certificate of Urgency and Bills which affect the defence, security, public safety, peace or good order of Singapore. Each Bill passed by Parliament will be sent to the President for his or her assent, and the Speaker will send an authenticated copy to the Presidential Council for Minority Rights for its consideration. The Council must consider the Bill and make a report to the Speaker within thirty days. This thirty-day limit may be extended if the Bill is particularly complex or difficult. If the Council presents no report within the time limit, it is presumed that no provision of the Bill contains a differentiating measure.

419. If the Council issues an adverse report, Parliament can either amend the Bill and resubmit it to the Council or proceed to present the Bill for the Presidential Assent in spite of the adverse report. The latter course of action is only feasible if Parliament passes the motion for presentation by 'an affirmative vote of not less than two-thirds of the total membership of Parliament'. If the report presented to Parliament is not adverse, then it goes to the President for his or her assent without further delay. Once the President assents to the Bill, it becomes an Act of Parliament, that is law. Of course, the President may, in areas where his or her personal discretion is invoked under the Constitution – such as budgets or the raising of loans or giving of guarantees by the Government – refuse to assent to a Bill duly passed by Parliament.

Part III. Citizenship and the Administration of Justice

Chapter 1. Rules Concerning Nationality and Relevance of Nationality

§1. Introduction

420. Generally speaking, a citizen is a member of the political community to which he or she belongs. Citizens are the people who comprise the State and have subjected themselves to the domination of the State for the promotion of their general welfare and for the protection of their individual and collective rights. As such, there are certain privileges and benefits to be gained from being a citizen of a particular state. At the same time, citizenship imposes certain responsibilities and obligations on the individual. In Singapore, for example, every male citizen is eligible for National Service.

421. There are a number of theories of citizenship. In ancient Greece, Aristotle saw citizenship as the privilege of the ruling class. In our more egalitarian times, citizenship has extended across the whole of society. Karl Marx, on the other hand, objected to modern democratic citizenship because it did not go far enough in emancipating the human race as a whole, rather than emancipating society as a political unit. The current leading works on citizenship have emerged as a result of various debates concerning a thought-provoking essay by TH Marshall entitled 'Citizenship and Social Class'[175] in which he argued that in the modern State, there are three distinct rights associated with citizenship: civil, political and social rights.

422. Briefly, the civil element comprises the rights necessary for individual freedom, while the political part of citizenship encompasses the right to participate in the political process and in the exercise of political power. Finally, the social aspect of citizenship (which is perhaps Marshall's most significant contribution to the study of this area) refers to the right to the prevailing standard of life and social heritage of a society. It is not within the scope of this chapter to discuss these various theories, but it is crucial to note that in constitutional law, the subject of citizenship is a very sensitive one and has more often than not been a source of controversy, especially since the state can always discriminate against a non-citizen.

---

175. *See* Citizenship and Social Class and Other Essays (T.H. Marshall ed., Cambridge U. Press 1950).

423. The concept of citizenship or nationality is also extremely important in international law. In particular, a person's nationality is crucial in the following instances:

(a) Diplomatic Protection. Each state has a right and duty to provide protection for its citizens and their rights at home and abroad.
(b) Deportation. A state does not generally refuse to take back one of its own nationals if he or she is being deported by another country.
(c) Allegiance. The citizen is expected to owe his or her allegiance to the state of which he or she is a national. He or she may, therefore, be expected to fulfil certain obligations, like military service. By the same measure, a citizen who swears allegiance to his or her state may not be banished from it.
(d) Extradition. Since a state is responsible for its nationals, it may refuse to extradite any of its nationals to another state who is requesting that extradition.
(e) Enemy Status. In times of war, enemy status is determined by the nationality of the person apprehended. Enemy aliens are eligible for protection under the Geneva Convention 1949.
(f) Jurisdiction. Jurisdiction for criminal offences is frequently exercised on the basis of nationality.

§2. Acquisition of Citizenship

424. Under the Singapore Constitution,[176] there are five main ways a person can acquire citizenship in these countries. Citizenship can be acquired by: (1) birth, (2) descent, (c) registration, (d) enrolment, and (e) naturalization.

I. Citizenship by Birth

425. The general principle followed by most countries in the world is that persons who are born in that country should be able to acquire the citizenship of that country. This is known as the doctrine of *jus soli*. There are, however, certain limitations to the application of this doctrine. While Article 121(1) of the Constitution provides that 'every person born in Singapore after 16 September 1963 shall be a citizen by birth', either of the child's parents must be a Singapore citizen (Article 121(2)(c)). Under Article 121(2), a person born in Singapore may not be a citizen if:

(a) his father, not being a citizen of Singapore, possessed such immunity from suit and legal process as is accorded to an envoy of a sovereign power accredited to the President; or
(b) his father was an enemy alien and the birth occurred in a place then under the occupation of the enemy.

---

176. On the evolution of Singapore's citizenship laws, *see* Visuvanathan Sinnadurai, *Singapore Citizenship Laws*, 12 Mal LR 160 (1970); and Goh Phai Cheng, *Citizenship Laws of Singapore* (Educ. Book Publishers 1970).

426. Notwithstanding the qualifications in Article 121(2), Article 121(3) gives the Government discretion to confer citizenship on a person born in Singapore 'where it considers it just and fair and having regard to all the circumstances prevailing at the time of the application'.

II. Citizenship by Descent

427. Even if a person is not born in Singapore, he or she can still become a Singapore citizen if one or both of his or her parents is a citizen. This is known as citizenship by descent or *jus sanguinis*. A person who is born outside Singapore may still be a Singapore citizen by descent if:

(a) his father is a citizen of Singapore by birth or registration (if born prior to 15 May 2004); or
(b) either parent is a Singapore citizen by birth, registration or descent (if born on or after 15 May 2004).

428. In the latter case, the parent concerned must have stayed in Singapore for a total period of 'at least five years before the child's birth', or 'at least two years out of the five years immediately before the child's birth'.

429. For a child to become a citizen by descent, his or her birth must be registered at the Registry of Citizens, or at a diplomatic or consular mission of Singapore within one year after his or her birth. A minor who becomes a citizen by descent must, upon the attainment of the age of 22 years, take the Oath of Renunciation, Allegiance and Loyalty if he or she wishes to remain a Singapore citizen.

III. Citizenship by Registration or Enrolment

430. Citizenship by registration is dealt with under Articles 123–126 of the Constitution. Persons who are likely to become citizens by registration are foreign-born wives and children of citizens. Generally, any person above the age of 21 years is eligible to register as a Singapore citizen. This is subject to certain conditions and restrictions such as residence, intention to reside in the country permanently, character and knowledge of the local language. The effective date of citizenship is the date of registration (Article 125). Generally, a person is not allowed to be registered until he or she has taken the Oath of Renunciation, Allegiance and Loyalty (*see* Article 123 and Second Schedule of the Constitution). A person who has previously 'renounced or has been deprived of citizenship' may not be registered as a citizen except with the Government's approval (Article 126(2)).

431. The acquisition of citizenship by enrolment is peculiar to Singapore and only applies to those persons who were not Singapore citizens prior to separation from Malaysia on 9 August 1965. At that time, many people living and working in Singapore were actually citizens of the Federation but not of the State of Singapore.

Likewise, there were many people who were Singapore citizens who became Malaysian citizens by virtue of merger (1963–1965). At separation, the latter category of persons lost their Malaysian citizenship while retaining their Singaporean citizenship, while those who were Malaysian citizens and who enrolled to be Singapore citizens under Article 53(1)(c) of the Singapore State Constitution (and this is acknowledged in Article 120(2)(c) of the present Constitution) continued to be Singapore citizens.

IV. Citizenship by Naturalization

432. In many ways, citizenship by naturalization is similar to citizenship by registration. A person may apply for and be granted a Certificate of Naturalization under Article 127 of the Constitution. The only differences between the conditions for naturalization and registration concern the knowledge of languages. The applicant for citizenship by registration is required to know *any* of the four official languages, while the applicant for citizenship by naturalization must have an elementary knowledge of the national language, Malay (Article 127(1)). Although the Constitution clearly provides for citizenship by naturalization, the Registry of Citizens does not in practice grant citizenship under these provisions. Instead, applicants are told to apply for citizenship by registration.

§3. Proof of Citizenship Status

433. Citizenship carries both privileges and obligations. For example, a citizen may not be banished from Singapore under Article 13 of the Constitution, and freedom of speech guarantees apply only to citizens. Under international law, a person who is a citizen or national of another country has the rights of a prisoner of war under the Geneva Convention 1949 if arrested by an alien enemy.

434. The burden of proving that a person is a citizen falls on the person asserting citizenship.[177] Section 17 of the Banishment Act provides that should any question arise as to whether a person is a Singapore citizen, the onus of proof falls on that person.

435. An interesting question arose in the Malaysian case of *Ooi Kee Hoi v. Public Prosecutor & Ooi Wan Yui v. Public Prosecutor.*[178] The appellant Ooi was charged with possession of a firearm, possession of ammunition and consorting with members of the Indonesian armed forces under the ISA. He argued that he was and therefore should be treated as a 'prisoner of war' under Article 4 of the Third Schedule of the Geneva Conventions Act 1962. Ong Hock Thye FJ held that the onus of proving that Ooi was not a member of the Indonesian armed forces lay on the prosecution and that it was not for Ooi to prove that he was not a Malaysian subject.

177. *See Re Hoon Tye Wan* [1965] 1 MLJ 90 (High Court, Malaysia).
178. [1966] 2 MLJ 183 (Federal Court, Malaysia).

The Federal Court's decision was overturned on appeal to the Privy Council. Lord Hodson distinguished between nationality and allegiance and held 'allegiance to be the governing principle' and that as Ooi owed an allegiance to Malaysia, he was not a 'prisoner of war'.

436. In *Lau Seng Poh v. Controller of Immigration, Singapore*,[179] the applicant was to be deported for entering Singapore illegally. Although the case did not involve any of the citizenship provisions, it is important that the High Court was prepared to undertake a review of the facts to determine whether the applicant had in fact been born in Singapore. Justice L.P. Thean (as he then was) held that on the totality of the evidence and on the balance of probabilities, the applicant had in fact been born in Singapore and therefore had not entered Singapore illegally.

§4. Loss of Citizenship

437. Generally speaking, a person can lose his or her citizenship in one of three ways: (i) renunciation, (ii) cancellation, and (iii) deprivation. Much of the case law generated arose out of issues concerning the deprivation of citizenship.

I. Renunciation

438. Under Article 128(1) of the Constitution, a person who is about to become a citizen of another country can renounce his or her citizenship by making a declaration to that effect. This declaration is registered by the Government, but the Government may refuse registration if the declaration is made during times of war. This is probably to discourage citizens from evading conscription in times of war.

II. Cancellation

439. This mode of losing one's citizenship applies only to Singapore and to those persons who acquired their citizenship by enrolment. Article 132 provides that their enrolment may be cancelled if the Government is satisfied that the enrolment was obtained by fraud, false representation or concealment of any material fact, or that it was affected by a mistake.

III. Deprivation

440. A citizen may be deprived of his or her citizenship in a number of instances (*see* Articles 133–137). It is not within the purview of this chapter to consider all these grounds in detail. Among other things, deprivation of citizenship can be made

179. [1985] 2 MLJ 250.

on grounds that the citizen has acquired the citizenship or exercised the exclusive rights of a citizen in a foreign country or if he or she has acquired and travelled on a foreign passport.

441. Prior to 2 January 1986, Singaporean citizens could lose their citizenship rights by either deprivation or termination. The provisions of the old Article 134 (termination of citizenship) were very similar to those of Article 135 (deprivation of citizenship), except that in the former, there is no right of notice and reference to a board of enquiry, whereas these rights existed in the latter. These provisions became the source of great confusion, and the Government amended the Constitution to do away with loss of citizenship by termination.

442. One unique feature of the deprivation provisions in Singapore is found under Article 135(1)(c). It provides that any citizen aged 18 years and above and has been 'ordinarily resident outside Singapore for a continuous period of ten years' and has not entered Singapore (by virtue of either a Certificate of Status or Singapore travel documents) or has not been in the employment of an international organization to which Singapore is a member may be deprived of his or her citizenship.

443. The major legal issue concerning the deprivation of citizenship is the extent to which the decision can be reviewed by the courts. Deprivation of citizenship is an executive administrative action and generally speaking, the same public law principles of judicial review ought to apply. However, section 2 of the Third Schedule provides that a decision of the Government under Part X 'shall not be subject to appeal or review in any court'.

444. The main question posed by section 2 is whether it precludes an applicant seeking an order of certiorari from the courts? In other words, can the High Court review the decision of the Government? The wording of section 2 is almost word-for-word the same as its counterpart in the Malaysian Constitution, and this question was posed in the case of *Mak Sik Kwong v. Minister of Home Affairs, Malaysia.*[180] Justice Abdoolcader (as he then was) held that section 2 did not 'preclude recourse to the courts by way of application for an order of certiorari' and quoting Lord Denning MR in *Tehrani & Anor v. Rostron*[181] he said:

> The modern cases establish this principle: when Parliament says that a decision of an inferior tribunal is to be 'final', it does so on the assumption that the tribunal will observe the law. Parliament only gives the impress of 'finality' to the decision on the condition that it is reached in accordance with law: and the Queen's courts will *see* to it that this condition is fulfilled. Accordingly if a tribunal goes wrong in law and the error appears on the face of the record, the High Court will interfere by certiorari to quash the decision. It is not to be

180. [1975] 2 MLJ 168 (High Court, Malaysia).
181. [1972] 1 QB 182.

deterred by the enactment that the decision is 'final'. The decision may be final on the facts, but it is not final on the law.

445. Justice Abdoolcader went on to add:

> I do not think that there can be any doubt now that it is settled law that a finality or privative clause does not restrict in any way whatsoever the power of the courts to issue certiorari to quash for jurisdictional defect, error of law on the face of the record or manifest fraud. The same process of reasoning has even permitted the courts to interpret ouster clauses expressly referring to prohibition and certiorari and taking away the right to apply for such remedies as still permitting the grant of those remedies for lack of jurisdiction or fraud but the lack of jurisdiction or the fraud must be manifest.

446. The second issue canvassed in *Mak Sik Kwong's* case was whether the act of making an order to deprive someone of his or her citizenship was a purely administrative or ministerial one or was it quasi-judicial in nature. Purely administrative acts are not subject to an order of certiorari. Justice Abdoolcader held that to constitute a quasi-judicial act, it was sufficient if the Minister had an obligation 'to decide questions of law or fact affecting individual rights and exercise a judicial or limited discretion' and that a purely administrative or executive function was 'one where there is no duty to afford a hearing to the parties interested, and where the decision can be made on the basis of policy considerations only'. In this case, the Minister was obliged by Article 27(2) of the Federal Constitution to refer *Mak's* case to a committee of enquiry, and this procedure is thus injected with quasi-judicial elements. As such, the Minister was in fact acting in a quasi-judicial capacity in making the order to deprive Mak of his citizenship and that the Minister was under a duty to determine the rights of individuals and thus under a duty to act fairly. Such orders are subject to the order of certiorari.

447. The decision in *Mak Sik Kwong* was followed in the Singapore High Court case of *Lau Seng Poh v. Controller of Immigration, Singapore*.[182] The principles of judicial review of administrative action enunciated in the landmark case of *Chng Suan Tze v. Minister for Home Affairs, Singapore & Ors and Other Appeals*[183] will no doubt be relevant in ascertaining the ambit of the court's role in judicial review.

---

182. [1985] 2 MLJ 250.
183. [1989] 1 MLJ 69. For a comment on *Chng Suan Tze*, *see* Sin Boon Ann, *Judges and Administrative Discretion – A Look at* Chng Suan Tze v. Minister of Home Affairs & Ors, 2 MLJ ci (1989).

Chapter 2. Fundamental Rights and Liberties

§1. The Protection of Human Rights in the Constitution[184]

448. One of the earliest legal documents safeguarding the rights of citizens against government abuse was the *Magna Carta* (1215) which the barons forced King John of England to sign. This document dealt specifically with abuses of the time, and guaranteed the freedom of the English Church from royal interference. It also protected the property and inheritance rights of heirs and widows, limited taxes, established standing and roving courts, required punishment to fit the crime, and forbade officials from stealing from citizens whether they be nobles or commoners. However, the *Magna Carta* never evolved into a written constitution. The earliest constitutional protection of rights is to be found in the American Bill of Rights (1791). The idea that all human beings had certain rights simply because they are human was spelt out by Thomas Jefferson in the Declaration of Independence (1776) when he wrote:

> We hold these truths to be self-evident, that all men are created equal, that they are endowed by their Creator with certain unalienable Rights, that among these are Life, Liberty and the pursuit of Happiness.

449. James Madison, one of the principal architects of the American Constitution and later America's fourth President, drafted the Bill of Rights (1789) and in 1791 they were passed as the first ten amendments to the American Constitution. Rights protected by these ten amendments include: (a) freedom of religion; (b) freedom of speech, press, petition and assembly; (c) freedom to bear arms; (d) privacy; (e) due process of law; (f) fairness of punishment; and (g) equality before the law.

450. Many constitutions drafted in the nineteenth and twentieth centuries drew heavily on the American example by incorporating various rights into their constitutions. Even the infamous 1936 Soviet Constitution included a whole chapter on 'Fundamental Rights and Duties of Citizens'. Of course, rights are not worth the paper they are written on unless the Government has the political will to honour these limits on their power or the people have some way to compel the Government to obey the Constitution.

451. The need to protect human rights legally gained prominence and urgency following the horrors of World War II and the Holocaust. At the international level, attempts to safeguard human rights culminated in the Universal Declaration of Human Rights (1948) and subsequently in the International Covenant on Civil and Political Rights (1966) and the International Covenant on Economic, Social and Cultural Rights (1966). Naturally, only parties who are parties to these Conventions are legally obliged to obey its terms. Singapore is not a signatory to either of these

184. *See* generally, Li-ann Thio, *Protecting Rights*, in *Evolution of a Revolution: Forty Years of the Singapore Constitution* 193–233 (Li-ann Thio & Kevin Y.L. Tan eds, RoutledgeCurzon 2009).

important human rights conventions. As we shall see, this does not mean that Singapore's Constitution contains no provisions relating to human rights.[185]

§2. Fundamental Liberties under Singapore's Constitution[186]

452. Part IV of Singapore's Constitution is entitled 'Fundamental Liberties' and contains guarantees on: (a) life and liberty; (b) prohibition of slavery and forced labour; (c) protection against retrospective criminal laws and repeated trials; (d) equality and equal protection of the law; (e) prohibition against banishment and freedom of movement; (f) freedom of speech, assembly and association; (g) freedom of religion; and (h) rights in respect of education. In this chapter and the next, we consider how these various liberties and rights have been articulated and limited by the courts. This Part of the Constitution was adopted (almost word-for-word) from the Federation of Malaysia Constitution 1957 by virtue of the Republic of Singapore Independence Act.

453. In framing the Malayan Federal Constitution, the Reid Commission (1957) recommended that the Constitution includes 'certain fundamental individual rights which are generally regarded as essential conditions for a free and democratic way of life'. Even though the Commission felt that the rights were already established throughout the region, they felt constitutional safeguards were necessary because of 'vague apprehensions about the future'.

454. Philosophically, the Malaysian and Singapore governments are pragmatists. For example, Lee Kuan Yew, Singapore's first Prime Minister, once argued that developing countries sometimes have to sacrifice certain liberties 'for the sake of development, security and to prevent communist oppression'. This led the Singapore Government to omit Article 13 of the Federal Constitution guaranteeing the right to property, upon separation on 9 August 1965 because the Government felt that it would impede economic progress and affect the legality of the Land Acquisition Act. Similarly, the Wee Chong Jin Commission (1966) recommended entrenching a provision to protect against torture and inhuman or degrading punishment or treatment, but this recommendation was not adopted as the death penalty would prove problematic otherwise.

455. The framers of the Constitution obviously felt some liberties to be more important than others. Some of them are absolute (e.g., Article 10(1) which states

---

185. *See* Kevin Y.L. Tan, *Fifty Years of the Universal Declaration of Human Rights: A Singapore Reflection*, 20 Sing LR 239–280 (1999).

186. For a general overview, *see* Thio Li-ann, *A Treatise on Singapore Constitutional Law* Chapter 11 (Academy Publishing 2012); Li-ann Thio, *Protecting Rights*, in *Evolution of a Revolution: Forty Years of the Singapore Constitution* 193–233 (Li-ann Thio & Kevin Y.L. Tan eds, RoutledgeCurzon 2009); and R.H. Hickling, *Law and Liberty in Singapore*, 21 Mal LR 1 (1979). *See also* Harry E. Groves, *Fundamental Liberties in the Constitution of the Federation of Malaysia*, in *The Constitution of Malaysia: Its Development, 1957–1977* (Mohamed Suffian, H.P. Lee & F.A. Trindade eds, Oxford U. Press 1978) for a comparative perspective.

that no person may be held in slavery). Others are qualified (e.g., the exceptions to equality under Article 12), or protect only citizens (e.g., freedom of speech, association and assembly under Article 14). The extent to which human rights are realized in Singapore depends on the degree to which these rights are constitutionally qualified, judicially interpreted and the ease with which they may be amended.

§3. Interpreting Fundamental Liberties[187]

456. No court can interpret a constitution without due regard to its historical background, or cognizance of the intention of its framers. To a large extent, constitutional interpretation is a philosophical exercise. Over the last two decades, a big debate has raged over what 'human rights' comprises and how they should be protected. The 'universalists' assert a uniform universal application of human rights norms, while the 'cultural relativists' argue that human rights are essentially a 'Western' construct and therefore inapplicable. 'Asian' or 'communitarian' approaches to human rights advocated by the so-called Singapore School advocate social harmony and group values over individual autonomy and rights.

457. Whichever way we view this debate, the fact is that in an imperfect world, there will be trade-offs. We need to strike a balance between an individual's liberty and the community's right to public order, health and morality. This balancing process is entrusted to the judiciary. How should the appropriate balance be struck? There is one further theoretical difficulty. How do we ascertain the content of human rights? The answer to this question turns on what we understand a human being to be. For example, does the right to life extend to an unborn child?

458. In interpreting the fundamental liberties provisions in the Constitution, the local courts adopt as their starting point Lord Diplock's admonition in *Ong Ah Chuan v. Public Prosecutor*[188] to give the liberties provisions 'a generous interpretation, avoiding what has been called "the austerity of tabulated legalism", suitable to give to individuals the full measure' of these liberties.[189] That said, the courts have at times also adopted a strict textualist reading of the rights provisions, such as in the case of *Chan Hiang Leng Colin v. Public Prosecutor.*[190] In that case, the court had to consider whether the Government's decision to deregister the Jehovah's Witnesses as a society violated Article 15 (freedom of religion) of the Constitution. In

187. *See* Jaclyn CL Neo ed., *Constitutional Interpretation in Singapore: Theory and Practice* (Routledge 2016); Thio Li-ann, *A Treatise on Singapore Constitutional Law* 538–570 (Academy Publishing 2012) ; Li-ann Thio, *Trends in Constitutional Interpretation: Oppugning Ong, Awakening* Arumugam, SJLS 240 (1997); and Li-ann Thio, *An 'I' for an 'I': Singapore's Communitarian Model of Constitutional Adjudication*, 27 Hong Kong L.J. 152 (1997) for insights into how Singapore courts contemplate and balance individual liberties and public policy. For a comparative perspective, *see* Arun K. Thiruvengadam, *Comparative Law and Constitutional Interpretation in Singapore: Insights from Constitutional Theory*, in *Evolution of a Revolution: Forty Years of the Singapore Constitution* 114–152 (Li-ann Thio & Kevin Y.L. Tan eds, Routledge-Cavendish 2009).

188. [19779–1980] SLR(R) 710 (Privy Council on appeal from Singapore).

189. *Ibid.*, at [23].

190. [1994] 3 SLR(R) 209 (High Court, Singapore).

the course of his judgment, Yong Pung How CJ held that the 'right of freedom of religion must be reconciled with the right of the State to employ the sovereign power to ensure peace, security and orderly living without which constitutional guarantee of civil liberty would be a mockery'. As such, the 'sovereignty, integrity and unity of Singapore' were 'undoubtedly the paramount mandate of the Constitution and anything, including religious beliefs and practices, which tend to run counter to these objectives must be restrained'.[191]

§4. Protection of Life and Liberty

459. Article 9(1) of the Constitution provides that 'No person shall be deprived of his life or personal liberty save in accordance with law.' This article looks simple enough, but there are serious definitional issues. What exactly do we mean when we use words like 'person', 'personal liberty' and 'law'? Does 'person' include an unborn foetus? If it does, then abortion would be considered illegal. In the following section, we consider how the local courts have interpreted this particular provision. Here, as elsewhere throughout this book, Malaysian decisions carry much persuasive weight, especially where the corresponding constitutional provisions are practically identical.

I. Meaning of 'Life' and 'Personal Liberty'

460. There is no local case interpreting the meaning of 'life' under Article 9(1) although most cases deal with this article on the basis that the word 'life' means physical life. However, it appears that the Malaysian Court of Appeal was prepared to adopt a broader definition of 'life' in the Malaysian Article 5(1) (which is identical to Singapore's Article 9(1)) in *Tan Tek Seng v. Suruhanjaya Perkhidmatan Pendidikan*,[192] which concerned the dismissal of a public servant. Gopal Sri Ram JCA held that the expression 'life' in the Constitution did not refer to mere existence but included 'all those facets that are an integral part of life itself and those matters which go to form the quality of life'. These included the right to seek and be engaged in lawful and gainful employment; to receive those benefits that society has to offer to its members; and the right to live in a reasonably healthy and pollution-free environment. This expansive view of the meaning of 'life' is, however, unlikely to be adopted by the Singapore courts.

461. The word 'personal liberty' in Article 9(1) has been given a restrictive meaning by the local courts. In *Government of Malaysia & Ors v. Loh Wai Kong*,[193] the Malaysian Federal Court held that 'personal liberty' only related to liberty concerning the body of the individual. As such, it did not include the right to leave the

---

191. *Ibid.*, at [64].
192. [1996] 1 MLJ 261 (Court of Appeal, Malaysia).
193. [1979] 2 MLJ 33.

country, the right to travel overseas, nor the right to a passport. 'Personal liberty' is thus restricted to physical incarceration of the individual, his or her punishment and suffering in body.[194]

II. Meaning of 'In Accordance with Law'

462. The meaning of the word 'law' in the phrase *in accordance with law* is one of the key issues in the interpretation of Article 9(1). Two alternatives are possible. 'Law' can either mean duly enacted law (whether the law be fair or not) or it could incorporate some substantive test of fairness. If the second interpretation is adopted, a duly enacted piece of legislation will fail as 'law' if it fell short of a certain standard of, for example, fairness.

463. Prior to 1981, the Singapore courts construed the phrase restrictively. All that the Constitution required was that the legislation be enacted in due form and within the legislature's competence. As such, the reasonableness of such law could not be called into question, no matter how arbitrary it was.[195]

464. In the seminal case of *Ong Ah Chuan v. PP*,[196] the Privy Council rejected this literal interpretation. Lord Diplock held that the word 'law' in any Westminster-based constitution, particularly in chapters relating to fundamental liberties, must refer to a system of law which incorporates the fundamental rules of natural justice:

> In a constitution founded on the Westminster model and particularly in that part of it that purports to assure to all individual citizens the continued enjoyment of fundamental liberties or rights, references to 'law' in such contexts as 'in accordance with law', 'equality before the law', 'protection of the law' and the like, in their Lordship's view, refer to a system of law which incorporates those fundamental rules of natural justice that had formed part and parcel of the common law of England that was in operation in Singapore at the commencement of the Constitution. It would have been taken for granted by the makers of the Constitution that the 'law' to which citizens could have recourse for the protection of fundamental liberties assured to them by the Constitution would be a system of law that did not flout those fundamental rules. If it were otherwise it would be misuse of language to speak of law as something which affords 'protection' for the individual in the enjoyment of his fundamental liberties, and the purported entrenchment of arts 9(1) and 12(1) would be little better than a mockery.

---

194. *See also Public Prosecutor v. Tengku Mahmood Iskandar & Anor* [1973] 1 MLJ 128 (High Court, Malaysia).
195. *See Arumugam Pillai v. Government of Malaysia* [1975] 2 MLJ 29 (Federal Court, Malaysia).
196. [1981] 1 MLJ 64. For a discussion on what might constitute natural justice in the Constitution, *see* A.J. Harding, *Natural Justice and the Constitution*, 23 Mal LR 226 (1981) which considers how courts interpret what constitutes 'natural justice' in the Constitution.

465. As to what is exactly covered by these 'fundamental rules of natural justice', the judges remain elusive. For example, in *Haw Tua Tau v. PP*,[197] the Privy Council held that it would 'be imprudent … to attempt to make a comprehensive list of what constitute fundamental rules of natural justice applicable to procedure for determining the guilt of a person charged with a criminal offence'.

466. Attractive as the concept of 'rules of natural justice' may be, the guidelines enunciated by the Privy Council do not make it sufficiently clear as to how we can go about identifying what these rules of natural justice are. Even so, Singapore courts have not dismissed this concept outright. In *PP v. Mazlan bin Maidun*,[198] for example, Chief Justice Yong Pung How referred to the concept but held that 'the right of silence [at trial] has never been regarded as subsumed under the principles of natural justice'.[199]

467. The case of *Jabar v. PP*[200] marked a return to the *Arumugam* positivist position. The question before the court was whether a five-and-a-half-year time lapse between the date of a death sentence conviction and the scheduled date of execution constituted such a prolonged delay such that carrying out the execution constituted cruel and inhuman punishment. Jabar argued such a cruel and inhuman punishment was not in accordance with law and was thus unconstitutional. Chief Justice Yong Pung How, sitting in the Court of Appeal, held that:

> Any law which provides for the deprivation of a person's life or personal liberty is valid and binding so long as it is validly passed by Parliament. The court is not concerned with whether it is also fair, just and reasonable as well.[201]

III. Death Penalty and Life Imprisonment

468. Is the deprivation of life through mandatory death penalties permitted under Article 9(1)? This was considered in the Malaysian Federal Court case of *Public Prosecutor v. Lau Kee Hoo*[202] and the Malaysian High Court in *Public Prosecutor v. Yee Kim Seng*.[203] In these two cases, that relevant law was the ISA 1960 of Malaysia. The courts have also been invited to adjudicate on the wisdom or

197. [1981] 2 MLJ 49.
198. [1993] 1 SLR 512.
199. *See* generally, Swati Jhaveri, *The Broader Case for Developing the Content of Fundamental Rules of Natural Justice under Article 9 of the Constitution: A Placeholder for a Proportionality-Type Adjudication?*, in *Constitutional Interpretation in Singapore: Theory and Practice* 188–209 (Jaclyn LC Neo ed., Routledge 2016).
200. [1995] 1 SLR 617.
201. *See* Thio Li-ann, *Trends in Constitutional Interpretation: Oppugning Ong: Awakening* Arumugam?, SJLS 240–290 (1997).
202. [1983] 1 MLJ 157 (Federal Court, Malaysia).
203. [1983] 1 MLJ 252 (High Court, Malaysia).

appropriateness of the death penalty and they declined. Both courts considered mandatory death penalties constitutional, and Ajaib Singh J in *Yee Kim Seng* held that the court was not concerned with the fairness or reasonableness of the law.

469. In the Singapore High Court case of *Public Prosecutor v. Nguyen Tuong Van*,[204] it was argued that hanging was 'cruel and unusual punishment' that violated Article 9(1) of the Constitution as well as the Universal Declaration of Human Rights. Justice Kan Ting Chiu held that as the Declaration was not an international treaty or convention with binding effect on Singapore and nor was it a codification of customary international law, the argument failed. This was affirmed by the Court of Appeal.[205]

470. The question of whether mandatory life imprisonment is prohibited by Article 9(1) was considered by the Federal Court in *Che Ani bin Itam v. Public Prosecutor*.[206] The issue was whether there was anything in the provision for mandatory life imprisonment that makes it unconstitutional on the grounds that it infringes the fundamental rules of natural justice. Lord President Raja Azlan Shah considered the Indian Supreme Court in *Maneka Gandhi v. Union of India*[207] where Bhagwati J held that procedure prescribed by law has to be 'fair, just and reasonable, not fanciful, oppressive or arbitrary', and held that there was nothing 'fanciful, oppressive or arbitrary' in the legislatively defined sentence for the specific offence in question under the Firearms (Increased Penalties) Act, 1971. This seems to suggest a willingness by the courts to consider the reasonableness of the legislative enactment.

§5. Rights of an Accused Person

471. Article 9(2), (3) and (4) of the Constitution contains constitutional protections for an arrested person. At this juncture, we will examine the protection offered by Clauses 2 and 3 of Article 9, that is, the writ of habeas corpus and the right to counsel.

I. Writ of Habeas Corpus

472. Article 9(2) provides that where a complaint is made to the High Court that a person is being unlawfully detained, the court must enquire into the complaint and, unless satisfied that the detention is lawful, must order him or her to be produced before the court and release him or her. The complainant applies by way of a writ of habeas corpus or Order for the Review of Detention (ORD). The complaint need not be brought by the person in custody himself or herself, but can be

204. [2004] 2 SLR 328.
205. [2005] 1 SLR(R) 103.
206. [1984] 1 MLJ 113 (Federal Court, Malaysia).
207. 1978 SC 597 (Supreme Court, India).

brought by someone else on his or her behalf. The nature of the ORD was noted by Mr Justice Choor Singh in *Re Onkar Shrian*[208] where he held:

> The writ of habeas corpus is of English origin and ... the writ is a prerogative process of securing the liberty of the subject by affording an effective means of immediate release from unlawful or unjustifiable detention, whether in prison or in private custody. By it the High Court and the judges of that court, at the instance of a subject aggrieved, command the production of that subject, and inquire into the cause of his imprisonment. If there is no legal justification for the detention, the party is ordered to be released. Release on habeas corpus is not, however an acquittal nor may the writ be used as a means of appeal. The writ is applicable as a remedy in all cases of wrongful deprivation of personal liberty. Where the detention of an individual is under process for criminal or supposed criminal causes the jurisdiction of court and the regularity of the commitment may be inquired into. Where the personal freedom of an individual is wrongly interfered with by another, the release of the former from illegal detention may be effected by habeas corpus. The illegal detention of a subject, that is a detention or imprisonment which is incapable of legal justification, is the basis of jurisdiction in *habeas corpus*.

473. Several issues regarding the right to ORD come up for consideration. First, what is the meaning of the word 'detention' in Article 9(2)? Is the writ of habeas corpus only available to someone who is in physical custody? Or does it extend to someone who is on bail? Can a person whose movements are restricted be considered to be under 'detention'? Second, who bears the burden of proof to show that the detention is unlawful? How does the burden shift, and what does the burden require the parties to prove in such an action? Third, are there restrictions on an applicant for habeas corpus? Will the court refuse to entertain an application for a prerogative writ unless the applicant has exhausted all alternative remedies? Finally, does the denial of the right to consult counsel warrant an application for habeas corpus?

474. In *Kamal Jit Singh v. Minister for Home Affairs*,[209] the SGCA made three important rulings on the ORD: (1) the writ would only issue on probable cause shown by affidavit; (2) the onus of showing probable cause falls on the applicant; and (3) once probable cause is shown, the court has no discretion to refuse the applicant the writ. Habeas corpus is not available to a person who is out on bail (*see Re Onkar Shrian*)[210] where the Singapore High Court held that:

> if a person is not detained in custody he is not entitled to a writ of habeas corpus. A person on bail cannot by any stretch of imagination be said to be detained in custody and is therefore not entitled to a writ of *habeas corpus*.

---

208. [1970] 1 MLJ 28.
209. [1993] 1 SLR 24.
210. [1970] 1 MLJ 28.

475. In the Malaysian case of *Yeap Hock Seng @ Ah Seng v. Minister for Home Affairs, Malaysia & Ors,*[211] the right to apply for habeas corpus was available even though the applicant had not exhausted other possible alternate remedies, provided he alleged that his fundamental rights had been abridged. However, a denial of the right to counsel did not entitle a detainee to apply for habeas corpus.[212]

§6. THE RIGHTS OF ARRESTED PERSONS: ARTICLE 9(3)

476. Article 9(3) of the Constitution reads:

> 9(3) Where a person is arrested, he shall be informed *as soon as may be* of the grounds of his arrest and shall be allowed *to consult and be defended by a legal practitioner of his choice.*

Under this provision, an arrested person has three related rights: (1) the right to be informed as soon as may be of the grounds of his or her arrest; (2) the right to consult counsel; and (3) the right to be defended by a lawyer of his or her choice. Let us consider each of these rights in turn.

I. The Right to Be Informed of the Grounds of Arrest

477. The main issue here is the meaning of 'as soon as may be' used in Article 9(3). In *Aminah v. Superintendent of Prison, Pengkalan Chapa, Kelantan,*[213] Wan Suleiman J held, following the Indian Supreme Court decision in *Tarapade v. State of West Bengal* (1959), that the words 'as soon as may be' mean 'as nearly as is reasonable in the circumstances of the particular case'. As to how the arrested person is to be informed, the court in *Re PE Long @ Jimmy*[214] held that this could be done orally although such evidence will be difficult to prove in court.

II. The Right to Consult Counsel[215]

478. When does the right to counsel arise, and when may it be exercised? In *Lee Mau Seng v. Minister for Home Affairs, Singapore & Anor,*[216] Chief Justice Wee Chong Jin held that the right to counsel arose the moment the person is arrested but was only 'entitled to have this constitutional right granted to him by the authority'

211. [1975] 2 MLJ 279 (High Court, Malaysia).
212. *Lee Mau Seng v. Minister for Home Affairs, Singapore & Anor* [1971] 2 MLJ 137.
213. [1968] 1 MLJ 92.
214. [1976] 2 MLJ 133 (High Court, Malaysia).
215. On the right to counsel, *see* Michael Hor, *The Right to Consult a Lawyer on Arrest*, 3 CLAS News 4 (1989), and 4 CLAS News 4 (1989); and Michael Hor, *The Right to Counsel – The Right to Be Informed*, 5 SALJ 141 (1993).
216. [1971] 2 MLJ 137. This position was affirmed in the subsequent High Court decision in *James Raj Arokiasamy v. Public Prosecutor* [2014] 3 SLR 750.

who has him in custody. Such right must be granted within a reasonable time after arrest. As such, the arrested person cannot exercise his or her right to counsel immediately but only after 'reasonable time' is given to the police to conduct their investigations. In the Singapore Court of Criminal Appeal case of *Jasbir Singh v. PP*,[217] Chief Justice Yong Pung How held that a two-week hiatus between the accused's arrest and his or her seeing his or her counsel was reasonable.

III. Ambit of the Right to Counsel

479. A problem that is likely to arise in practice is: how does this right to counsel relate to the person detained? The prisoner is often unaware of his or her right to consult counsel or has no way of nominating counsel when he or she does not know of any particular counsel. In many cases, the family will engage counsel on the prisoner's behalf. Problems arise when counsel tries to gain access to the prisoner. Does the constitutional right to counsel extend to require the detaining authority to admit the lawyer even though the prisoner is unaware of his or her right to consult counsel or appoint such a lawyer to represent him or her? In this situation, it becomes a case of the counsel claiming the right to see his or her client. Can counsel claim the benefit on behalf of his or her client who has not appointed him or her? These issues were canvassed in the case of *Rajeevan Edakalvan v. Public Prosecutor*[218] where Yong Pung How CJ held that Article 9(3) did not confer on an accused, a 'constitutional right to be informed of one's right to counsel'.[219]

480. Another dilemma the courts face is where counsel has been instructed by the prisoner but fails to turn up or is not willing to represent the prisoner. Can the prisoner claim that his or her constitutional right to counsel has been violated and as such any proceedings against him or her are rendered null and void? The right to counsel does give the prisoner the right to demand that a particular lawyer represents him or her. The right is designed to make him or her aware of his or her rights as a prisoner and to receive the benefit of proper legal advice while in detention and while under interrogation.

481. Can the prisoner insist on being defended by a particular lawyer? After all, Article 9(3) states that he or she should be 'allowed to consult and be defended by a legal practitioner of his choice'. In *Re Seed Nigel John QC*,[220] the applicant Seed, a Queen's Counsel (QC) with extensive experience in ecclesiastical practice, sought ad hoc admission as an advocate and solicitor under section 21 of the Legal Professions Act to represent Father Joachim Kang, a Catholic priest charged with criminal breach of trust. In rejecting his application, Justice Tay Yong Kwang held that the prisoner's right under Article 9(3) was subject to: (a) the lawyer's willingness and ability to act for him or her; and (b) the lawyer being properly admitted under

217. [1994] 2 SLR 18.
218. [1998] 1 SLR(R) 10 (High Court, Singapore).
219. *Ibid.*, at [21].
220. [2003] 3 SLR 407.

the Legal Professions Act. The law does not require the court to admit any QC chosen by the prisoner. The court concluded that while Seed had the special qualifications for the purposes of the case, the case was not of sufficient complexity to warrant his admission.

IV. Conclusion

482. The rights to life and liberty are often considered the most important of all the rights enumerated in the Constitution. The general ideal underlying these constitutional provisions is that a man is innocent till proven guilty. It also imports the corollary idea that if a person is to be deprived of his or her life or liberty, the strictest adherence to the letter of the law must be required. As can be seen, the courts have generally been conservative and positivist in their approach to construing the ambit of an individual's constitutional rights and guarantees. In the rare instance that the court ventured to adopt an object test in the determination of ministerial 'satisfaction', the legislature moved swiftly to restore the equilibrium in favour of the executive. Over the years, laws relating to criminal procedure and sentencing have been regularly amended to make it easier for the prosecution to prove their case. In many instances, there are built-in assumptions of guilt and a corresponding shift in the burden of proof to the accused. Even the safeguard of having two judges preside over trials where the death penalty is involved has been removed. As the foregoing discussion shows, the balance between the efficient prosecution of criminals and the desirability of mounting pre-emptive strikes against potential subversives seems to have prevailed over the need to maximize and safeguard individual liberty.

§7. Protection Against Slavery and Forced Labour: Article 10

483. There are three parts to Article 10: (i) prohibition against slavery, (ii) exception for forced labour for national purposes, and (iii) labour while serving a prison sentence.

I. Slavery

484. Article 10(1) provides that 'No person shall be held in slavery.' This is the most absolute among all the fundamental liberties listed in Singapore's Constitution. No 'ifs'; no 'buts': slavery is absolutely forbidden. What happens if someone does in fact hold another in slavery? What is considered 'slavery'? There has been no litigation on this point, and one can only surmise that the natural ordinary dictionary of 'slave' and 'slavery' will be used to interpret this article. The *Oxford Compact Dictionary* defines *slave* as 'a person who is the legal property of another and is forced to obey them' and *slavery* as 'the state of being a slave' and 'the practice or system of owning slaves'.

485. This definition is broad, and the court will probably consider the much broader definition in the Supplementary Convention on the Abolition of Slavery, the Slave Trade, and Institutions and Practices Similar to Slavery 1957, to which Singapore is a party. This definition includes the following:

(a) Debt bondage, that is to say, the status or condition arising from a pledge by a debtor of his personal services or of those of a person under his control as security for a debt, if the value of those services as reasonably assessed is not applied towards the liquidation of the debt or the length and nature of those services are not respectively limited and defined.
(b) Serfdom, that is to say, the condition or status of a tenant who is by law, custom or agreement bound to live and labour on land belonging to another person and to render some determinate service to such other person, whether for reward or not, and is not free to change his status.
(c) Any institution or practice whereby:
   - a woman, without the right to refuse, is promised or given in marriage on payment of a consideration in money or in kind to her parents, guardian, family or any other person or group; or
   - the husband of a woman, his family, or his clan, has the right to transfer her to another person for value received or otherwise; or
   - a woman on the death of her husband is liable to be inherited by another person.
(d) Any institution or practice whereby a child or young person under the age of 18 years is delivered by either or both of his natural parents or by his guardian to another person, whether for reward or not, with a view to the exploitation of the child or young person or of his labour.

486. Section 370 of the Penal Code makes it an offence for anyone to buy, dispose or keep anyone as a slave. An offender may be jailed for up to seven years, fined and have his or her property confiscated under the Corruption, Drug Trafficking and Other Serious Crimes (Confiscation of Benefits) Act.[221] It is likewise an offence to kidnap or abduct a person for slavery.[222] Punishment for the latter offence is imprisonment for up to ten years, fine and caning.

II. Forced Labour

487. The second part of Article 10 provides that:

> All forms of forced labour are prohibited, but Parliament may by law provide for compulsory service for national purposes.

---

221. Cap 84A, Singapore Statutes.
222. Section 367, Penal Code (Cap 224), Singapore Statutes.

This provision is designed to absolve the Government from any charges of slavery or forced labour when it legislates for compulsory military service or civil defence service. In this respect, the key legislation is the Enlistment Act.[223]

III. Prison Sentences

488. The third part of Article 10 provides that 'work incidental to the serving of a sentence of imprisonment imposed by a court of law' shall not be regarded as 'forced labour'.

§8. Protection Against Retrospective Criminal Laws: Article 11

489. Ex post facto or retrospective criminal laws are inherently undesirable as they violate the notion of fair notice and the rule of law. It is unfair to punish a person for doing an act which was not a crime at the time he or she did it, but was then retrospectively made a crime. Article 11(1) provides:

> No person shall be punished for an act or omission which was not punishable by law when it was done or made, and no person shall suffer greater punishment for an offence than was prescribed by law at the time it was committed.

490. Article 11(1) has two limbs. It forbids the retrospective: (a) creation of offences; and (b) increase in the punishment for existing offences. This ban on retrospective laws applies only to criminal offences, and the operative time of this provision is the time of the act or omission, or the time the offence was committed.

491. What about pending actions? As a general rule, statutes that come into force while an action is pending and which alter the substantive law do not affect the rights of the parties. The action is then disposed of according to the law existing at the time the offence was committed. This appears to be the position unless the statute explicitly intends rights to be affected.

492. It is well recognized that statutes are interpreted in a manner that respects vested rights. The basis of this rule is the presumption that the legislature does not intend to alter or interfere with existing rights. Where the statute is ambiguous, the courts lean towards an interpretation that maintains the status quo. It is to be noted that in relation to repealing acts, section 16 of the Interpretation Act[224] provides specifically that any rights vested should not be disturbed by the coming into force of such acts and the proceeding should continue with such rights being observed and respected, that is as it would proceed under the law before the change occurred.

223. Cap 93, Singapore Statutes.
224. Cap 1, Singapore Statutes.

Since there is no vested right in procedure, this presumption does not apply to statutes which merely alter or affect procedural matters or matters of the practice of the courts. However, there is a notable exception to this rule. This relates to statutes which take away a right of appeal. The Privy Council held, in *Colonial Sugar Refining Co. v. Irving*,[225] that in a pending action, the deprivation of a party's right of appeal was the removal of substantive right, not a procedural one.

I. Amending the Constitution Retrospectively

493. What if the Constitution is amended with retrospective effect? Flowing from the presumption that the legislature does not intend what is unjust, there is a common law rule of statutory interpretation that presumes that a statute is not intended to have retrospective effect, unless there is a clear legislative intent otherwise. Courts will thus lean towards construing any statute as operating only in cases or facts that come into being after the statute is enacted.

II. Retrospective Changes in Procedure

494. Is a change in trial procedure void under Article 11(1) if it is made after the offence was committed? These changes take various forms, for example, changes in the mode of trial from a trial before judge and jury to a trial before judge alone;[226] abolishing the accused's right to make unsworn statements from the dock;[227] or making a hitherto non-extraditable offence extraditable.[228]

495. The words of Article 11(1) only extend to the retrospective *creation of offences* and the retrospective increase in punishment for existing offences. The courts have consistently drawn a clear distinction between substance and procedure, holding that Article 11(1) only protects substantive changes to law, for example, creation of a new offence as opposed to procedural matters like changes to the mode of trial.

III. Removal of Sentencing Discretion

496. Many statutory provisions give the court discretion to choose between two forms of punishment. What happens if a statute is amended to remove this discretion? If the prescribed mandatory punishment is the more severe of the two forms of punishment the court had previous discretion over, does such an amendment violate Article 11(1)?

---

225. [1905] AC 643.
226. *Lim Sing Hiaw v. Public Prosecutor* [1965] 1 MLJ 85 (Federal Court, Malaysia).
227. *Haw Tua Tau v. Public Prosecutor* [1981] 2 MLJ 49.
228. *Chua Han Mow v. Superintendent of Pudu Prison* [1979] 2 MLJ 70.

497. In the Malaysian High Court case of *Public Prosecutor v. Mohamed Ismail*,[229] the accused was convicted of trafficking in a dangerous drug, contrary to section 39B(1) of the Dangerous Drugs Act, 1952. On the day he was convicted, section 39B(1) was amended by section 14 of the Dangerous Drugs (Amendment) Act, 1983 which removed the court's discretion to impose either life imprisonment or the death penalty. Instead, the death sentence became mandatory. The issue before the court was the material date for determining sentence for such offences. Was it the date of the offence or the date of the conviction? If the relevant date was the date of conviction, would Article 11(1) operate to strike down the amendment in this particular case? Mr Justice Edgar Joseph Jr (as he then was) held that the amendment violated Article 7(1) of the Federal Constitution (which is identical to Singapore's Article 11(1)), and that where the offence was committed prior to the date of the amending law, the judge retained discretion on the matter of sentencing.

498. In *Public Prosecutor v. Hun Peng Khai & Ors*,[230] the question before the Malaysian High Court was whether sections 15 and 16 of the Dangerous Drugs (Amendment) Act 1983 violated Article 7(1) of the Federal Constitution. The amendment effectively removed the Sessions Courts' jurisdiction and its discretion to impose sentences of either life imprisonment and/or whipping; it also made the death penalty mandatory. Justice Edgar Joseph Jr (as he then was) held that the amendments were not retrospective either by express enactment or by necessary implication. As such, once an accused is charged and his or her case fixed for hearing in the Sessions Court, that gave them a vested right to trial in that court.

499. In *PP v. Tan Teck Hin*,[231] the respondent Tan was convicted by a District Court for driving under the influence of drink under section 67(1) of the Road Traffic Act on 28 July 1991. The offence was committed on 9 June 1991. Tan had previously been convicted of a similar offence on 5 March 1990. Section 67(1) of the Road Traffic Act was amended on 2 April 1990 to increase the punishment for both first time and repeat offenders. Justice Warren Khoo, sitting in the Singapore Court of Criminal Appeal, held that Tan must be dealt with as a first offender under the amended section 67(1) for to treat him 'as a second offender under the re-enacted section is to apply the re-enacted section to him retrospectively', and this was contrary to Article 11(1).

500. In *Harry Lee Wee v. Public Prosecutor*,[232] the appellant Wee was charged under section 213 of the Penal Code with eight charges of obtaining restitution in consideration of the concealment of the offence of criminal breach of trust committed by his legal assistant, and of attempting to obtain such restitution. The District Court convicted him and imposed fines amounting to SGD 30,000. The offences were committed in 1976, and the trial was conducted in 1978. At the time of the offences, section 17 of the Criminal Procedure Code empowered the District Court

229. [1984] 2 MLJ 219.
230. [1984] 2 MLJ 318.
231. [1992] 2 SLR 841.
232. [1980] 2 MLJ 56.

to impose punishments to the limit of its jurisdiction on each charge brought before it, as long as the aggregate fine imposed in respect to the several charges did not exceed double the amount of its jurisdiction on fines for a single offence. In 1977, section 17 was amended to remove this limit. Under the amended provision, so long as the District Court keeps within its jurisdiction for each offence, there is no ceiling on the aggregate amount of the fine that it could impose. Wee argued that this amendment infringed the second limb of Article 11(1). Mr Justice Choor Singh held that the punishment prescribed under section 213 of the Penal Code was not changed by the amendment. The amendment only affected the District Court's powers to impose fines, and as such, no ex post facto legislation was enacted or altered, nor was any punishment under section 213 of the Penal Code increased.

IV. Protection Against Double Jeopardy

501. Article 11(2) of the Constitution provides:

> A person who has been convicted or acquitted of an offence shall not be tried again for the same offence except where the conviction or acquittal has been quashed and a retrial ordered by a court superior to that by which he was acquitted or convicted.

This provision embodies the principle that no person should be tried or punished more than once on the same accusation, based on the same set of facts. This principle is commonly known as the rule against double jeopardy and extends only to criminal proceedings.

502. This constitutional principle is further buttressed by section 239 of the Criminal Procedure Code:

> 239. A person who has once been tried by a court of competent jurisdiction for an offence and convicted or acquitted of that offence shall, while the conviction or acquittal remains in force, not be liable to be tried again for the same offence nor on the same facts for any other offence for which a different charge from the one made against him might have been made under section 172 or for which he might have been convicted under section 173 or 174.

503. However, section 239 further provides that a person who has been acquitted or convicted of any offence may still be 'tried for any distinct offence for which a separate charge might be made against him'.

504. A dismissal of a complaint or a discharge of the accused is not an 'acquittal' under the Criminal Procedure Code:

> The first issue under Article 11(2) is: what amounts to a 'conviction' or an 'acquittal'? An accused who is acquitted by a competent court cannot again be

tried for the same offence. However, if the first trial is quashed as a nullity – the effect being that there was never such a trial – can the prosecution bring the same charge for the same offence against him? If a retrial is ordered, there would be no difficulty, but can the accused challenge a fresh proceeding if no retrial is ordered? What if the accused was convicted but the trial later declared a nullity. Can he challenge a subsequent attempt by the prosecution to bring the same charges against him?

505. In *Fan Yew Teng v. Public Prosecutor*,[233] the appellant Fan was convicted of sedition. On appeal, his conviction was quashed as a nullity and Fan was subsequently rearrested, charged and convicted with the same offence. The issue before the court was whether the second conviction infringed Article 7(2) of the Federal Constitution (which is identical to Singapore's Article 11(2)). A subsidiary issue was whether the new trial initiated on the same charge infringed the same article. Lee Hun Hoe CJ (Borneo) held that when Fan's earlier trial was declared a nullity, he was never in any jeopardy. As such, he was 'not a person who has been convicted of an offence' within the meaning of Article 11(2). Where a trial is declared a nullity, there was in fact no trial. As such, the trial court could neither convict nor acquit, and Fan's retrial and conviction did not contravene Article 7(2).

506. The same principles applied if a joint trial was subsequently nullified. This occurred in *Sau Soo Kim v. Public Prosecutor*[234] where the appellant Sau and another person were jointly charged and tried in the High Court. Sau was acquitted while the other person was convicted. The convicted person appealed, and the Malaysian Federal Court set aside his conviction, declaring the trial a nullity. Subsequently, both the accused were separately recharged and retried. Although Sau pleaded guilty and was convicted, he appealed to the Federal Court to set aside his conviction. He argued that as there was no appeal against his initial acquittal, it remained in force even after his co-accused's appeal, and as such, his retrial contravened Article 7(2). Lee Hun Hoe CJ (Borneo) held that when the joint trial was nullified, the High Court could not either convict or acquit. Consequently, Sau must be regarded as having only been discharged, and his retrial did not violate Article 7(2).

V. Meaning of 'Same Offence'

507. The Constitution does not define the meaning of the words 'same offence' under Article 11. Must the 'offence' relate to a court action? In *Jamali Bin Adnan v. Public Prosecutor*[235] (1986), the appellant Jamali was arrested, and he led the police to a place where two revolvers and several rounds of ammunition were recovered. After police investigations, he was separately charged for four counts of robbery

233. [1975] 2 MLJ 235 (Federal Court, Malaysia).
234. [1975] 2 MLJ 134 (Federal Court, Malaysia).
235. [1986] 1 MLJ 163.

with a deadly weapon. He pleaded guilty to all counts and was sentenced to a total of six years' imprisonment and five strokes of the cane. While Jamali was still serving out his sentence, he was again charged, but this time for unlawful control of the two revolvers and twenty-nine rounds of ammunition under the ISA 1960. He was sentenced to death for one of the charges.

508. The question of law referred to the Malaysian Supreme Court was: can Jamali be charged for an offence under the ISA 1960 even after he had been charged, tried and convicted and then sentenced for four robberies with a deadly weapon under the Penal Code? The court held that 'same offence' was one in which 'the ingredients are the same', and that a comparison of the charges indicated that the essential ingredients of the two offences were not the same:

> as armed robbery can be regarded as an aggravated form of theft causing fear of instant death or hurt on the intended victim voluntarily by means of a deadly weapon. On the other hand, the essential ingredients under the Internal Security Act 1960 are simply control of firearms and/or ammunitions without lawful authority.

509. What if parallel proceedings are brought in domestic tribunals and courts? With the growth of the administrative state, it is not uncommon to find a public employee subjected to disciplinary proceedings instituted by his or her statutory body as well as criminal proceedings in the courts. Do disciplinary proceedings that parallel criminal proceedings infringe Article 11(2)? Are these in fact proceedings for 'the same offence'?

510. This question came up for consideration in the Singapore High Court in *Mohamed Yusoff bin Samadi v. Attorney-General*[236] where the plaintiff Yusoff was charged with five counts of outraging the modesty of his students. Yusoff was acquitted, but the Public Service Commission commenced disciplinary proceedings against him with a view to dismissing him. He applied to the High Court for a declaration that Regulation 11 of the Public Service (Disciplinary Proceedings) Regulations 1970, under which the disciplinary proceeding proceeded, was void as being in violation of Article 11(2). Justice FA Chua held that the word 'offence' means 'any act or omission punishable by law' and that the charges against Yusoff before the Committee of Enquiry were for 'misconduct with outraging the modesty of certain of his girl pupils'. He was thus not being tried for the 'same offence' since professional misconduct is not an offence against the law.

VI. Preventive Detention

511. Does Article 11(2) apply to preventive detention cases? What happens if a person is subject to a fresh detention order after the initial order expires? Can he or

236. [1975] 1 MLJ 1.

she challenge the subsequent order by arguing that he or she had already been punished once before by the first order, and that the second order would be to punish him or her a second time for the same offence? What happens if the authorities employ preventive detention powers (e.g., under the Criminal Law (Temporary Provisions) Act) to detain criminals against whom they are unable to gather sufficient evidence? The accused may be discharged from the trial or even acquitted, but subsequently served with a detention order. Can the accused challenge the validity of his or her detention on the basis that he or she is being subject to the peril of legal sanctions twice for the same offence?

512. In *Public Prosecutor v. Musa*,[237] the respondent Musa was detained under section 8(1)(a) of the ISA and subsequently served with a restriction order under section 8(1)(b) of the same Act. The issue before the Malaysian High Court was whether the detention or restriction order was equivalent to a conviction for an offence for the purposes of Article 7(2) of the Malaysian Constitution (which is the same as Singapore's Article 11(2)). Justice Syed Othman held that:

> the Minister's decision to detain someone under the Internal Security Act was not a conviction for an offence or crime and the detention or restriction order is not a punishment for the purpose of Article 7 of the Constitution.

513. In *Yeap Hock Seng @ Ah Seng v. Minister for Home Affairs, Malaysia & Ors*,[238] the appellant Yeap was arrested along with six others and charged with murder. Due to a lack of evidence, the accused were discharged, but as the seven of them walked out of the courthouse, they were immediately arrested and served with a detention order made by the Minister under the emergency (Public Order and Prevention of Crime) Ordinance, 1969. Yeap argued that the detention order was null and void as it infringed the rule against double jeopardy embodied in Article 7(2) of the Federal Constitution. Justice Abdoolcader (as he then was) held that as the whole essence of preventive detention was incarceration without trial, with no offence proved or charge formulated, it did not constitute a 'trial'. As such, the detention order made against Yeap following his discharge by the court did not violate the Constitution.

VII. Common Law Doctrine of Autrefois Convict

514. An important question is whether Article 11(2) is an exclusive statement of the doctrine of double jeopardy. Can it be argued that it is only part of a wider common law doctrine of double jeopardy? The fact that the doctrine is constitutionally provided under Article 11(2) does not preclude the existence of a wider common law doctrine. An enunciation of this wider common law doctrine is found in the

237. [1970] 1 MLJ 101 (High Court, Malaysia).
238. [1975] 2 MLJ 279 (High Court, Malaysia).

judgment of Lord Morris of Borth-y-Gest in the House of Lords decision of *Connelly v. Director of Public Prosecutions*[239] which held that:

> one test as to whether the rule applies is whether the evidence which is necessary to support the second indictment, or whether the facts which constitute the second offence, would have been sufficient to procure a legal conviction upon the first indictment either as to the offence charged or as to an offence which, on the indictment, the accused could have been found guilty.

This proposition is clearly wider than that pronounced in *Jamali Bin Adnan's* case[240] (discussed above). Although the court in *Jamali Bin Adnan's* case declined to refer to *Connelly*'s case and preferred to restrict itself to the words of the Constitution, there is really nothing to prevent the court from looking to the common law doctrine as well for the reasons stated above.

515. Moreover, such an approach is consistent with that taken in the Privy Council opinion in *Harry Lee Wee v. Law Society of Singapore*.[241] In that case, the Law Society suspended the appellant Wee from legal practice for two years for professional misconduct. Following his conviction on a criminal charge which arose from identical facts, the Law Society proceeded to convene and subject Wee to a second disciplinary proceeding. Wee argued that this amounted to an abuse of process. One should note that in this instance, the argument was not based on Article 11(2) since Wee was challenging a disciplinary proceeding by a professional body rather than a trial by a court of law. The Privy Council held that the common law principles of *autrefois acquit* and *autrefois convict* applied to disciplinary proceedings, and that there was in fact an abuse of process in *Wee's* case.

§9. Equality Before the Law and Equal Protection of the Law: Article 12

I. Introduction

516. Article 1 of the Universal Declaration of Human Rights 1948 declares:

> All human beings are born free and equal in dignity and rights. They are endowed with reason and conscience and should act towards one another in a spirit of brotherhood.

239. [1964] AC 1254.
240. [1986] 1 MLJ 163 (Supreme Court, Malaysia).
241. [1985] 1 MLJ 1.

517. This universal commitment to equality as part of the rule of law is reflected in Article 12 of the Constitution[242] which comprises three parts. Article 12(1) is the most general and applies to everyone:

> 12(1)All persons are equal before the law and entitled to the equal protection of the law.

518. The second part deals expressly with discrimination against Singapore citizens:

> 12(2)Except as expressly authorised by this Constitution, there shall be no discrimination against citizens of Singapore on the ground only of religion, race, descent or place of birth in any law or in the appointment to any office or employment under a public authority or in the administration of any law relating to the acquisition, holding or disposition of property or the establishing or carrying on of any trade, business, profession, vocation or employment.

519. The third part is a saving provision, listing out exceptions to the first two parts. In particular, the safeguards against discrimination under Article 12 do not apply to 'any provision regulating personal law'. Neither does it apply to 'any provision or practice restricting office or employment connected with the affairs of any religion, or of an institution managed by a group professing any religion, to persons professing that religion'.

II. Meaning of Discrimination

520. The law recognizes the need for a state to discriminate between its subjects. In itself, discrimination is neither morally objectionable nor unlawful. Common bases of the discrimination are gender, age and even educational qualifications. For example, males are required to serve full-time National Service while females are not. Similarly, persons below the age of 18 are not allowed to purchase alcohol while those above that age may.

---

242. On constitutional discrimination in Singapore, *see* S.M. Huang-Thio, *Constitutional Discrimination Under the Malaysian Constitution*, 6 Mal LR 69 (1964); and S.M. Huang-Thio, *Legal Aid: A Facet of Equality before the Law*, 12 ICLQ 1133 (1963); Tania Li, *Malays in Singapore: Culture, Economy and Ideology* (Oxford U. Press 1989); M.P. Lee, *Breeding the Best and the Brightest*, 11 J. Malaysian & Comp. L. 11 (1984). On gender discrimination *see* generally *Singapore Women: Three Decades of Change* (Aline K. Wong & Leong Wai Kum eds, Times Academic Press 1993); *Women in Singapore Country Report* (Ministry Community Dev. 1995); Geraldine Heng & Janadas Devan, *State Fatherhood: The Politics of Nationalism, Sexuality and Race in Singapore*, in *Nationalisms and Sexuality* (Andrew Parker et al. eds, Routledge 1992); and Li-ann Thio, *The Impact of Internationalisation on Domestic Governance: Gender Egalitarianism and the Transformative Potential of CEDAW*, 1 SJICL 278 (1997). On sexual orientation, *see* Jack Lee, *Equal Protection and Sexual Orientation*, 16 Sing LR 228 (1995).

521. The key to legal discrimination is the concept of classification. In *PP v. Su Liang Yu*,[243] the Malaysian High Court stated that the dominant idea behind the idea of 'equal before the law' and 'equal protection under the law' was that of equal justice. Legislative discrimination or selective application of the law was necessary to deal with 'the complex problems arising out of an infinite variety of human relations'. As such, the central issue concerns the examination of when discrimination is constitutionally permissible or desirable.

III. The Problem of Classification[244]

522. Article 12(1) consists of two propositions: first, that all persons are 'equal before the law' and second, that all persons are 'entitled to the equal protection of the law'. These are two different but related concepts, but the Singapore courts have typically treated them as one and the same. The first concept that all persons are equal before the law derives from the English common law, while the second concept of equal protection of the law comes from the 14th Amendment of the US Constitution.[245] The plain words of Article 12(1) thus require that where the subjects are equal, they should be treated equally. For example, where crimes are concerned, men and women should be treated equally since persons of either gender are equally capable of committing a crime.[246] In such an instance, since there is 'no objective difference between males and females in the context of the criminal', a criminal law that discriminates against one class of persons 'on the basis of sex or gender does not conform to the fundamental right of equality before the law'.[247] Former Chief Justice Chan Sek Keong writing extrajudicially offers this analysis:

> If equality before the law is not absolute, a differentiating law based on sex or gender must have a rational basis for the classification. It is suggested that the basis should be whether it advances or serves a legitimate state interest that justifies curtailing the fundamental right of equality before the law. Suppose Parliament enacts a law that makes it an offence for women to smoke cigars in public or in private. Such a law would violate women's right to equality with men before the law, that is, their equal freedom to smoke cigars .... If Parliament bans women, but not men, from smoking cigars, equality for all persons under Article 12(1) requires the State to justify the reasonableness of the ban. The Government may try to justify it on health grounds that women are more prone to cancer than men, or die earlier than men. If medical research shows that women are ten times more likely to contract lung cancer from

243. [1976] 2 MLJ 128 (High Court, Malaysia).
244. On the problem of classification, *see* Joseph Tussman & Jacobus TenBroek, *The Equal Protection of the Laws*, 37 California L. Rev. 341 (1949); and S.M. Huang-Thio, *Equal Protection and Rational Classification*, Pub. L. 412 (1963).
245. *See Lim Meng Suang & Anor v. Attorney General* [2013] 3 SLR 118, at [35]–[36] (High Court, Singapore).
246. This example was given in Chan Sek Keong, *Equal Justice Under the Constitution and Section 377A of the Penal Code: The Roads Not Taken*, 31 Singapore Acad. L.J. 773–844 at 821 (2019).
247. *Ibid.*, at 821–822.

smoking cigars than men, that would be a good reason for the ban, as there is a legitimate state interest in safeguarding their health, and also in reducing the economic costs of having to treat them. But if the reason for banning women from smoking cigars is that Parliament considers it unseemly or undignified for women to smoke cigars, the court will have to consider whether Parliament's disapproval is a legitimate ground on the basis of whether it advances or serves any state interest.[248]

523. The Singapore courts have hitherto not adopted the approach to the first clause of Article 12(1) argued by the former Chief Justice. Instead, both clauses are conflated and presume the constitutionality of unequal treatment, focusing instead on whether the discrimination satisfies the 'reasonable classification' test.

524. Equal treatment under the law does not imply that all persons should be treated alike. People differ in terms of abilities, personalities and culture. For example, it makes no sense to treat a child in the same manner as an adult when it comes to matters of voting or criminal culpability. All the law requires is that like persons in like circumstances should be treated alike. Under the doctrine of classification, one may in certain instances discriminate *between* classes, but no one *within* a particular class should be singled out for discriminatory treatment. Let us consider some cases.

525. The leading local authority is the Court of Appeal's 1998 decision in *Public Prosecutor v. Taw Cheng Kong*[249] which adopted the test first enunciated in the Malaysian Federal Court case of *Datuk Haji bin Harun Idris v. Public Prosecutor.*[250] In the latter case, the appellant was convicted of three charges of corruption and sentenced to a total of three years' imprisonment. He was also ordered to pay Malaysia Ringgit (MYR) 225,000 to UMNO Selangor on whose behalf he accepted the bribes. One of his arguments was that section 418A of the Criminal Procedure Code (which allowed his case to be transferred from the State Court to the High Court) violated Article 8(1) of the Federal Constitution (which is identical to Singapore's Article 12(1)). In a now-classic judgment, Lord President Mohamed Suffian laid down the principles in interpreting the equality provisions. He held that 'equality before the law' did not mean that 'all laws must be general in character or universal in application', and that Parliament could make law in respect of a group or class of persons provided that : (a) the classification is rational; (b) the classification is founded on an intelligible differentia (distinguishing mark) which distinguishes persons that are grouped together from others that are left out of the group; and (c) there must be a reasonable nexus between the basis of classification and the

248. *Ibid.*, at 822.
249. [1998] 2 SLR 410.
250. [1977] 2 MLJ 155 (Federal Court, Malaysia).

object of the discriminatory legislation. This test has been followed in all subsequent cases. This test has been affirmed by the SGCA in *Lim Meng Suang v. Attorney-General*.[251]

526. One question which the court has thus far been reluctant to rule on is this: can the court question the legality of the legislative object? This matter was discussed in *Lim Meng Suang v. Attorney-General*, where among other things, the Court of Appeal was asked to consider if the legislative object – in this case, to prosecute only male homosexuals for 'gross indecency' – was legitimate. The Court of Appeal refused to consider this argument, stating emphatically:

> To permit the court the power – over and above its power of scrutinising legislation pursuant to the 'reasonable classification' test – to declare a statute inconsistent with Art 12(1) (and, therefore, unconstitutional under Art 4) because the object of that statute is illegitimate would precisely be to confer on the court a licence to usurp the legislative function in the course of becoming (or at least acting like) a 'mini-legislature'. Put another way, only the Legislature has the power to review its own legislation and amend legislation accordingly if it is of the view that this is necessary. The courts, in contrast, have no such power – nor ought they to have such power.[252]

527. Two problems arise in using the rational nexus test for determining the constitutionality of discriminatory legislation. First, classification can be either underinclusive or overinclusive. Second, if the legislature defines its objectives very narrowly, the courts will find it difficult to find fault with the classification. If the objectives are themselves discriminatory, for example, based on race or religion, or descent, then the test of classification is impotent and cannot be used to strike down the discriminatory legislation.

528. This problem is illustrated by the contrasting approaches taken by the High Court and the Court of Appeal in the local case of *Public Prosecutor v. Taw Cheng Kong*.[253] In this case, the respondent Taw – a manager of the Governing of Singapore Investment Corporation Pte Ltd (GIC) based in Hong Kong – was alleged to have received some 'incentive fees' from one Kevin Lee of Rockerfeller & Co. Inc to make GIC purchases of certain shares in Hong Kong and Australia under Lee's instigation. He was charged under section 37(1) of the PCA which provides:

---

251. [2015] 1 SLR 26. For a commentary of this case, *see* Jaclyn C.L. Neo, *Equal Protection and the Reasonable Classification Test in Singapore after* Lim Meng Suang v. Attorney-General, SJLS 95–117 (2016); and Jack Tsen-Ta Lee, *The Limits of Liberty: The Crime of Male Same-Sex Conduct and the Rights to Life and Personal Liberty in Singapore:* Lim Meng Suang v. Attorney-General *[2015] 1 SLR 26*, Hong Kong L.J. 47 (2016).

252. [2015] 1 SLR 26, at 56.

253. [1998] 3 SLR 410. *See* generally, C.L. Lim, *Singapore Crimes Abroad*, SJLS 494 (2001); and Tan Yock Lin, *Equal Protection, Extra-Territoriality and Self-Incrimination*, 19 Sing LR 10 (1998). Tan's arguments were endorsed by the High Court in *Lim Meng Suang v. Attorney-General* [2013] 3 SLR 118, 131–145.

> The provisions of this Act have effect, in relation to citizens of Singapore, outside as well as within Singapore; and where an offence under this Act is committed by a citizen of Singapore in any place outside Singapore, he may be dealt with in respect of that offence as if it had been committed in Singapore.

529. In the High Court,[254] Karthigesu JA held section 37(1) to be unconstitutional as section 37(1) of the PCA was both overinclusive and under-inclusive. He held that as the main object of the PCA as disclosed in its long title was 'the more effectual prevention of corruption'. That being the case, section 37(1) was overinclusive because it would include persons not contemplated by the PCA, such as a Singapore citizen who is a foreign permanent resident, employed in a foreign country by a foreign government, receiving a bribe paid in foreign currency by a foreign payor. It was also under-inclusive in failing to include persons contemplated by the PCA, such as a Singaporean permanent resident or foreigner working for the Singapore Government agreeing to take a short trip outside Singapore to receive a bribe in Singapore dollars in relation to an act he or she would then do in Singapore. In light of this, 'citizenship' provided an illogical criteria for discrimination.

530. The Court of Appeal reversed Karthigesu JA's decision and held that:

> in view of the all-encompassing ambit of s 37(1), which would have captured all corrupt acts independently of harmful consequences in Singapore, we unanimously concluded that it was rational to draw the line at citizenship and leave out non-citizens so as to observe international comity and the sovereignty of other nations.

531. Chief Justice Yong Pung How further held that so long as the differentiation was 'justified and permissible', the fact that the PCA was overinclusive or under-inclusive was not fatal. In this case, the differentiation was between Singapore citizens and non-citizens, and such a distinction was logical. So long as all citizens as a class are treated alike, section 37(1) of the PCA was constitutional. This approach was criticized in the High Court in the case of *Lim Meng Suang v. Attorney-General*[255] where Quentin Loh J opined that the Court of Appeal applied a tautologous logic to interpreting Article 12 and that had the court been 'less fixated' with the idea of classes and more focused on 'the fundamental rubric that "like should be treated alike"', it may well have arrived at a different decision.

IV. Equality in Criminal Prosecutions

532. Two main issues arise for consideration here. First, is the mandatory death penalty contrary to Article 12? Which offences should carry the mandatory death

254. *See Taw Cheng Kong v. PP* [1998] 1 SLR 943.
255. [2013] 3 SLR 118 (High Court, Singapore).

sentence and which should not? Can Parliament's decision to make some offences punishable with the death penalty unconstitutional? The second issue concerns the AG's prosecutorial discretion. If the AG has an option to charge an accused with two possible offences (based on the same set of facts) and chooses to charge him or her with one which carries a heavier penalty, is this unconstitutional?

533. The leading local case is *Lee Keng Guan & Ors v. Public Prosecutor.*[256] In that case, the appellants were convicted under section 4 of the Arms Offences Act 1973 and sentenced to death. They argued that section 4 of the Arms Offences Act violated the equal protection clause under Article 12(1) of the Constitution as their acts were also punishable under section 324 of the Penal Code where the punishment was imprisonment or fine. The Singapore Court of Criminal Appeal held that there was no discrimination under Article 12.

V. Non-discrimination Against Citizens

534. Article 12(2) of the Constitution prohibits discrimination against citizens: (a) in any law or in the appointment to any office or employment under a public authority; or (b) in the administration of any law relating to the acquisition, holding or disposition of property; or (c) the establishing or carrying on of any trade, business, profession, vocation or employment. The prohibited grounds of discrimination are: (a) religion, (b) race, (c) descent, or (d) place of birth.

535. There are two qualifiers to this prohibition. First, it applies only to citizens, and second that the words used in Article 12(2) 'on the ground only' suggest that a combination of the prohibited criteria would be permissible. For example, a class of persons that is discriminated on the basis of race *and* religion cannot argue that such discrimination violates Article 12(2).

VI. Positive Discrimination under the Constitution[257]

536. Some constitutions may prescribe *positive discrimination* or *affirmative action* to recognize formal equality as well as to implement substantive equality. Positive discrimination attempts to remedy past discrimination or injustices. Singapore's Constitution contains no specific affirmative action clauses but does single out certain groups for distinction. For instance, Article 152(2) recognizes the Malays to be 'the indigenous people of Singapore', and Article 153A(2) specifies

256. [1977] 2 MLJ 95.
257. On the history of the evolution of Art. 152, *see* Kevin Y.L. Tan, *The Legal and Institutional Framework and Issues of Multiculturalism in Singapore*, in *Beyond Rituals and Riots: Ethnic Pluralism and Social Cohesion in Singapore* 98–113 (Lai Ah Eng ed., Eastern U. Press 2004).

Malay to the 'national language' even though Article 153A(1) recognizes four official languages (Malay, Mandarin, Tamil and English). Article 153 empowers Parliament to 'make provision for regulating Muslim religious affairs and for constituting a Council to advise the President in matters relating to the Muslim religion'.

537. Some read Article 152 as an affirmative action clause. This first part of this clause states that it shall be the Government's responsibility 'to care for the interests of the racial and religious minorities in Singapore'. The second part reads:

> 152(2) The Government shall exercise its functions in such manner as to recognise the special position of the Malays, who are the indigenous people of Singapore, and accordingly it shall be the responsibility of the Government to protect, safeguard, support, foster and promote their political, educational, religious, economic, social and cultural interests and the Malay language.

538. Article 152 has never been invoked, challenged or questioned in a court of law. As such, its impact, if any, has been largely psychological rather than legal. From a constitutional perspective, it is doubtful whether a literal reading of the document imposes on the Singapore Government the duty to protect Malay *rights* as such. Indeed, nowhere are the words 'right' or 'rights' used throughout the article, only the word 'interests'. The Constitution does not require the Government to safeguard, support, foster or promote the political, educational, religious, economic, and social interests of any other ethnic group in Singapore. Viewed in that light, Article 152 may be seen as an affirmative action clause. However, the word 'interests' is vague and is not defined in the Constitution. The constitutional responsibility of the Government to promote Malay interest does not forbid the promotion of the interests of any other ethnic group. It merely charges the Government with this task. It is more of a reminder to the Government not to neglect Malay interests, rather than a mandate to buttress Malay interests.

539. Nonetheless, the inclusion of this provision signifies a conscious attempt to entrench and honour the Malays as the indigenous people of the land through the Constitution. It also requires the Government to safeguard and protect their economic, social, cultural and linguistic interests. Unlike the Malaysians who have opted for affirmative action in favour of Malays, the Singapore Government has interpreted its constitutional duty as providing opportunities for Malays to compete on equal terms with the rest of the population by providing assistance wherever needed. This has largely been the field of education, where up to recently, free education became one of the cornerstones of the Government's policy.

540. One major criticism of this approach has been that the idea of promoting Malay interests is totally at odds with the Government's policy of meritocracy that is pursued aggressively. On the other hand, a number of better-educated Malays feel that Article 152 is no longer needed and should be removed. Leaving Article 152 in the Constitution serves only to cultivate a 'crutch mentality', the idea that Malays, no matter what their abilities, have succeeded on account of their race alone. Personally, I would urge that Article 152 be retained. It is symbolic rather than legal and will constantly remind Singaporeans of their multiracial heritage, and of the special position of the Malays in our historical development.

541. Singapore is a party to the International Convention for the Elimination of All Forms of Discrimination Against Women of CEDAW (1979)[258] which seeks to eradicate discrimination on the basis of gender. There is, however, no specific provision in the Singapore Constitution that forbids discrimination on the basis of gender.

§10. Freedom of Speech and Expression[259]

I. Introduction

542. Speech gives expression to our ideas and is the outward expression of our free conscience. Not all forms of speech merit constitutional protection. For example, crying fire in a crowded theatre creates more harm than good and cannot, from a public policy perspective, be regarded as worthy of legal protection. Speech may be political, artistic, commercial, pornographic, racist or even incite hatred. Speech may also be symbolic. Courts constantly try to strike a balance between giving an individual wide latitude for expression and safeguarding the public interest.

II. Constitutional Provisions and Qualifications

543. Under Article 14(1), the right to free speech and expression extends only to citizens. These rights are not absolute and are expressly qualified by Article 14(2)(a) under which Parliament is empowered to impose any restrictions on it:

---

258. *See* generally, Li-ann Thio, *The Impact of Internationalization on Domestic Governance: Gender, Egalitarianism and the Transformative Potential of CEDAW*, 1 SJICL 278 (1997).

259. *See* generally, Michael Hor & Colin Seah, *Selected Issues in the Freedom of Speech and Expression in Singapore*, 12 Sing LR 298 (1991); and Li-ann Thio, *Human Rights and the Media in Singapore, in Human Rights and the Media* (Robert Haas ed., AIDCOM 1996); Li-ann Thio, *The Virtual and the Real: Article 14, Political Speech and the Calibrated Management of Deliberative Democracy in Singapore*, SJLS 25–57 (2008); Ang Peng Hwa, *The Media and the Flow of Information*, in *Singapore in the New Millennium: Challenges Facing the City-State* 243–263 (Derek da Cunha ed., Inst. S.E. Asian Stud. 2002); Tsun Hang Tey, *Singapore's Jurisprudence of Political Defamation and Its Triple-Whammy Impact on Political Speech*, Pub. L. 452 (2008); Garry Rodan, *Asian Crisis, Transparency and the International Media in Singapore*, 13 The Pac. Rev. 217 (2000); and Mark Cenite, *Too Much Legislation, Too Little Expression*, in *Asia's March Towards Freedom of Expression and Development* 167–198 (Kalinga Seneviratne & Suganthi Singarayar eds, AMIC 2006).

considers necessary or expedient in the interest of the security of Singapore or any part thereof, friendly relations with other countries, public order or morality and restrictions designed to protect the privileges of Parliament or to provide against contempt of court, defamation or incitement to any offence.

544. The derogation provisions under Article 14(2)(a) are in two parts with the words 'necessary or expedient' applying only to: (a) the interest of the security of Singapore or any part thereof; (b) friendly relations with other countries; (c) public order; or (d) morality. Parliament is not required to justify restrictions 'designed to protect the privileges of Parliament'; or to provide against: (i) contempt of court; (ii) defamation; or (iii) incitement to any offence, on the grounds that they are either 'necessary' or 'expedient'.

545. Under Article 149, any law dealing with subversive elements, such as the ISA (1960), may legally contradict these rights. Furthermore, Article 14 rights may be suspended under any emergency declared under Article 150. It is the courts' role to determine the ambit of constitutional protection under Article 14 and to determine whether any particular legislation contravenes this article. Aside from challenging the legislation, it is also possible to challenge acts of restraint apparently authorized by such legislation. In interpreting the free speech clause, one important issue is whether the common law defences to laws limiting free speech such as libel laws are overridden or preserved.

546. In *X Pte Ltd & Anor v. CDE,*[260] the Singapore High Court stated that the law relating to confidence and the tort of conspiracy as restrictions on freedom of speech embodied in the common law had been preserved by the Constitution. This approach has been followed in cases dealing with contempt of court and defamation. Theoretically, constitutional liberties are given greater protection than a residual common law liberty.

III. Regulating Speech Through Licensing

547. Most governments use licensing to control and regulate activities it considers potentially harmful to society. For example, you need a licence before you can make a public address in Singapore. Section 3 of the Public Entertainments and Meetings Act provides that no public entertainment shall be provided except in an approved place and according to a licence issued by the relevant authority, who may impose such conditions as he or she thinks fit (section 10).

548. Generally, a licensing law can be challenged at two levels: (1) one can challenge the law giving the official the power to grant or refuse licences as being unconstitutional; and (2) one can accept the validity of the law, but challenge the exercise of the power under the law. In his *Commentaries on the Law of England*

260. [1992] 2 SLR 996.

(1765–1769), Sir William Blackstone (1723–1780) commented that although the state could punish an expressed opinion through the subsequent imposition of penal sanctions, no law could validly restrain the articulation of that opinion.

549. In *JB Jeyaretnam v. Public Prosecutor,*[261] the accused Jeyaretnam proceeded to conduct a public meeting even though he was denied a licence to do so. One argument advanced in the High Court was whether the licensing requirement under the Public Entertainment Act contravened Article 14. Justice Chan Sek Keong (as he then was) dismissed the argument but held that if the licensing officer is given absolute and untrammelled discretion to grant licences, it may be argued that the licensing scheme was unconstitutional, since the licensing officer would be vested with arbitrary power to deprive a citizen of his or her constitutional right to freedom of speech and expression contrary to the objects of Article 14(2). A similar argument was made in *Chee Soon Juan v. Public Prosecutor*[262] in respect of the Public Entertainment and Meetings Act which Chief Justice Yong Pung How held to be constitutional.

IV. Freedom of the Press[263]

550. There is no express reference to the freedom of the press in Singapore's Constitution although that right broadly falls under the freedom of speech. In Singapore, the Government has always demanded that the press exercises 'responsible journalism' which requires the press to be an instrument of nation-building rather than a check on political power. Singapore laws exercise extensive control over publications in general. For example, section 5 of the Official Secrets Act (OSA) prohibits the communication of official secrets, and section 20(1) of the ISA authorizes the prohibition of any publication which appears to the Minister-to-be likely to cause violence, disobedience, a breach of peace or feelings of hostility between different races or classes of the population. In addition, the Newspaper and Printing Presses Act controls the press through its licensing and shareholding provisions.

551. Press control started in 1920 with the Printing Presses Ordinance which required licences for printing press owners. In 1939, this legislation was amended to require a permit for printing or publishing a newspaper in the country. Today, the main legislation is the Newspapers and Printing Presses Act (NPPA). Under section 3 of this Act, the Minister may 'in his discretion' grant or withdraw a licence to own

261. [1990] 1 MLJ 129.
262. [2003] 2 SLR 278.
263. For a history of the press in Singapore, *see* Tan Yew Soon & Soh Yew Peng, *The Development of Singapore's Modern Media Industry* 1–61 (Times Academic Press 1994). On the role of the press, *see* generally, Roger Mitton, *What Role for the Press: Singapore's Answers*, Asiaweek, 44–55 (25 Sep. 1992); Chua Beng Huat, *Communitarian Ideology and Democracy in Singapore* (Routledge 1995); Tsun Hang Tey, *Confining the Freedom of the Press in Singapore: A 'Pragmatic' Press for 'Nation-Building'?*, 30 Hum. Rights Q. 876 (2008); and Tan Teng Lang, *The Singapore Press: Freedom, Responsibility and Credibility*, Institute of Policy Studies Occasional Paper No. 3 (Times Academic Press 1989).

and operate a printing press. Section 15 NPPA requires permits for circulating newspapers printed in Malaysia and in Singapore, while section 15A requires a permit for dealing in offshore newspapers in Singapore.

552. In 1974, the Government felt that some newspapers were being manipulated by foreign elements[264] and further amended the NPPA to require newspaper companies publish in Singapore to have two kinds of shares: (1) management shares and (2) ordinary shares. Management shares carry two hundred votes each, compared to one vote per ordinary share. Furthermore, only citizens or corporations who or which are approved by the Minister can hold management shares. Transfers of management shares must also be approved by the Minister.

553. The Singapore Government is extremely wary of foreign journalists whom they perceive to be seeking to influence and manipulate the local populace. Apart from expelling foreign journalists, or merely refusing to renew their work permits, or citing them for contempt of court, Singapore's press laws provide a powerful means to directly control the business of the foreign papers in Singapore. By controlling newspaper company ownership, foreign influence in the local newspaper scene is much reduced. Foreign funds coming into newspaper companies must also be declared and approved by the relevant Minister.

554. In 1986, the NPPA was further amended to empower the Minister to declare a newspaper published outside Singapore as 'engaging in domestic politics', thus restricting its circulation in Singapore. This amendment came about after a foreign paper refused to publish replies by government officials to articles that the Government argued contained inaccurate misrepresentations. The newspapers argued that freedom of the press did not encompass a right to reply. The Government decided that since the primary motivation of the foreign press was pecuniary, it would cut the local circulation of the foreign press. To reinforce this point, Parliament in 1988 amended section 17 of the NPPA to allow anyone to apply for the Minister's approval to reproduce and circulate a gazetted foreign publication without infringing the publisher's copyright. However, such approval is at the Minister's absolute discretion.

555. In 1990, section 15A was inserted to make it compulsory for anyone wishing to sell, distribute or import 'offshore' newspapers to obtain a permit from the Minister. An 'offshore' newspaper is one whose editorial policies are decided outside Singapore, and which are published at least weekly and deal with politics and current affairs of Southeast Asia, and whose circulation in Singapore is three hundred copies or more. This does not include newspapers printed in Malaysia as there is a separate provision for it. The Minister may grant or refuse the permit without

---

264. On the Singapore Government's attitude towards the foreign press, *see* Lee Kuan Yew, *Singapore and the Foreign Press*, in *Press Systems in Asean States* 117–124 (Achal Mehra ed., AMIC 1989); and *How the Press Can Best Serve Singapore: PM*, *Sun. Rev.* 4 (16 Jul. 1995).

assigning any reason. There is no avenue for appeal. The Minister may impose conditions in granting the yearly licence, including requiring the proprietor of the newspaper to furnish a security deposit. The Minister may also control the number of copies sold or distributed in Singapore.

556. Section 16 of the NPPA came up for consideration in *Dow Jones Publishing Company (Asia) Inc v. Attorney General.*[265] In this case, the *Asian Wall Street Journal* published a series of articles questioning the Singapore Government's motives in setting up a second stock exchange (SESDAQ). When the paper refused to publish a government reply, the Minister declared the publication to be 'engaging in the domestic politics of Singapore' and reduced its circulation from five thousand to four hundred copies. One issue concerned the meaning of 'engaging in the domestic politics of Singapore'. In the Court of Appeal, Justice Chan Sek Keong (as he then was) held that:

> Whatever else that expression may comprehend, it is wide enough, according to the *Longman Dictionary of the English Language* to include political practices or policies. In the context of Singapore, domestic politics would, in our view, include the political system of Singapore and the political ideology underpinning it, the public institutions that are a manifestation of the system and the policies of the government of the day that gave life to the political system. In other words, the domestic politics of Singapore relate to the multitude of issues concerning how Singapore should be governed in the interest and for the welfare of its people. In this broad sense, the political, social and economic policies of the government of the day are part and parcel of the domestic politics of Singapore.

V. Express Constitutional Grounds for Enacting Derogating Laws

557. The Government may restrict free speech because of its objectionable content. For example, such speech may promote racist ideas or deviant sexual practices or pornography. Even so, such restrictions must fall within one of the constitutionally stipulated grounds in Article 14(2). Regulation is often justified in the name of state or community interest.

VI. Restrictions Under the Criminal Law

558. The freedom of speech and expression is specifically restricted by the Penal Code, which was introduced to the Straits Settlements – of which Singapore was a constituent part – in 1872. Chapter XV, which covers offences relating to religion or race, makes it an offence for any person to 'utter any word' or make any sound or gesture 'with deliberate intention of wounding the religious or racial feelings of any

265. [1989] 2 MLJ 385.

person'.[266] It is also an offence to promote or attempt to promote 'on grounds of religion or race, disharmony or feelings of enmity, hatred or ill-will between different religious or racial groups' by 'words, either spoken or written, or by signs'.[267]

559. Section 267C of the Penal Code makes it offence for a person to 'utter any words' or make 'any sign or visible representation … containing any incitement to violence, counselling disobedience to the law or to the lawful order of a public servant' or is 'likely to lead to any breach of the peace' if that person does so 'intending for violence, disobedience to the law or such lawful order, or breach of the peace to occur' or has reason to believe that such 'violence, disobedience to the law or such lawful order, or breach of the peace' is like to occur as a result. Any person who 'transmits or communicates' information which he knows to be false or fabricated, and 'contains a reference to the presence in any place or location or in any conveyance or means of transportation of any thing that is likely to cause hurt or damage to property by any means'.[268]

560. Section 499 of the Penal Code criminalizes defamation. Whoever, 'by words either spoken or intended to be read, or by signs, or by visible representations, makes or publishes any imputation concerning any person, intending to harm, or knowing or having reason to believe that such imputation will harm' the reputation of that person.

VII. Free Speech in Parliament

561. There is no constitutional provision in Singapore to protect free speech in Parliament. Article 63 merely allows Parliament to regulate its own privileges, immunities and powers. It is in section 5 of the Parliamentary (Privileges, Immunities and Powers) Act[269] that one finds the proverbial privileged free speech provisions in parliamentary debates. This section provides that there shall be freedom of speech and debate in Parliament, which cannot be impeached or questioned anywhere outside of Parliament.

VIII. Official Secrets

562. Section 5 of the OSA[270] forbids, on pain of imprisonment, anyone from communicating any official secret which is defined as 'any secret official code word, countersign or password, or any photograph, drawing, plan, model, article, note, document or information' which: (a) relates to or is used in a prohibited place; (b) relates to munitions of war; (c) has been made or obtained in contravention of the

266. Section 298, Penal Code (Cap 224).
267. Section 298A, Penal Code (Cap 224).
268. Section 268A, Penal Code (Cap 224).
269. Cap 217, Singapore Statutes.
270. Cap 213, Singapore Statutes.

Act; (d) has been entrusted in confidence by any person holding office under the Government; or (e) has been obtained by such person owing to his position as a person who holds office under the Government.

563. In *Public Prosecutor v. Phua Keng Tong*,[271] the constitutionality of section 5 of the OSA was challenged as being contrary to Article 14. One of the accused was charged for passing confidential information to another who in turn used it to speculate in the foreign exchange market. The latter was charged with receiving an official secret. In the Singapore High Court, Justice L.P. Thean (as he then was) held that as the OSA was enacted 'in the interest of security of Singapore', it did not violate Article 14.

564. In *Bridges Christopher v. Public Prosecutor*,[272] the SGCA held that the *mens reas* necessary for an offence under section 5 are:

(a) an intention to communicate the information;
(b) knowledge that the information was obtained by the communicator in contravention of the Act; and
(c) knowledge of the communicator that he had no authority to communicate the information to the person to whom he communicated it or that he had no duty to communicate it to the person he communicated it.

IX. Defamation

565. A person's reputation is enforced through the law of defamation which in Singapore is based on common law principles. Although Article 14(2) provides that Parliament may impose 'such restrictions … to provide against … defamation', no such legislation has been passed. Instead, the local courts have held that the Defamation Act (originally enacted as the Defamation Ordinance 1960) – which is not a codification of the rules governing the tort of defamation but simply modifying some of these rules – was such a statute that was passed to enable the common law of defamation to restrict free speech and expression.[273] The Court of Appeal further held, in the case of *Review Publication v. Lee Hsien Loong & Anor Appeal*,[274] that Article 105(1) of the Constitution of the State of Singapore (1963) – which provided for all pre-independence laws to continue in force and required them to be construed 'with such modifications, adaptations, qualifications and exceptions as may be necessary' to bring them into conformity' with the Constitution – had the effect of restricting citizens' constitutional rights of free speech and expression by

271. [1986] 2 MLJ 279.
272. [1997] 1 SLR 406.
273. *See Lee Kuan Yew v. Jeyaretnam Joshua Benjamin* [1990] 1 SLR(R) 709 (High Court, Singapore).
274. [2010] 1 SLR 52 (Court of Appeal, Singapore).

providing for continued application of the common law of defamation.[275] This reading of Article 14(2)(a) is almost certainly wrong as the common law must necessarily be read in a manner that brings it in line with the constitutional guarantee and not the other way around.[276]

566. Under the common law, in order for a defamation action to succeed, the plaintiff must show that the words complained of has: (a) disparaged him or her in his or her office, profession, calling, trade or business; (b) exposed him or her to hatred or ridicule; (c) caused him or her to be shunned or avoided; or (d) lowered him or her in the estimation of right-thinking members of society generally. Much local case law on defamation is concerned with the appropriate reading of the words, and whether the words complained of either 'in their ordinary or natural meaning' or through innuendo defames the plaintiff.

567. One important issue is whether public officials or politicians should be given the same level of protection as a private citizen. The logic is based on the idea that there exists a strong community interest in discussing the behaviour of public officials and politicians. The rule was laid down by the United States Supreme Court in *New York Times v. Sullivan*[277] and holds that a person is not liable for defaming a public figure unless 'actual malice' is proven.

568. This argument was advanced and rejected in the SGCA case of *JB Jeyaretnam v. Lee Kuan Yew*.[278] It was argued that qualified privilege attaches to defamatory publications concerning public officials relating to their official conduct or the performance of their public duties by those who have an honest and legitimate interest in the matter to those who have a corresponding and legitimate interest. Justice L.P. Thean (as he then was) held that the *New York Times* case was inapplicable as Article 14 of Singapore's Constitution differs materially from the First and Fourteenth Amendments under the American Constitution, as well as from Article 10 of the European Convention on Human Rights. Furthermore, it was implicit that the right of free speech under Article 14 was subject to the common law of defamation as modified by the Defamation Act.

569. The Singapore courts have also rejected the qualified privilege advanced in the 2001 UK House of Lords case of *Reynolds v. Times Newspaper Ltd*[279] and the argument based on the right to receive political communication articulated by the Australian High Court in the 1997 case of *Lange v. Australian Broadcasting Corporation*.[280]

---

275. *Ibid.*, at [168].
276. *See* Kevin Y.L. Tan, *Besmirching Honourable Men: The Defamation of Politicians in Singapore*, Indian Y.B. Comp. L. (2020).
277. (1964) 376 US 254 (US Supreme Court).
278. [1992] 2 SLR 310. For a critical appraisal of *JB Jeyaretnam v. Lee Kuan Yew*, *see* Michael Hor, *The Freedom of Speech and Defamation*, SJLS 542 (1992).
279. [2001] 2 AC 127 (House of Lords, UK).
280. (1997) 145 ALR 96 (High Court, Australia).

X. Contempt of Court

570. *See* Chapter 6, paragraphs 400–403.

XI. Public Morality

571. Freedom of speech and expression may be restricted in the name of public morality under Article 14(2)(a). This restriction stems from the paternalistic concern that moral values may be eroded if certain types of speech are permitted. A long list of legislation regulates public morality in Singapore. For example, we have film censorship under the Films Act; prohibition of local and foreign publications that are contrary to public interest under the Undesirable Publications Act; prohibition against sale and distribution of obscene material and even the singing of obscene songs in public under the Penal Code. Advertising is largely left to professional self-regulation, though the Indecent Advertisements Act prohibits indecent advertisements relating to the treatment of sex-related diseases. The same Act also prohibits the sticking of indecent posters and Bills in places within public view.

§11. Freedom of Assembly

572. Article 14(1)(b) guarantees that all citizens 'have the right to assemble peaceably and without arms'. This is subject to Article 14(2)(b) which allows Parliament to restrict the right in the interest of the security of the country or public order. Given the language of the restrictions, our discussion in the context of *Freedom of Expression* applies equally here.

573. This freedom has its roots in the tradition of petitioning to the legitimate government for redress within the democratic process. The United States Supreme Court has said that '[t]he very idea of government, republican in form, implies a right on the part of its citizens to meet peaceably for consultation in respect of public affairs and to petition for a redress of grievances'.[281] However, the American courts have not restricted the right of assembly to the petition process. The right extends to any assembly for lawful discussion, so long as there is no incitement to violence or crime.

574. Singapore's Constitution is also not restricted in terms of the right of petition. However, restrictive legislation exists in the form of: the Penal Code (unlawful assembly); the Miscellaneous Offences (Public Order and Nuisance) Act (empowering the Minister to make rules regulating public meetings and processions in public places); the Public Entertainment and Meetings Act (regulating the licensing for public entertainment including lectures, talks, addresses, debates and discussions in a public place); the Societies Act (which renders a meeting of an unlawful

281. *See United States v. Cruikshank* (1875) 92 US 542 (US Supreme Court).

society an offence) and the Public Order (Preservation) Act and the Preservation of Peace Act (which gives the authorities power to disperse assemblies in gazetted areas in the interest of public order).

575. The Singapore courts adopt a generous reading of the restrictive clauses under Article 14 and have generally exercised careful restraint in striking down restrictive legislation on the grounds of the freedom of expression under the Constitution. In *Chee Siok Chin & Ors v. Minister for Home Affairs*,[282] the appellants challenged the constitutionality of the Miscellaneous Offences (Public Order and Nuisance) Act[283] on the grounds that their constitutional rights in relation to free speech and assembly under Article 14 had been infringed. V.K. Rajah J (as he then was) held that the Miscellaneous Offences Act was enacted to uphold public order and was thus 'necessary and expedient' within the meaning of Article 14(2) of the Constitution.

§12. Freedom of Association

576. The right to freedom of association under Article 14(1)(c) is historically connected with the right to free speech. Political parties will often try to convince the electorate that they carry the correct viewpoints, and pursuant to this, we see the similarities in the rationales underlying free speech and association. Freedom of association allows like-minded individuals to band together to further a cause. Without it, effective opposition can be eliminated through curfews or laws forbidding meetings or targeted specifically at certain political opponents.

577. Exceptions to this right are found in Article 14(2)(c) which allows Parliament to impose laws restricting this right where it considers it necessary or expedient in the interest of the security of the country or public order or morality. The language of restriction is in terms similar to Article 14(2)(a), and our earlier discussion in the context of *Freedom of Expression* applies equally here. However, Article 14(3) appears to be more widely worded since restrictions may be imposed by any law, so long as they relate to labour or education.

282. [2006] 1 SLR 582.
283. Cap 184, Singapore Statutes.

§13. FREEDOM OF RELIGION[284]

I. Introduction

578. Religious freedom is an internationally recognized human right. Article 18 of the Universal Declaration of Human Rights reads:

> Everyone has the right to freedom of thought, conscience and religion; this right includes the freedom to change his religion or belief, and freedom, either alone or in community with others and in public or private, to manifest his religion or belief in teaching, practice, worship and observance.

579. The main function of law with respect to religious freedom is to create and maintain an environment where different faiths may be peaceably practised. The law affords equal protection to all religions and refrains from judging the merits of any religion. There is no 'state religion' in Singapore. Indeed, the Constitution does not demand that anyone profess a religion. We are concerned with two primary issues here: (i) the relationship between state and religion; and (ii) the content of religious liberty.

580. In Singapore, race and religion tend to be conflated (e.g., a Malay is by definition also a Muslim), and the cleavage lines are drawn rather sharply. Because riots have broken out in the past over insensitivities to race and religion, the Government is especially concerned that the freedom of religion does not result in one religious group offending another through its proselytizing activities or insensitive actions.

---

284. *See* Thio Li-ann, *A Treatise on Singapore Constitutional Law* (Academy Publishing 2012) Chapter 15 'Freedom of Religion'; Li-ann Thio, *Rule of Law, Religious Liberty and Harmony: Multiculturism, Legal Pluralism, and the Singapore Model of Accommodative Secularism*, J.L., Religion and State 254–291 (2017); Thio Li-ann, *The Secular Trumps the Sacred: Constitutional Issues Arising from* Colin Chan v. Public Prosecutor, 16 Sing LR 26 (1995); Li-ann Thio, *Religion in the Public Sphere of Singapore: Wall of Division or Public Square?*, in *Religious Pluralism and Civil Society: A Comparative Analysis* 73–104 (Bryan Turner ed., Bardwell Press 2008); and Thio Li-ann, *Control, Co-optation and Co-operation: Managing Religious Harmony in Singapore*, 33 Hastings Const. L.Q. 197–253 (2006); Noor Aisha Abdul Rahman, *Muslim Personal Law and Citizens' Rights: The Case of Singapore*, 7(1) Asian J. Comp. L. Article 14 (2012); Jaclyn L. Neo, *Secular Constitutionalism in Singapore: Between Equality and Hierarchy*, Oxford J. of L. & Relgn. 1–26 (2016).

II. Historical Flashpoints in Race-Religion Relations[285]

581. One of the earliest instances of incidents triggered by religion was the Sepoy Mutiny of 1915. One apparent cause of the revolt was the rumour that the Indian Muslims were going to be dispatched to fight the Muslim Turks. Consequently, the Colonial Office set up the Muhammedan Advisory Board to advise the British Colonial Government on Islamic matters. In December 1950, the decision in *Maria Hertogh's* case[286] sparked off riots in Singapore. The court declared invalid the minor's Muslim marriage and removed her from her adoptive Muslim family to a Catholic convent. Since the Muslims felt that Islam was being attacked, they retaliated, and a matter of child custody exploded into a maelstrom of anti-colonial nationalism and religious chauvinism.

582. When Singapore became part of the Federation of Malaysia in 1963, the Malays in Singapore expected to enjoy the special privileges found in the 1957 Federal Constitution even though this was never part of the merger agreement. They were deeply disappointed when the Singapore Government announced that these privileges did not apply to them and this led to demonstrations. The situation was exacerbated by the Confrontation with Indonesia, and in 1964, riots broke out during the Prophet's Birthday. It lasted five days, and a total of 22 people died and 109 were injured.

583. In 1987, the Singapore Government apprehended under the ISA a number of people engaged in the so-called Marxist conspiracy who were accused of using religion as a front to subvert law and order.

---

285. On the role religion played in the politics of Singapore, *see* Kho Ee Moi, *Religion and State in Singapore* (1959–1978), Unpublished academic exercise, Department of Sociology (U. Sing. 1979); Lim Hwee Hoon, *Religion and Politics in Secular State: A Case Study of Singapore, Academic Exercise, Department of Political Science* (Natl. U. Sing. 1989–1990); Trevor Ling, *Religion*, in *Management of Success: The Moulding of Modern Singapore* (KS Sandhu & Paul Wheatley eds, Inst. S.E. Asian Stud. 1989). For religious trends in Singapore, *see* Eddie Kuo & Tong Chee Kiang, *Religion in Singapore, Census of Population 1990*, Monograph No. 2 (Sing. Natl. Printers 1995); White Paper for the *Maintenance of Religious Harmony Bill* (Cmd. 21 of 1989); Joseph Tamney, *Religion and State in Singapore*, 30 J. Church & St. 109 (1988); and Joseph Tamney, *The Struggle over Singapore's Soul: Western Modernization and Asian Culture* (Walter de Gruyter 1996); Tay Eng Soon, *Religion and Politics in the Singapore Context*, in *Church and Society: Singapore Context* (Bobby Sng ed., Graduate Christians Fellowship 1989). On the legal issues raised in connection with the right to religion, *see* Li-ann Thio, *The Secular Trumps the Sacred: Constitutional Issues Arising out of* Colin Chan v. PP, 16 Sing LR 26 (1995); and V.S. Winslow, *The Separation of Religion and Politics: The Maintenance of Religious Harmony Act 1990*, 32 Mal LR 327 (1990).

286. *See In re Maria Huberdina Hertogh, Adrianus Petrus Hertogh & Anor v. Aminah bte Mohamed & Ors*, [1951] MLJ 12 (High Court); and *Re Maria Huberdina Hertogh, Inche Mansor Adabi v. Adrianus Petrus Hertogh & Anor* [1951] 1 MLJ 164 (Court of Appeal).

III. Constitutional Safeguards

584. Singapore's post-independence government continued the British policy of not interfering in communal affairs and instead concentrated on economic development. However, it took steps to ensure that the racial, religious and linguistic minorities were not neglected. In 1969, the Presidential Council for Minority Rights was established with the general function to 'consider and report on such matters affecting persons of any racial or religious community in Singapore as may be referred to the Council by Parliament or the Government', and the specific function of drawing attention to any bill or subsidiary legislation that discriminates against any racial or religious community (Article 76(2) of the Constitution).

585. In 1990, the MRHA was passed.[287] The rationale behind the MRHA was avowedly to prevent the mixing of religion and politics and to prevent those holding religious offices from using them as a platform to mount political agitation and make inflammatory political speeches. The MRHA is pre-emptive in nature, and was, as then First Deputy Prime Minister Goh Chok Tong noted, introduced 'more in sorrow than with joy'. Under Section 8 of the MRHA, the Minister may make a 'restraining order against any priest, monk, pastor, imam, elder, office-bearer or any other person who is in a position in any religious group or institution or any member thereof' if the Minister is satisfied that that person has committed or is attempting to commit the following acts:

(a) causing feelings of enmity, hatred, ill-will or hostility between different religious groups;
(b) carrying out activities to promote a political cause, or a cause of any political party while, or under the guise of, propagating or practising any religious belief;
(c) carrying out subversive activities under the guise of propagating or practising any religious belief; or
(d) exciting disaffection against the President or the Government while, or under the guise of, propagating or practising any religious belief.

586. Such an order may restrain him from addressing (either orally or in writing) any 'congregation, parish or group of worshippers or members of any religious group of institution on any subject, topic or theme'. This order may extend to retraining the religious leader from 'printing, publishing, editing, distributing or in any way assisting or contributing to any publication produced by any religious group' and from 'holding office in any editorial board or a committee of a publication of any religious group'.

587. All orders by the Minister shall be referred to the Presidential Council for Religious Harmony for its deliberation and consideration. The Council must, within thirty days, make its recommendations to the President. All orders shall cease to

287. For a comment on this legislation, *see* V.S. Winslow, *The Separation of Religion and Politics: The Maintenance of Religious Harmony Act 1990*, 32 Mal LR 327 (1990).

have effect unless it is confirmed by the President within thirty days from the date the Council presents its recommendations.[288]

588. The MRHA regulates religious harmony in Singapore by creating a Presidential Council for Religious Harmony, and prohibiting certain forms of behaviour. Essentially, it prohibits two types of acts: (i) those that directly cause disharmony between different religions; and (ii) those that indirectly cause disharmony, when religion and politics are mixed. The Council's responsibility is to report on such matters pertaining to religious harmony in Singapore as are referred to it by the Minister or by Parliament, and to consider and make recommendations on prohibition orders made by the Minister.

IV. The Meaning of 'Religion'

589. Since only religions qualify for protection under Article 15, it is important for us to define 'religion'. No attempt has been made by a Singapore court to define what is 'religion' within the meaning of Article 15. In one of the best known and oft-cited attempts by an English court, Dillon J. held in the case of *In re South Place Ethical Society*[289] that religion was concerned with man's relationship with God, and that it required two elements: (i) faith and (ii) worship. In other words, 'faith in a god and worship of that god'. In *Church of New Faith v. Commissioner for Pay-Roll Tax*,[290] the Australian High Court held 'religion' to comprise: (a) belief in a supernatural Being, Thing or Principle; and (b) the acceptance of canons of conduct in order to give effect to that belief.

590. This question came up for consideration locally in *Nappalli Peter Williams v. Institute of Technical Education*.[291] The appellant Williams was a Jehovah's witness and taught for several years at the Institute of Technical Education (ITE). Like all schools in Singapore, all staff and students attend a daily flag-raising, national anthem singing and pledge-taking ceremony. A circular requiring staff to do so was also issued in 1988 by the authorities. Williams refused to take part in these daily ceremonies on the grounds that they were religious ceremonies and such ceremonies were only reserved for God. He argued that the 1988 circular violated his constitutional rights under Article 16(3) of the Constitution which provides that:

> No person shall be required to receive instruction in or to take part in any ceremony or act of worship or a religion other than his own.

591. The Court of Appeal held that 'religion' is about 'a citizen's faith in a personal God' or supernatural being, and not about 'a system of belief in one's own

288. Section 11, Maintenance of Religious Harmony Act (Cap 167A).
289. [1980] 1 WLR 1565.
290. (1984) 49 ALR 65 (High Court of Australia).
291. [1999] 2 SLR 569.

country'. Chief Justice Yong Pung How further added that as 'the State commands no any supernatural existence in a citizen's personal belief system', Williams' constitutional rights were not violated. He concluded with these observations:

> Obviously, not every conviction or belief, including those held with what ironically may best be described as religious fervour, qualifies as a religious belief. Indeed, we were inclined to agree with the view of the lower court in *Thomas v Review Board of the Indian Employment Security Division* (1981) 450 US 707 that such beliefs would best be philosophical choices rather than religious beliefs. In other words, although the pledge ceremony does not demand worship of the flag as a symbol, if a person held that understanding, that perception was a philosophical choice. It seemed clear to us that the appellant's interpretation of the pledge and anthem ceremony as a religious ceremony was a distortion of secular fact into religious belief. It is not accepted as a religious belief and is not entitled to protection under the Constitution of Singapore.[292]

V. The Protection of Minors

592. Under Article 15, 'everyone' is protected but does 'everyone' include a minor? Can a minor (i.e., someone under the age of 21 years) claim the right to the freedom of religion under Article 15? This question has never been litigated in Singapore, but the Malaysian courts had occasion to consider this in *Re Susie Teoh*.[293] In that case, Susie Teoh, a 17-year-old girl, ran away from home and converted to Islam. Her father sought a declaration that he could decide her religion, and that her conversion to Islam (having been made without his consent) was null and void. Justice Abdul Malek held that the father had no right under the Guardianship of Infants Act 1961 to choose a religion for his daughter, and that in any event she had a right under Article 11(1) of the Malaysian Constitution to choose her own religion.

593. It is doubtful if the same conclusion would be reached if a Singapore court were to have decided the same case. The common law age of majority in Singapore is 21, and the age to consent of marriage is 18. Furthermore, Article 16(3) of the Constitution provides that:

> No person shall be required to receive instruction in or to take part in any ceremony or act of worship of a religion other than his own.

Article 16(4) goes on to provide that for the purposes of Article 16(3), 'the religion of a person under the age of 18 years shall be decided by his parent or guardian'.

---

292. *See Nappalli Peter Williams v. Institute of Technical Education* [1999] 2 SLR 569, at 576.
293. [1986] 2 MLJ 228 (High Court, Malaysia).

VI. Content and Extent of Religious Liberty

594. The Constitution protects religious practices but reserves the right to curtail them as well. As Karthigesu JA declared in the Court of Appeal decision of *Chan Hiang Leng Colin v. Minister for Information and the Arts* (1996):

> There is no provision in either the Societies Act or the Undesirable Publications Act which prohibits the holding of a religious belief. It is … not illegal to profess the beliefs of Jehovah's Witnesses *per se*, nor is it an offence to be a Jehovah's Witness. A citizen's right to profess, practice or propagate his religious belief, even as a Jehovah's Witness, has not been taken away. It is the manner of carrying out these activities that are circumscribed by the relevant orders. The relevant orders provide that in pursuing these activities, Jehovah's Witnesses may not be a member of the SCJW or any other unregistered society and they may not have access to the prohibited publications.[294]

595. Society has a clear right to guard against activity infringing on the rights of other members of society. For example, the Japanese Aum Shinrikyo cult leader Shoko Asahara has been charged with murder in June 1995 in connection with the March 1995 sarin gas attack in a Tokyo subway. Acts done in the name of religion are not immune from the regulation of general laws. It has been said that 'The first and most fundamental duty of every Government is the preservation of order, since order is the condition precedent to all civilization and the advance of human happiness.'[295]

596. This is constitutionally recognized by Article 15(4) of the Constitution which states that religious liberty does not authorize any act contrary to any general law relating to public order, public health or morality. This is an important consideration in the light of the turbulent history of religious conflict in this region. Hence, like other fundamental liberties, religion is not absolute. Article 11 distinguishes between the *practice* and *propagation* of religion: Article 11 allows states to enact laws restricting propagation of any religious doctrines among persons professing Islam.

597. The Singapore Government has a comprehensive arsenal of general laws that may be used to limit religious freedom. For example, the Societies Act may be used to outlaw certain religious groups such as the Jehovah's Witnesses. If the Registrar refuses registration or cancels the existing registration of a religious group, this will make it an unlawful society. Anyone who attends any such meeting would be liable to be punished. The Minister may also dissolve any registered society if it is used for purposes 'prejudicial to public peace, welfare or good order'.

---

294. *Chan Hiang Leng Colin & Ors v. Minister for Information and the Arts* [1996] 1 SLR 609, at 615.
295. *See Reg v. Alexander Martin Sullivan* (1867-71) 11 Cox CC 44.

The Undesirable Publications Act gives the Government power to ban 'undesirable' religious material, while the draconian ISA 1960 and the Sedition Act are potential and potent tools to use against the overzealous. The Penal Code criminalizes the utterance of words that are intended to wound another's religious feelings.

Chapter 3. Judicial Control of Administrative Action

§1. Administrative Law Under a Written Constitution

598. The Constitution does not regulate every sphere of government activity. Under the Westminster parliamentary model of government, the executive commands a great deal of power and possesses much discretion. Regardless of how wide a discretion the executive might have, it is still necessary to ensure that they do not act illegally or capriciously. This role is reserved for the judiciary as the final arbiters of what the law is. The case law that developed over the last fifty years in this regard now constitutes a specialized field of study known as *administrative law*. Strictly speaking, administrative law is not considered to be part of the rubric of constitutional law. However, the two areas of law share many commonalities which will become evident in the course of this chapter.

599. In England, administrative law developed in the absence of a written constitution and thus forms part and parcel of what a British student might study in a course on constitutional law. This body of judge-made law has been transplanted into Singapore which has a written constitution providing for the judiciary as final arbiter of limits to legislative power. The power of Singapore's Parliament is limited, and the courts may strike down Acts of Parliament which contravene the Constitution (*see* Article 4).

600. Furthermore, the courts are constitutionally responsible for ensuring that the executive branch does not overstep its legal powers. In the case of *Chng Suan Tze v. The Minister of Home Affairs*, the Court of Appeal affirmed that:

> the notion of a subjective or unfettered discretion is contrary to the rule of law. All power has legal limits and the rule of law demands that the courts should be able to examine the exercise of discretionary power.[296]

601. The rule of law requires that administrative bodies should not be the final arbiters on the legality of their own decisions. Instead, they should be subject to correction or supervision by the courts. Many facets of the rule of law find explicit expression in Singapore constitutional law. For example, Article 12 of the Constitution mandates that all persons are *equal before the law* and entitled to the *equal protection of the law*, while Article 9 provides a person may not be deprived of life or liberty arbitrarily but *in accordance with law*.

602. For a decision to be subject to judicial review, it must be one made by a public authority in the exercise of a public power. To determine if the decision is one that falls under the rubric of public law, we look at both the source of the power being exercised and the nature of the power being exercised. The 'source of power'

296. [1988] SLR 132, at 156.

approach was developed in England in the leading cases of *Council of Civil Service Unions & Others v. Minister for the Civil Service*[297] and *R v. Panel on Take-Overs and Mergers, ex parte Datafin plc & Anor*[298] and adopted by the SGCA in *Public Service Commission v. Lai Swee Lin Linda.*[299]

603. Courts cannot substitute their decisions for those of the executive. That would be overstepping its role under the constitutional separation of powers. What the court must do is to pronounce on the *legality* or *process* of decision-making rather than the *substance* or merits of a decision. Two constitutional justifications are offered for the courts' intervention in executive decision-making: (a) courts implement Parliament's will by confining the decision-maker within his or her statutory allocation of power; and (b) this forms part of the checks and balances under the separation of powers doctrine.

I. Controlling Delegated Legislation

604. Under Article 58 of the Constitution, legislative power is exercised by Parliament through the laws it passes. Parliament may also confer executive functions on any persons under Article 23(2). Section 36 of the Interpretation Act provides that the Minister may subdelegate his or her powers to another official 'with the approval of the President and by notification in the *Gazette*', provided there is no written law to the contrary. However, the Minister must personally exercise the power to make delegated legislation; he or she cannot delegate it.

605. Time constraints and other practicalities mean that over the years, the legislature has increasingly delegated its lawmaking function to ministers and non-elected administrative agents. Acts of Parliament are general in coverage, and details are left to be fleshed out by administrative officials according to law. This is done through rules, orders and regulations – all of which come under the rubric of 'subordinate' or 'delegated' legislation. This process is simpler, much more flexible and less time-consuming than the normal legislative process.

606. Under section 2 of the Interpretation Act, 'subsidiary legislation' is defined as:

> any order in council, proclamation, rule, regulation, order, notification, by-law or other instrument made under any Act, Ordinance or other lawful authority and having legislative effect.

297. [1985] 1 AC 374 (House of Lords, UK).
298. [1987] QB 815.
299. [2001] 1 SLR 644.

607. Any subsidiary legislation must be laid before Parliament and published in the *Gazette* (section 23 of the Interpretation Act). Failure to publish renders it void. Laws must be accessible and made known to the public at large so that they may order their lives accordingly.

608. The validity of subsidiary legislation may be challenged on substantive and procedural grounds. For a start, a piece of subsidiary legislation may be challenged if it violates any constitutional provision. If it is constitutional, it may still be invalid if it conflicts with the parent statute. A statutory instrument may be considered substantially ultra vires (enacted outside jurisdiction) if the parent Act does not confer the executive power to pass that particular instrument. The Singapore courts have adopted Lord Diplock's three-step approach in *McEldowney v. Forde* which requires that the court:

> first, to determine the meaning of the words used in the Act of Parliament itself to describe the subordinate legislation which that authority is authorised to make; secondly, to determine the meaning of the subordinate legislation itself and finally to decide whether the subordinate legislation complies with that description.[300]

609. A statutory instrument may be procedurally ultra vires if the procedure laid down by the parent Act is ignored or violated.

II. Informal Rules or Guidelines

610. While both primary and subsidiary legislation must be laid before Parliament and published in the *Gazette*, there is no legal requirement for informal rules or quasi-delegated legislation to be published. How then can the court ensure that such administrative rules or guidelines are adhered to and that they do not prejudice the common man. The status and legal effect of administrative guidelines arose in the High Court case of *Lines International Holding Pte Ltd v. Singapore Tourist Promotion Board and Port of Singapore Authority.*[301]

611. In this case, the plaintiff Lines International, who operated cruises, was denied berthing rights for failing to comply with guidelines which the Singapore Tourist Promotion Board (STPB) and the Port of Singapore Authority (PSA) issued in 1995. These guidelines, which were orally communicated to local cruise operators, stated that 'Cruises to Nowhere' (CNW) should not exceed 30% of the voyages undertaken by a cruise vessel. At the time the guidelines were made, Lines International had contracted to maintain a 66% CNW schedule. It was widely known that the chief form of entertainment of a CNW was casino gambling. Lines

300. [1971] AC 632 at 658 (House of Lords, UK).
301. [1997] 2 SLR 584.

International argued that the relevant administrative bodies had no power to issue these guidelines, and as such, they were ultra vires and unenforceable.

612. Judith Prakash J held that the PSA had power to control the use of berths and could thus rely on the guidelines to justify denying Lines' vessel a berth even though these guidelines were never officially promulgated. She further identified four conditions that validated the adoption of a general policy: (1) the adoption of a general policy must not fetter the authority's discretion to deal with exceptional cases; (2) the guidelines must be made known to all those affected; (3) the policy must not be unreasonable in the limited *Wednesbury* sense;[302] and (4) in considering what 'reasonableness' constituted, the courts would be vigilantly cognizant that they were not to impose or substitute their views on how the discretion should be exercised.

III. Judicial Review of Administrative Action

613. Judicial *review* is concerned not with the correctness or substantive merits of a decision but its legality. If a decision is illegal, the court quashes it (i.e., renders it a nullity) and directs the relevant public authority to decide the issue again. The merits of a case can only be heard on an *appeal.* In conducting judicial review, courts are more willing to intervene in questions of law rather than questions of fact. Of course, the court will not hesitate to intervene if a tribunal's factual findings are so seriously flawed, in that there is no evidential support for its conclusion. Similarly, if a tribunal has reached a totally unreasonable conclusion on the basis of certain facts, the court can intervene.

§2. Precedent or Jurisdictional Facts

614. Courts will scrutinize more stringently cases where precedent or jurisdictional facts are involved. A *precedent fact* is one upon which the exercise of an administrative power depends. The court will determine if the administrative body or tribunal has made a correct or right finding. For example, a statute may give a Minister discretion to order the temporary detention of anyone 'who is a repeat offender'. The precedent fact in this instance would be whether the subject is indeed a 'repeat offender' or not. It would be insufficient if the Minister *suspects* him or her to be a 'repeat offender'. The question as to whether a precedent fact has been satisfied involves a true/false proposition rather than a reasonable opinion.

615. Here, the court had to enquire whether the facts justified the decision. Where a non-precedent fact is involved, a less rigorous standard is applied: the issue is whether one can reasonably come to a decision on the evidence. In reviewing this, the court must enquire into the existence of the facts upon which the evaluation was

302. *See Associated Provincial Picture Houses v. Wednesbury Corporation* [1948] 1 KB 223.

made. In *Cheong Seok Leng's* case,[303] Chan Sek Keong J (as he then was) cited with approval what Lord Wilberforce said in the *Secretary of State for Education and Science v. Tameside MBC*[1977] AC 1014:

> If a judgment requires, before it can be made, the existence of some facts, … the court must inquire whether those facts exist and have been taken into account, whether the judgment has been made upon a proper self-direction as to those facts, whether the judgment has not been made upon other facts which ought not to have been taken into account. If these requirements are not met, then the exercise of judgment, however bona fide it may be, becomes capable of challenge.

§3. Errors of Law

616. Traditionally, a distinction was drawn between jurisdictional errors of law and non-jurisdictional errors of law. A jurisdictional error said to *go to jurisdiction* (or affect jurisdiction) is ultra vires since it affects the tribunal's power to act. However, when an error is committed *within jurisdiction*, the court will decline to interfere unless there is an *error of law on the face of the record*: one which is evident just from an examination of the record.

617. However, recent decisions from the English courts have eradicated this distinction. One of the first such decisions was the House of Lords decision of *Anisminic v. Foreign Compensation Commission*[304] in which Lord Reid made a distinction between 'narrow' and 'broad' definitions of jurisdictional errors. Lord Denning went one step further in the Court of Appeal decision in *Pearlman v. Keepers and Governors of Harrow School*[305] where he held that 'no court or tribunal has any jurisdiction to make an error of law on which the decision of the case depends'.

618. The current approach is that adopted in *Page v. Hull University Visitor*[306] which was followed by the Malaysian Court of Appeal in *Syarikat Kenderaan Melayu Kelantan Bhd v. Transport Workers' Union*[307] where Gopal Sri Ram JCA quoted with approval the following words of Lord Browne-Wilkinson in *Page v. Hull*:

> In my judgment, the decision in *Anisminic* … rendered obsolete the distinction between errors of law on the face of the record and other errors of law by extending the doctrine of ultra vires. Thenceforward it was to be taken that Parliament had only conferred on the decision-making power on the basis that it was to be exercised on the correct legal basis: a misdirection in law in making the decision therefore rendered the decision ultra vires.

303. *Cheong Seok Leng v. PP* [1988] 2 MLJ 481.
304. [1969] 2 AC 147 (House of Lords, UK).
305. [1979] QB 56 (Court of Appeal, UK).
306. [1993] AC 682.
307. [1995] 2 MLJ 317.

I. The Control of Substantive Discretion

619. Any discretionary power is limited and subject to judicial review. However, not every decision is subject to judicial review. The decision-maker must be empowered by public law to make decisions leading to administrative action. An improper exercise of discretion arises in several instances. First, the exercise of discretion suggests the application of the official's own mind to the matter. If that official is merely acting under someone else's instruction or has simply delegated this discretion to another, the decision may be impugned. At the same time, if the exercise of discretion has been fettered, for example, by too rigid an adherence to a policy or set of guidelines, that would also be invalid.

II. The Grounds of Judicial Review

620. In a now-classic judgment in the *Council of Civil Service Unions v. Minister for the Civil Service* (the '*GCHQ* case'),[308] Lord Diplock categorized the grounds for the judicial review of government action as: (a) illegality, (b) irrationality, (c) procedural impropriety, and (d) possibly proportionality. This categorization was expressly adopted by the SGCA in *Chng Suan Tze v. Minister of Home Affairs.*[309] A contravention of any of these grounds will render a decision ultra vires. Let us consider each of these grounds briefly.

§4. Illegality

621. Illegality occurs when a public authority exercises a power he or she does not possess. The same can be said if he or she acted in a manner contrary to the policy and objects of the Act in question. Naturally, the wider the object of a legislation is framed, the wider the powers of the executive authority. In Singapore, the courts adopted a broad approach to the 'purpose test' in *PP v. MM Pillay*,[310] where the High Court held that an administrative measure need not directly relate to the statutes' purpose but need only be 'incidental thereto'.

§5. Irrationality

622. By 'irrationality', Lord Diplock was referring to what can be succinctly called '*Wednesbury* unreasonableness'. In *Associated Pictures v. Wednesbury*,[311] Lord Greene MR held that the authority exercising discretion must take into consideration relevant factors set out in the statute, ignore irrelevant collateral matters,

308. [1985] 1 AC 374 (House of Lords, UK).
309. [1989] 1 MLJ 69. For a comment on *Chng Suan Tze*, *see* Sin Boon Ann, *Judges and Administrative Discretion – A Look at* Chng Suan Tze v. Minister of Home Affairs & Ors, 2 MLJ ci (1989).
310. [1977] 1 MLJ 228.
311. [1948] 1 KB 223 (Court of Appeal, UK).

have due regard for public policy and not be 'unreasonable'. The kind of unreasonable decision referred to by Lord Greene is one:

> which is so outrageous in its defiance of logic or of accepted moral standards that no sensible person who had applied his mind to the question to be decided could have arrived at it.

623. In *Ng Hock Guan v. Attorney-General,*[312] the plaintiff Ng was a senior investigation officer of the Anti-Vice Branch of the Criminal Investigation Department (CID) of the Police Force. He was charged for allegedly slapping three Filipina suspects, and disciplinary proceedings were preferred against him. After a fifteen-day hearing involving nineteen witnesses, the Authorized Officer found Ng guilty and Ng was dismissed from the Police Force. Ng sought judicial review of the Authorized Officer's decision. Justice Lai Kew Chai held that the manner in which the Authorized Officer arrived at his decision, especially his prejudicial attitude towards some key witnesses, was 'irrational and one which no rational and fair-minded arbiter properly directing himself would have made'.

§6. Procedural Impropriety

624. 'Procedural impropriety' refers to instances when executive action fails to comply with: (a) common law principles of *natural justice*; and (b) statutorily requirements of procedural fairness. Natural justice, in this context, refers to two procedural rules: (i) the rule against bias (*nemo iudex in causa sua*); and (ii) the right to a fair hearing (*audi alteram partem*). In *Stansfield Business International Pte Ltd v. Minister for Manpower,*[313] Warren Khoo J explained the nature of the rules of natural justice:

> Rules of natural justice are not some arcane doctrine of law. They represent what the ordinary man expects and accepts as fair procedure for the resolution of conflicts and disputes by a decision-making body that affects his interest. The ordinary man will feel he has not been fairly heard if he has not been allowed a reasonable opportunity to present his case. He will equally feel that he has not been fairly heard if he has not been fully informed of what his opponent has to say or if he has not been given an opportunity to answer it or correct it. He will similarly feel aggrieved if a point is taken by the tribunal and he has not been given an opportunity to answer it or correct it. So the rules of natural justice require simply, first, that a party is told of the case he has to meet and of the allegations made against him; secondly, that he is given not only a fair opportunity to put his own case, but also a fair opportunity to correct or

312. [2004] 1 SLR 415.
313. [1999] 3 SLR 742.

contradict the case and the allegations of the other party; thirdly, if a significant point is to be taken against him by the tribunal, he should have a similar opportunity.

625. The rule against bias requires that a person may not be a judge in a case in which he or she has a personal or pecuniary interest. In *Chiam See Tong v. Singapore Democratic Party*,[314] for example, the court held the members of the SDP's Central Executive Committee to be biased in view of its members' confrontational and hostile tone. Two major tests have been developed to determine the extent of bias necessary to disqualify an adjudicator: (a) reasonable suspicion of bias; and (b) real likelihood of bias.

626. Both these tests were considered in *De Souza Lionel Jerome v. AG*.[315] Lim Teong Quee JC examined the two tests and favoured the more stringent 'reasonable suspicion of bias' test as seen through the eyes of a reasonable person with knowledge of all matters before the court.

627. 'Fair hearing' requires that an accused be given due notice of the charges made against him or her and the right to be heard before an unbiased tribunal. An accused must be given adequate notification of the date, time and place of the hearing as well as detailed notification of the case he or she is to meet. In *Chiam See Tong v. Singapore Democratic Party*, Chiam was never told the real nature of the grievance against him and was thus not fully apprised of the case against him.

628. The hearing must also be conducted fairly and properly. In *Tan Boon Chee David v. Medical Council of Singapore*,[316] the members of the Medical Council were found to be very slipshod in their attendance at the disciplinary hearings. Some of them did not even stay through the whole proceeding and thus did not hear all the oral evidence and submissions made. The court held that this conduct substantially prejudiced the appellant Tan and constituted a fundamental breach of natural justice.

629. A right to a fair hearing does not automatically import the right to legal representation. Tribunals have discretion to admit or bar legal counsel, depending on the circumstances, including: (a) the seriousness of the charge and of the potential penalty; (b) whether any points of law were likely to arise; (c) the capacity of a particular accused to present his or her own case; (d) procedural difficulties faced by accused in conducting their own defence, for example, lack of access to potential witnesses; (e) the need for reasonable speed in making the adjudication; and (f) the need for fairness as between the accused and between accused and accusers.

---

314. [1994] 1 SLR 278.
315. [1993] 1 SLR 882.
316. [1994] 1 SLR 278.

630. Tribunals must also give reasons for their decisions. This will enable an aggrieved individual to know the possible grounds the decision may be challenged. This also helps ensure that decisions are carefully thought through. In *Re Siah Mooi Guat*,[317] the High Court held that there was no common law duty requiring an authority or administrative tribunal to give reasons. The House of Lords held in *Doody v. SS for the Home Department*[318] that while there was no general duty at common law to give reasons for an administrative decision, 'it is equally beyond question that such a duty may in appropriate circumstances be implied'.

§7. PROPORTIONALITY?

631. In addition to Lord Diplock's 'Three "I"s', the ground of proportionality has been invoked in some local cases. Proportionality is concerned with the balance between the objects of the statute and the means by which the objects are to be achieved. In *PB Chapman v. Deputy Registrar of Companies*,[319] the court held that the appellant Chapman's acts were not dishonest or criminal and as such did not merit the extreme penalty of permanently being disqualified from holding a securities dealer's licence. The doctrine of proportionality was discussed by the Court of Appeal in *Chan Hiang Leng Colin & Ors v. Minister for Information and the Arts*;[320] *Chng Suan Tze v. Minister of Home Affairs*[321] and *Kang Ngah Wei v. Commander of Traffic Police*,[322] even though it was subsumed under 'irrationality'.

§8. LEGITIMATE EXPECTATIONS

632. While the principle of legitimate expectation has long been recognized as a separate head of judicial review in several jurisdictions, it was recognized as such in Singapore in 2013 in *Chiu Teng @ Kallang Pte Ltd v. Singapore Land Authority*.[323] In this case, the applicant challenged the respondent's assessment of the differential premium payable for the lifting of title restrictions for two plots of land. In the course of his judgment, Justice Tay Yong Kwang entered into a detailed discussion of the concept of legitimate expectation and held that it should be recognized as a separate head of judicial review in Singapore and operate as follows:

> In my opinion, the doctrine of legitimate expectation should be recognised in our law as a stand-alone head of judicial review and substantive relief should be granted under the doctrine subject to certain safeguards. Having regard to the case law from the various common law jurisdictions and applying some

317. [1980] 2 MLJ 116.
318. [1992] 2 MLJ 337.
319. [1993] 3 All ER 92 (House of Lords, UK).
320. [1977] 2 MLJ 5.
321. [1996] 1 SLR 609.
322. [1989] 1 MLJ 69.
323. [2013] SGHC 262.

commonsensical principles, I believe the doctrine can operate effectively and fairly in the following manner without the court overstepping its judicial role:

a. The applicant must prove that the statement or representation made by the public authority was unequivocal and unqualified:
   - If the statement or representation is open to more than one natural interpretation, the interpretation applied by the public authority will be adopted; and
   - The presence of a disclaimer or non-reliance clause would cause the statement or representation to be qualified.
b. The applicant must prove that the statement or representation was made by someone with actual or ostensible authority to do so on behalf of the public authority;
c. The applicant must prove that the statement or representation was made to him or to a class of persons to which he clearly belongs;
d. The applicant must prove that it was reasonable for him to rely on the statement or representation in the circumstances of his case:
   - If the applicant knew that the statement or representation was made in error and chose to capitalize on the error, he will not be entitled to any relief;
   - Similarly, if he suspected that the statement or representation was made in error and chose not to seek clarification when he could have done so, he will not be entitled to any relief;
   - If there is reason and opportunity to make enquiries and the applicant did not, he will not be entitled to any relief.
e. The applicant must prove that he did rely on the statement or representation and that he suffered a detriment as a result;
f. Even if all the above requirements are met, the court should nevertheless not grant relief if:
   - Giving effect to the statement or representation will result in a breach of the law or the state's international obligations;
   - Giving effect to the statement or representation will infringe the accrued rights of some member of the public;
   - The public authority can show an overriding national or public interest which justifies the frustration of the applicant's expectation.

I. Limits to Judicial Review

633. The ongoing tension between the judicial and executive branches of government in respect of administrative decision-making has resulted in various efforts by the legislature to curtail the courts' judicial review jurisdiction. These limits may be categorized as follows: (a) constitutional exclusion of judicial review, (b) statutory exclusion of judicial review through *ouster clauses*, and (c) non-statutory exclusion of judicial review.

§9. Constitutional Limitation on Judicial Review

634. Certain provisions in the Constitution explicitly exclude judicial review. For example, Article 100(4) of the Constitution provides that 'no Court shall have jurisdiction to question the opinion' of the Special Tribunal while Article 149(3) of the Constitution prohibits the courts from applying any law in reviewing detentions under the ISA except that provided by section 8B of the Act itself. It has been argued, albeit unsuccessfully, in *Teo Soh Lung v. Minister of Home Affairs*[324] that this legislative enactment and constitutional amendment violated the basic features of the Singapore Constitution.

§10. Statutory Exclusion of Judicial Review: Ouster Clauses

635. Ever since the great English Chief Justice Sir Edward Coke (1552–1634) told King James I (1566–1625) that he was not above the law and that he could not sit in judgment in his own courts, Parliament has sought to limit the power of courts to review legislation and the decisions of statutory tribunals. In Singapore, Parliament has attempted to curtail or preclude judicial review through statutory ouster clauses, for example, under the ISA and the MRHA. The clause may stipulate that any determination by an administrative body is 'final and conclusive' or 'shall not be called into question in a court of law'. Typically, the following devices are used: (a) Finality Clauses, (b) 'No Certiorari' Clauses, (c) 'Shall Not Be Questioned' Clauses, and (d) 'As If Enacted' and 'Conclusive Evidence' Clauses.

636. Typically, *Finality Clauses* provide that a Minister's decision shall be 'final', or that a tribunal's decision shall be 'final'. The idea behind this tactic is to render the decision unreviewable or unassailable. The courts have not been deterred. In the seminal case of *R v. Medical Appeal Tribunal Ex Parte Gilmore*,[325] Denning LJ (as he then was) held that the only effect of the finality clause was to prevent an appeal, and did not preclude judicial review of decisions made ultra vires:

> In stopping this abuse the statutes proved very beneficial, but the court never allowed those statutes to be used as a cover for wrongdoing by tribunals. If tribunals were to be at liberty to exceed their jurisdiction without any check by the courts, the rule of law would be at an end.

637. Even when the right to certiorari has been expressly taken away through 'non-certiorari clauses', the courts will invoke their power of judicial review on the assumption that Parliament could not possibly have intended that tribunal of limited jurisdiction be permitted to exceed its authority without the possibility of direct correction by a superior court. Again, Denning LJ in ex parte *Gilmore* said:

324. [2002] 1 SLR 213.
325. [1989] 2 MLJ 449.

> the remedy by *certiorari* is never to be taken away by any statute except by the most clear and explicit words. The word 'final' is not enough. That only means 'without appeal'. It does not mean 'without recourse to *certiorari*. It makes the decision final on the facts, but not final on the law. Notwithstanding that the decision is by a statute must final', *certiorari* can still issue for excess of jurisdiction or for error of law on the face of the record.[326]

638. Another method used by the legislature to exclude the courts is a *shall not be questioned clause* which was encountered in *Southeast Asia Firebricks Sdn Bhd v. Non-Metallic Mineral Products Manufacturers Employees Union*,[327] and it may or may not be used in conjunction with a 'no certiorari' clause.

639. Finally, *as if enacted* and *conclusive evidence clauses* may be employed. This device typically runs like this: this statutory order shall have effect 'as if enacted in this Act' or that confirmation by the Minister 'shall be conclusive evidence that the requirements of the Act have been complied with, and that the order has been duly made and is within the powers of the Act'. These clauses are meant to exclude judicial review of ministerial decisions and by-laws which have been made previously.

640. The courts have tried constantly to grapple with the problems of review and its limits. In Singapore, it would appear that as far back as 1978, the High Court adopted a generous view of its supervisory powers in the face of ouster clauses. In *Re Application by Yee Yut Ee*,[328] the High Court had to consider the effect of section 46 of the Industrial Relations Act which read:

> Subject to the provisions of this Act an award shall be final and conclusive, and no award or decision or order of a Court or the President or a referee shall be challenged, appealed against, reviewed, quashed, or called in question in any court and shall not be subject to certiorari, prohibition, mandamus or injunction in any court on any account.

641. Choor Singh J held that this clause did not preclude the High Court from exercising its jurisdiction to issue certiorari to the Industrial Arbitration Court to quash its decision if the tribunal:

> was improperly constituted, or if it lacked or exceeded jurisdiction, or failed to comply with essential preliminaries, or if a conviction or order had been procured by fraud or collusion, or where there has been a breach of the rules of natural justice.

---

326. *R v. Medical Appeal Tribunal Ex Parte Gilmore* [1957] 1 QB 574 (Court of Appeal, UK).
327. *Ibid.*, at 583.
328. [1980] 2 MLJ 165.

642. Chan Sek Keong CJ, in an extrajudicial speech, suggested that in a constitutional supremacy like Singapore, where the judicial power is vested in the judiciary under separation of powers, any attempt by the legislature to limit the court's powers of judicial review through privative clauses might prima facie be an interference with the court's judicial powers and thus void.[329]

I. Subjective Powers

643. The legislature may try to limit judicial review by conferring powers on an administrative body framed in terms of 'if the minister is so satisfied'. However, the courts have held that even absolute discretion is reviewable as 'the notion of a subjective or unfettered discretion is contrary to the rule of law'. In *JB Jeyaretnam v. Public Prosecutor*,[330] the constitutionality of the Public Entertainment Act was challenged as an unjustifiable interference with the right to freedom of speech under Article 14 of the Constitution. Chan Sek Keong J (as he then was) noted that while the licensing officer had discretion in refusing to issue licences, it would be unconstitutional to give arbitrary powers to an officer to deprive of a citizen of his or her constitutional rights.

II. Conclusion

644. In administrative law, more than anywhere else, one sees the separation of powers doctrine at work. The growth of a large administrative service and bureaucracy is a fact of modern life, and this has been matched with the correspondence growth of administrative law. Courts are charged with the constitutional duty of pronouncing on the law, its limits and whether the other branches have acted within the law. In Singapore, the development of administrative law is still in its infancy. The jurisprudence of Singapore's courts closely mirrors developments in England. The courts are also extremely practical in orientation and are prepared to give administrative authorities a wide berth. In the areas of public order and national security, the courts are especially sympathetic to executive and national concerns. There is thus a general reluctance to vigorously apply and develop tests to control executive discretion, or to develop administrative law according to fundamental values and principles as evinced in the Constitution.

329. Chan Sek Keong, *Judicial Review: From Angst to Empathy: A Lecture to Singapore Management University Second Year Law Students*, 22 SALJ 469, at 477 (2010).
330. [1978] 2 MLJ 142.

Chapter 4. Emergency Laws

§1. Special Powers Against Subversion and Emergency Powers

645. As a result of communist insurgency, the British proclaimed a state of emergency throughout the whole of Malaya and Singapore in 1948. These subversive activities continued for over a decade, and in 1957, the Reid Commission recommended including Article 149 in the Constitution to give Parliament wide powers to combat the communists by allowing it to enact legislation which may contravene other parts of the Constitution. Most notable among the laws passed under this provision is the ISA 1960. In Singapore, the ISA remained in the statute books as an inheritance from Malaysia after 9 August 1965.

646. Part XII of the Constitution gives special powers to the legislature and the executive to deal with emergencies and subversion. Article 149 – which is primarily directed against subversion – gives Parliament the power to make laws that even contravene the fundamental liberties of the person. This occurs primarily in the area of preventive detention or detention without trial. This fundamental derogation is justified by the extraordinary need to secure Singapore's internal security and public order.

647. In an emergency, Article 150 confers powers on both the legislature and executive to make laws that may contradict the Constitution. Article 151 lays down specific procedural guidelines to be followed when a person is incarcerated by preventive detention laws passed under this part.

I. The ISA: Constitutional Issues[331]

648. Under section 74 of the ISA, a police officer may, without a warrant, arrest a person if he or she has 'reason to believe' that there are grounds which would justify his or her detention under section 8, and that the person has acted or is about to act or is likely to act in any manner prejudicial to the security of the country. A person may be detained for up to thirty days provided the detention is duly authorized by officers of suitable rank under the provisions, and other procedural safeguards. A person so detained is deemed to be in lawful custody.

649. The Minister for Home Affairs may order a person to be detained for up to two years if the President 'is satisfied' that it is necessary to prevent that person from acting in any manner prejudicial to the security of, or to the maintenance of public order or essential services in, the country, under section 8(2). This order may be extended up to two years at a time for an indefinite period. Let us now consider some of the constitutional issues relating to preventive detention under the ISA.

331. [1990] 1 MLJ 129.

§2. The Recital

650. For Parliament to lawfully enact legislation under Article 149, that legislation must recite that:

> action has been taken or threatened by any substantial body of persons, whether inside or outside the country to cause, or to cause a substantial number of citizens to fear, organized violence against persons or property, to excite disaffection against the Head of the nation or the government, to promote hostility between races or different classes of the population, to procure an unlawful alteration of anything established by law, or which is generally prejudicial to the security of the nation.

651. Such a recital is to ensure that the law is valid notwithstanding any inconsistency with the Constitution. Two major issues arise for consideration: (1) can the court go behind the legislation and ask if it was in fact designed to stop or prevent such action, or is the recital conclusive? and (2) to what extent can the court question whether a decision under the Act was in fact made for the purposes of the Act?

652. In *Teo Soh Lung v. The Minister for Home Affairs and Anor*,[332] the amendments (Internal Security (Amendment) Act No. 2 of 1989) to the ISA (Cap 143, 1985 ed) were challenged on the basis that they were not made to prevent subversive actions, and thus fell outside the scope of Article 149. Justice Chua held that the question as to whether any law was enacted pursuant to Article 149 was non-justiciable.

§3. Inconsistency with Other Provisions

653. Laws enacted under Article 149 may legally contravene the following articles in the Constitution: Articles 9 (personal liberty), 11 (retrospective criminal laws), 12 (equality), 13 (freedom of movement) and 14 (freedom of speech, assembly and association). Article 149(3) further exempts laws relating to judicial review of executive action from complying with Article 93 (judicial power). However, courts adopt a strict construction when personal liberty is at stake. Express words must be used in the statute before the court will consider a fundamental right to be superseded. Thus, the right to counsel in the second limb of Article 9(3), though not

332. On the legal issues involved in preventive detention, *see* Tan Yock Lin, *Some Aspects of Preventive Detention in Malaysia and Singapore*, 29 Mal LR 237 (1987); and Kevin Y.L. Tan, *Recent Developments in the Law and Practice of Preventive Detention*, in *Public Law in Contemporary Malaysia* 293–315 (Wu Min Aun ed., Longman 1999). For a review of the role of habeas corpus in relation to preventive detention, *see* H.F. Rawlings, *Habeas Corpus and Preventive Detention in Singapore and Malaysia*, 25 Mal LR 324 (1983). As to how internal security laws are applied in Singapore, *see* Francis T. Seow, *To Catch a Tartar: A Dissident in Lee Kuan Yew's Prison*, Monograph 42 Yale S.E Asia Stud., Yale Ctr. Intl. & Area Stud. (1994); and *Silencing All Critics: Human Rights Violations in Singapore, An Asia Watch Report* 13–31 (USA 1989).

spelt out in the ISA, remains a fundamental right of a detainee arrested under the ISA (*see Lee Mau Seng v. Minister for Home Affairs, Singapore*).[333]

I. Judicial Review of Executive Detention

654. Let us now consider the constitutional issues related to judicial review of decisions and actions made under preventive detention laws. The major issues are: (a) What rights does a person have upon arrest? (b) To what extent can the court look into the executive's decision to detain a person? (c) What are the procedural grounds for challenging a detention?

§4. Rights on Initial Arrest

655. An arrest under section 74 of the ISA cannot be separated from the subsequent detention. As such, the principles of judicial review that apply to a detention under section 8 of the ISA apply with equal force during the arrest stage. In *Re Ong Yew Teck*,[334] the Singapore High Court held that an arrest was not justiciable since the arresting officer cannot be compelled to give information to the court which he or she considers to be prejudicial to the public interest.

656. A person arrested under the ISA has the right to counsel under Article 9(3) (*see* above), and he or she has the right to be informed of the grounds of arrest as soon as possible. However, because of the nature of preventive detention, the detainee's right to know the grounds of his or her arrest cannot be unqualified. In the Malaysian High Court case of *Chong Kim Loy v. Timbalan Menteri Dalam Negeri, Malaysia & Anor*,[335] Edgar Joseph Jr J (as he then was) held:

> all that an arrested person is entitled to demand for, is to be informed, at the earliest possible moment, not in detail and not necessarily in strict legal terminology, but only in general terms, by virtue of what power he is being arrested and of the grounds of his arrest. But, enough must be made known to him to afford him 'the opportunity of giving an explanation of any misunderstanding or of calling attention to other persons for whom he may have been mistaken with the result that further enquiries may save him from the consequences of a false accusation'.

---

333. [1989] 2 MLJ 449.
334. [1971] 2 MLJ 137.
335. [1960] MLJ 67.

§5. Bad Faith or *Mala Fides*

657. In *Karam Singh v. Menteri Hal Ehwal Dalam Negeri, Malaysia,*[336] the Malaysian Federal Court held that a detention can be challenged on the grounds that the decision was made in bad faith or *mala fides*. What amounts to *mala fides*? In *Yeap Hock Seng @ Ah Seng v. Minister for Home Affairs, Malaysia & Ors,*[337] Abdoolcader J (as he then was) held that the onus of proving the detaining authority's *mala fides* lay on the applicant and what was required was 'proof of improper or bad motive' and 'not mere suspicion'.

§6. 'Satisfaction': Subjective or Objective Test?[338]

658. The question as to whether the detaining authority – in this case, the Minister for Home Affairs, acting on the President's satisfaction – was properly 'satisfied' that the subject posed a security threat was first dealt with in the Malaysian Federal Court case of *Karam Singh v. Menteri Hal Ehwal Dalam Negeri, Malaysia.*[339] In that case, the Malaysian Federal Court held that the Minister's 'satisfaction' and the facts upon which he made his decision to detain the subject were non-justiciable. Such 'satisfaction' was subjective and not objective in nature, and the Constitution left it to the executive, and not the judiciary, to decide what national security required. This decision was followed in the Singapore High Court case of *Lee Mau Seng v. Minister of Home Affairs, Singapore.*[340]

659. In the 1980s, courts in both Singapore and Malaysia began adopting modern English principles of objective judicial review. The change finally came in the SGCA decision in *Chng Suan Tze v. The Minister of Home Affairs & Ors and Other Appeals*[341] where it was held that *Karam Singh* and its progeny 'can no longer be said to be good law' and that the objective test should apply to the review of the exercise of discretions under sections 8 and 10 of the ISA. Further, the court held that:

> Sections 8 and 10 of the ISA are exceptions to the fundamental rights guaranteed by arts 9, 13 and 14 of the Constitution and should therefore be narrowly construed so as to derogate as little as possible from such fundamental rights: *Liew Sai Wah v. PP* [1969] 1 AC 295 and *Ong Ah Chuan v PP* [1981] AC 648. The concept of 'Law' in arts 9 and 12(1) includes both the common law principles of natural justice and *fairness (Ong Ah Chuan v. PP*) and also the right contained in s 3 of the Habeas Corpus Act 1816 which right is also contained in art 9(2). Thus the legislative powers of Parliament must not be exercised in a manner which authorizes or requires the exercise of arbitrary power, or the

336. [1989] 3 MLJ 121 (High Court, Malaysia).
337. [1969] 2 MLJ 129 (Federal Court, Malaysia).
338. [1975] 2 MLJ 279 (High Court, Malaysia).
339. [1969] 2 MLJ 129 (Federal Court, Malaysia).
340. [1971] 1 MLJ 137.
341. [1988] 1 SLR 132, at 154.

exercise of power in breach of fundamental rules of natural justice: *Ong Ah Chuan*. Article 149(1) protects the validity of ss 8 and 10 against any inconsistency with art 9, 13 or 14, but not against inconsistency with art 12(1). Further, under art 93 judicial power is vested exclusively in the Supreme Court and Subordinate Courts of Singapore. Therefore, ss 8 and 10 of the ISA would be consistent with arts 12 and 93 of the Constitution, and consequently valid, only if the powers which they confer do not authorize arbitrary powers of detention, and only if the courts can review the exercise of these powers. Applying the subjective test to the exercise of discretion under ss 8 and 10 of the ISA would mean giving the executive arbitrary powers of detention, thereby rendering such powers unconstitutional and void.

660. In the wake of the decision in *Chng Suan Tze v. Minister for Home Affairs and Ors*, Parliament moved quickly to curb what it perceived as the judiciary's *volte facie*. The Constitution of the Republic of Singapore (Amendment) Act 1989 (Act 1 of 1989) came into effect on 27 January 1989, inserting Article 149(3). The effect of this amendment was that any question concerning the validity of any executive decision or act pursuant to powers conferred by an Act passed under Article 149 must be determined according to any law passed by Parliament for this purpose. Such law will not be invalidated by Article 93. Article 149(1) was also amended by including Article 11 (protection against retrospective criminal legislation) and Article 12 (right to equality) in the list of articles which laws passed under Article 149 are permitted to contravene.

661. Pursuant to that, the Internal Security (Amendment) Act (Act 2 of 1989) came into effect on 30 January 1989. New sections were inserted. Section 8A defines what amounts to judicial review. Section 8B(1) fixes the law governing such review to be that declared in Singapore on 13 July 1971 (which is the date of the judgment in *Lee Mau Seng v. Minister for Home Affairs, Singapore & Anor*)[342] to the exclusion of any Commonwealth decisions relating to judicial review, be they decided before, on or after that date. Section 8B(3) confines judicial review in courts to questions relating to compliance with the procedural requirements of the Act. Section 8C excludes appeals to the Privy Council in respect of such judicial decisions.

662. Four important questions arise with respect to these developments: (1) Are these constitutional amendments valid? (2) If so, are the legislative amendments pursuant to the amended Article 149 valid? (3) If so, does section 8B(2) of the ISA exclude judicial review of the executive decision altogether? (4) If not, does the test

342. [1971] 2 MLJ 137.

laid down in section 8B(1) (accepted to be that enunciated in *Lee Mau Seng*) exclude judicial review of the executive decision altogether?[343]

§7. Procedural Grounds of Challenge

663. A detention under the ISA can also be challenged on procedural grounds. Several grounds have been argued before the courts. The first pertains to the action of the Advisory Board. Under Article 151(1)(b) 'no citizen of Singapore shall be detained' under the ISA 'for a period exceeding three months unless an advisory board constituted' under Article 151(2) 'has considered any representations made by him' and 'made recommendations thereon to the President'. In *Re Tan Boon Liat @ Allen & Anor et al; Tan Boon Liat v. Menteri Hal Ehwal Dalam Negeri & Ors and Other Appeals*,[344] the applicants were detained under the Emergency (Public Order and Prevention of Crime) Ordinance, 1969. The Advisory Board failed to make recommendations within the three-month period, and the applicants challenged their detention as being unlawful. The Malaysian Federal Court held that as a 'condition precedent has not been satisfied' (i.e., the Advisory Board making the recommendation within three months), their continued detention was unlawful since it was not 'in accordance with law'.

664. Statutes depriving individuals of their liberty must be strictly complied with. As such, irregularities in the detention order have been held to invalidate the detention. For example, the detention is not lawful if the detention order is not signed by the proper authority (*see Lim Hock Siew & Ors v. The Minister of the Interior and Defence*).[345] Where the applicant was served a copy of the detention order which only bore a seal and rubber stamp, without a signature, the detention was also held to be illegal (*see Yit Hon Kit v. Minister of Home Affairs, Malaysia & Anor*).[346]

665. Is there, however, a minimum content of what should appear on the detention order? The Malaysian High Court considered this question in *Chong Kim Loy v. Timbalan Menteri Dalam Negeri, Malaysia & Anor*[347] and Justice Edgar Joseph Jr J (as he then was) held that it is essential that:

> the detention order contains at least so much of the belief of the Minister in regard to a detainee as will inform him, in general terms, of the reasons for his detention so as to enable him to exercise, as soon as reasonably possible, his right to make representation to an advisory board.

---

343. For a comment on the role of judges in reviewing administrative decisions, *see* C.M. Chinkin, *Abuse of Discretion in Malaysia and Singapore*, in *The Common Law in Singapore and Malaysia* 259 (A.J. Harding ed., Butterworths 1985); and Rowena Daw, *A Comment on Lee Mau Seng*, 14 Mal LR 276 (1972).
344. [1977] 2 MLJ 108.
345. [1968] 2 MLJ 219.
346. [1988] 2 MLJ 639 (High Court, Malaysia).
347. [1989] 3 MLJ 121 (High Court, Malaysia).

Selected Bibliography

The most thorough bibliographical review of writings on the Singapore Constitution is to be found in Kevin Y.L. Tan. 'Writing the Constitution: Forty Years of Singapore Constitutional Scholarship'. In *Evolution of a Revolution: Forty Years of the Singapore Constitution*, edited by Li-ann Thio & Kevin Y.L. Tan. London: Routledge-Cavendish, 2009, 288–322. What follows is just a select list of useful references.

§1. General Works (Historical)

Braddell, Sir Roland St John. *The Law of the Straits Settlements: A Commentary*. 2nd edn. 2 vols. Singapore: Kelly & Walsh, 1931 & 1932.

Kyshe, James William Norton. 'A Judicial History of the Straits Settlements 1786–1890', which was originally published as the Preface of his four-volume work Cases Heard and Determined in Her Majesty's Supreme Court of the Straits Settlements, 1808–1890, reprinted with an introduction by M.B. Hooker in *Malaya Law Review* 11, no. 1 (1969).

Napier, Sir Walter. *An Introduction to the Study of the Law Administered in the Colony of the Straits Settlements*. Singapore: Fraser & Neave, 1898. This rare volume was later reproduced in with an introduction in *Malaya Law Review* 16, no. 1 (1974): 4–51.

Sheridan, L.A. (ed.). *Malaya and Singapore, The Borneo Territories: The Development of Their Laws and Constitutions*. London: Stevens & Sons, 1961.

Winstedt, R.O. *The Constitution of the Colony of the Straits Settlements and of the Federated and Unfederated Malay States*. London: Royal Institute of International Affairs, 1931.

§2. General Works

Chan, Sek Keong, et al. 'Administrative and Constitutional Law'. *Halsbury's Laws of Singapore*. Vol. 1. Singapore: Butterworths Asia, 1999.

Jayakumar, S. *Constitutional Law (with Documentary Materials)*. Singapore: Malaya Law Review, 1976.

Tan, Kevin Y.L. *The Constitution of Singapore: A Contextual Analysis*. Oxford: Hart, 2015.

Tan, Kevin Y.L. *Introduction to Singapore's Constitution*. 3rd edn. Singapore: Talisman, 2013.

Thio, Li-ann & Kevin Y.L. Tan (eds). *Evolution of a Revolution: Forty Years of the Singapore Constitution*. London: Routledge-Cavendish, 2009.

Thio, Li-ann. *A Treatise on Singapore Constitutional Law*. Singapore: Academy Publishing, 2011.

§3. Casebook

Kevin Y.L. Tan & Li-ann Thio. *Constitutional and Administrative Law in Singapore*. Singapore: Academy Publishing, 2021.

§4. Singapore's Constitutional Development

Ahmad, I. 'The Position of Singapore in Malaysia'. *Malayan Law Journal* (1964): cxi.
Harding, A.J. 'Parliament and the Grundnorm in Singapore'. *Malaya Law Review* 25 (1983): 351.
Hickling, R.H. 'The Origins of Constitutional Government in Singapore'. In his *Essays in Singapore Law*. Kuala Lumpur: Peladuk Publications, 1992, 1–51.
Pillai, Philip N. & Kevin Tan Yew Lee. 'Constitutional Development'. In *Management of Success: The Moulding of Modern Singapore*, edited by K.S. Sandhu & P. Wheatley. Singapore: ISEAS, 1989, 647–668.
Sadka, Emma. 'Singapore and the Federation: Problems of Merger'. *Asian Survey* 1, no. 11 (1962): 17–25.
Sheridan, L.A. 'Constitutional and Legal Implications and Problems in the Separation of Singapore from Malaysia'. *Fiat Justitia* 1 (1966): 47.
Sheridan, L.A. 'Constitutional Problems of Malaysia'. 13 *International & Comparative Law Quarterly* 13 (1964): 1349.
Sheridan, L.A. 'From the Federation of Malaya to Malaysia'. *J du Droit International* 14 (1965): 543.
Turnbull, C.M. 'Constitutional Development 1819–1968'. *In Modern Singapore*, edited by Ooi Jin Bee & Chiang Hai Ding. Singapore: University of Singapore, 1969, 181–196.
Tan, Kevin Y.L. 'Foundational Moments: The "Singapore Constitution"'. In *Constitutional Foundings in Southeast Asia*, edited by Kevin Y.L. Tan & Bui Ngoc Son. Oxford: Hart, 2019, 161–190.
Tan, Kevin Y.L. 'The Evolution of Singapore's Modern Constitution: Developments from 1945 to the Present Day'. *Singapore Academy of Law Journal* 1 (1989): 1.
Tan, Kevin Y.L. 'A Short Legal and Constitutional History of Singapore'. In *The Singapore Legal System*, edited by Kevin Y.L. Tan. 2nd edn. Singapore: Singapore University Press, 1999, 26–66.
Tan, Kevin Y.L. 'A Short Legal and Constitutional History'. In *Essays in Legal History*, edited by Kevin Y.L. Tan. Singapore: Singapore Academy of Law & Marshall-Cavendish Academic, 2005, 27–72.
Tan, Kevin Y.L. *The Development of Constitutional Government in Singapore*. Unpublished JSD dissertation. New Haven: Yale Law School, 1995.

§5. Constitutional Interpretation

Lee, Jack Tsen-Ta. 'Shall the Twain Never Meet? Competing Narratives and Discourses of the Rule of Law in Singapore'. *Singapore Journal of Legal Studies* (2012): 298–330.

Neo, Jaclyn C.L. *Constitutional Interpretation in Singapore: Theory and Practice*. London: Routledge, 2016.

Neo, Jaclyn C.L. & Swati Jhaveri. 'The Many Facets of Constitutional Dialogue: The Case of Singapore'. *Australian Journal of Asian Law* (2017) 18(1): 1–14.

Thio Li-ann, '"It Is a Little Known Legal Fact": Originalism, Customary Human Rights Law and Constitutional Interpretation'. *Singapore Journal of Legal Studies* (2010) 558–570.

Thio, Li-ann. '"Beyond the Four Walls" in an Age of Transnational Judicial Conversations: Civil Liberties, Rights Theories and Constitutional Adjudication in Malaysia and Singapore'. *Columbia Journal of Asian Law* 19, no. 2 (2006): 428–518.

Thio, Li-ann. 'Trends in Constitutional Interpretation: Oppugning Ong, Awakening Arumugam?'. *Singapore Journal of Legal Studies* (1997): 240–290.

Thiruvengadam, Arun K. 'Comparative Law and Constitutional Interpretation in Singapore: Insights from Constitutional Theory'. In *Evolution of a Revolution: Forty Years of the Singapore Constitution*, edited by Li-ann Thio & Kevin Y.L. Tan. London: Routledge-Cavendish, 2009, 114–152.

§6. Rule of Law

Frank, Beatrice S., et al. 'The Decline of the Rule of Law in Singapore and Malaysia: A Report of the Committee of Human Rights of the Association of the Bar of the City of New York. New York: The Association, 1990; and B.S. Frank, et al'. The Decline of the Rule of Law in Malaysia & Singapore. The Record 46, no. 1 (1991): 5–63.

Lee, Jack Tsen-Ta. 'Constraint or Restraint? Singapore's Constitution at 50'. In *Singapore: Negotiating State and Society, 1965–2015*, edited by Jason Lim & Terence Lee. New York: Routledge, 2016, 15–34.

Neo, Jaclyn L.C. 'All Power has Legal Limits: The Principle of Legality as a Constitutional Principle of Judicial Review'. *Singapore Academy of Law Journal* 29 (2017): 667–689.

Tan, Eugene Kheng-Boon. 'Law and Values in Governance: The Singapore Way'. *Hongkong Law Journal* 30 (2000): 91.

Thio, Li-ann. 'Lex Rex or Rex Lex? Competing Conceptions of the Rule of Law in Singapore'. *UCLA Pacific Basin Law Journal* 20 (2002–2003): 1–76.

Thio, Li-ann. 'Rule of Law Within a Non-liberal "Communitarian" Democracy: The Singapore Experience'. In *Asian Discourses of the Rule of Law: Theories and Implementation of the Rule of Law in Twelve Asian Countries, France and the US*, edited by Randall Peerenboom. London & New York: Routledge, 2004, 183–224.

Thio, Li-ann. 'Apology & Apogee: The "Rule of Law" Beyond the Rules of Law in Singapore'. *Singapore Journal of Legal Studies* (2012).

§7. Institutions

Blöchlinger, Karen. 'Primus Inter Pares: Is the Singapore Judiciary First Among Equals?'. *Pacific Rim Law & Policy Journal* 9, no. 3 (2000): 591–618.

Selected Bibliography

Chan, Sek Keong. 'Working Out the Presidency: No Passage of Rights – In Defence of the Opinion of the Constitutional Tribunal'. *Singapore Journal of Legal Studies* (1996): 1.

Mutalib, H. 'Constitutional-Electoral Reforms and Politics in Singapore'. *Legislative Studies* 27, no. 4 (2002): 659–672.

Jayakumar, S. 'Protection of Civil Servants: The Scope of Article 135(1) and (2) of the Malaysian Constitution as Developed Through the Cases'. *Malayan Law Journal* 2 (1969): liv.

Jhaveri, Swati, 'Localising Administrative Law in Singapore: Embracing Inter-Branch Equality'. *Singapore Academy of Law Journal* (2017): 828–855.

Lee, Jack Tsen-Ta. 'Fundamental Constitutional Concepts and the Roles of the Branches of Government'. In *The Legal System of Singapore: Institutions, Principles and Practices*, edited by Gary Chan Kok Yew & Jack Tsen-Ta Lee). Singapore: LexisNexis, 2015, 47–88.

Lee, Yvonne C.L. 'Under Lock and Key: The Evolving Role of the Elected President as a Fiscal Guardian'. *Singapore Journal of Legal Studies* (2007): 290–322.

Malik, Waleed Haider. *Judiciary-Led Reforms in Singapore: Framework, Strategies, and Lessons*. Washington DC: World Bank, 2007.

Neo, Jaclyn L. & Swati Jhaveri. *Constitutional Changes in Singapore: Reforming the Elected Presidency*. London: Routledge, 2020.

Seow, Francis T. *Beyond Suspicion? The Singapore Judiciary*. New Haven: Yale Southeast Asian Studies, 2006.

Smith, T.E. 'The Effect of Recent Constitutional Changes on the Public Service in the Federation of Malaya and Singapore'. *Public Administration* 37 (1959): 267.

Tan, Kevin Y.L. 'The Singapore Judiciary'. In *Asia-Pacific Judiciaries: Independence, Impartiality and Integrity*, edited by H.P. Lee & M. Pittard. Cambridge: Cambridge University Press, 2017, 284–304.

Tan, Kevin Y.L. 'As Efficient as the Best Businesses: Singapore's Judicial System'. In *Asian Courts in Context*, edited by Jiunn-rong Yeh & Wen-chen Chang. Cambridge: Cambridge University Press, 2015, 228–265.

Tan, Kevin Y.L. 'Parliament and the Making of Law in Singapore'. In *The Singapore Legal System*, edited by Kevin Y.L. Tan. 2nd edn. Singapore: Singapore University Press, 1999, 123–159.

Tan, Kevin Y.L. 'Legislating Dominance: Parliament and the Making of Singapore's Governance Model'. In *The Limits of Authoritarian Governance in Singapore's Developmental State*, edited by Lily Zubaidah Rahim & Michael D Barr. Singapore: Palgrave MacMillan, 2019, 257–275.

Tan, Kevin Y.L. 'Delineation and Discretion: The Drawing of Electoral Boundaries'. In *Voting in a Time of Change: Singapore's 2020 General Election*, edited by Kevin Y.L. Tan & Terence Lee. Singapore: Ethos Books, 2021, 87–120.

Tan, Kevin Y.L. 'Constitutional Implications of the 1991 Singapore General Election'. *Singapore Law Review* 13 (1992): 1.

Tan, Kevin Y.L. 'Is Singapore's Electoral System in Need of Reform'. *Commentary* 14 (1997): 109–117.

Tan, Kevin Y.L. 'The Presidential Executive System in Singapore: Problems and Prospects'. In *The Powers and Functions of Executive Government: Studies from the Asia Pacific Region*, edited by Graham Hassell & Cheryl Saunders. Melbourne: Centre for Comparative Constitutional Studies, The University of Melbourne, 1994, 37–53.

Tan, Kevin Y.L. & Lam Peng Er (eds). *Managing Political Change in Singapore: The Elected Presidency*. London: Routledge, 1997.

Thio, Li-ann. 'The Right to Political Participation in Singapore: Tailor-Making a Westminster-Modelled Constitution to Fit the Imperatives of "Asian" Democracy'. *Singapore Journal of International & Comparative Law* 6 (2002): 181–243.

Thio, Li-ann. 'The Post-Colonial Constitutional Evolution of the Singapore Legislature'. *Singapore Journal of Legal Studies* (1993): 80.

Thio, Li-ann. 'Choosing Representatives: Singapore Does It Her Way'. In *The People's Representatives: Electoral Systems in the Asia-Pacific Region*, edited by Graham Hassell & Cheryl Saunders. Sydney: Allen & Unwin, 1997, 38–58.

Thio, Li-ann. 'Singapore: (S)electing the President: Diluting Democracy?'. *ICON* 5 (2007): 526–543.

Thio, Li-ann. 'Working Out the Presidency: The Rites of Passage'. *Singapore Journal of Legal Studies* (1995) 509.

Trindade, F.A. 'The Security of Tenure of Public Servants in Malaysia and Singapore'. In *Malaya Law Review Legal Essays*, edited by G.W. Bartholomew. Singapore: Malaya Law Review, 1975, 256.

Winslow, Valentine. 'Electing the President: The Presidential Elections Act 1991'. *Singapore Journal of Legal Studies* (1991): 476–481.

Winslow, V.S. 'The Public Service and Public Servants in Malaysia'. In *Constitution of Malaysia: Its Development, 1957–1977*, edited by Mohamed Suffian, H.P. Lee & F.A. Trindade. Kuala Lumpur: Oxford University Press, 1978, 262.

Worthington, Ross. 'Between Hermes and Themis: An Empirical Study of the Contemporary Judiciary in Singapore'. *Journal of Law & Society* 28, no. 4 (2001): 490–519.

§8. Rights and Civil Liberties

Boo, King Onn. 'Right to Counsel and Missing Lawyers'. *Malayan Law Journal* 2 (1986): lxxiv.

Chan, Cassandra. 'Breaking Singapore's Regrettable Tradition of Chilling Free Speech with Defamation Laws'. *Loyola LA International & Comparative Law Review* 26 (2003–2004): 315–339.

Chan, Sek Keong. 'Equal Justice Under the Constitution and Section 377A of the Penal Code: The Roads Not Taken'. *Singapore Academy of Law Journal* 31 (2019): 773–844.

Chew, Melanie. 'Human Rights in Singapore: Perceptions and Problems'. *Asian Survey* 34, no. 11 (1994): 933–948.

Chinkin, C.M. 'Abuse of Discretion in Malaysia and Singapore'. In *The Common Law in Singapore and Malaysia*, edited by A.J. Harding. Singapore: Butterworths, 1985, 259.

Goh, Phai Cheng. *Citizenship Laws of Singapore*. Singapore: Educational Book Publishers, 1970.

Harding, A.J. 'Natural Justice and the Constitution'. *Malaya Law Review* 23 (1981): 226–236.
Harding, A.J. 'The Right to Counsel – A Privy Council View'. *Malaya Law Review* 22 (1980): 160.
Hickling, R.H. 'Liberty and Law in Singapore'. *Malaya Law Review* 21 (1979): 1.
Hor, Michael & Colin Seah. 'Selected Issues in the Freedom of Speech and Expression in Singapore'. *Singapore Law Review* 12 (1991): 298.
Hor, Michael. 'The Death Penalty in Singapore and International Law'. *Singapore Yearbook of International Law* 8 (2004): 105.
Hor, Michael. 'The Freedom of Speech and Defamation'. *Singapore Journal of Legal Studies* (1992): 542.
Hor, Michael. 'The Presumption of Innocence: A Constitutional Discourse for Singapore'. *Singapore Journal of Legal Studies* (1995): 365.
Hor, Michael. 'The Privilege Against Self-incrimination and Fairness to the Accused'. *Singapore Journal of Legal Studies* (1993): 35–56.
Hor, Michael. 'The Right to Consult a Lawyer on Arrest'. *CLAS News* 3 (1989): 4, and *CLAS News* 4 (1989): 4.
Hor, Michael. 'The Right to Counsel – The Right to Be Informed'. *Singapore Academy of Law Journal* 5 (1993): 141.
Huang-Thio, S.M. 'Constitutional Discrimination under the Malaysian Constitution'. *Malaya Law Review* 6 (1964): 69.
Huang-Thio, S.M. 'Equal Protection and Rational Classification'. *Public Law* (1963): 412.
Huang-Thio, S.M. 'Legal Aid: A Facet of Equality Before the Law'. *International & Comparative Law Quarterly* 12 (1963): 1133.
Iyer, T.K.K. 'Article 9(1) and Natural Justice'. *Malaya Law Review* 23 (1981): 213–225.
Jayakumar, S. 'Deprivation of Citizenship'. *Malaya Law Review* 6 (1964): 178.
Jhaveri, Swati, 'Advancing Constitutional Justice in Singapore: Enhancing Access and Standing in Judicial Review Cases'. *Singapore Journal of Legal Studies* (2017): 53–76.
Jhaveri, Swati, 'The Doctrine of Substantive Legitimate Expectations: The Significance of Chiu Teng @ Kallang Pte Ltd v. Singapore Land Authority'. *Public Law* (2016) 1: 1–9.
Jones, Eric. 'Asia's Fate: A Response to the Singapore School'. *The National Interest* (Spring 1994): 18.
Kausikan, Bilahari. 'An East Asian Approach to Human Rights'. *Buffalo Journal of International Law* (1995–1996): 273.
Kausikan, Bilahari. 'Asia's Different Standard'. *Foreign Policy* (Fall 1993): 24.
Kausikan, Bilahari. 'Governance that Works'. *Journal of Democracy* (1997): 26.
Kausikan, Bilahari. 'An Asian Approach to Human Rights'. *Proceedings of the American Society of International Law* (1995): 147.
Kausikan, Bilahari. 'The Singapore School'. *The National Interest* (Summer (1994): 107.
Lee, Mei Pheng. 'Breeding the Best and the Brightest'. *Journal of Malaysian & Comparative Law* (1984): 11.

Lee, Jack. 'Equal Protection and Sexual Orientation'. *Singapore Law Review* 16 (1995): 228.

Lee, Jack Tsen-Ta. 'The Limits of Liberty: The Crime of Male Same-Sex Conduct and the Rights to Life and Personal Liberty in Singapore: Lim Meng Suang v. Attorney General [2015] 1 SLR 26'. *Hong Kong Law Journal* 46, no. 1 (2016): 49–70.

Lee, Jack Tsen-Ta. 'Equality and Singapore's First Constitutional challenges to the Criminalization of Male Homosexual Conduct'. *Asia-Pacific Journal of Human Rights and the Law*, 16 nos 1–2 (2015) 150–185.

Lee, Jack Tsen-Ta, 'According to the Spirit and Not the Letter: Proportionality and the Singapore Constitution'. *Vienna Journal of International Constitutional Law* 8, no. 3 (2014): 276–304.

Lim, C.L. 'The Constitution and the Reception of Customary International Law: Nguyen Tuong Van v. Public Prosecutor'. *Singapore Journal of Legal Studies* (2005): 218.

Mahbubani, Kishore. 'An Asian Perspective on Human Rights and Freedom of the Press'. UN General Assembly, A/Conf 157/PC/63/Add 28, 4 May 1993.

Mahbubani, Kishore. 'The Pacific Way'. *Foreign Affairs* (1995): 100.

Mahbubani, Kishore. 'The West and the Rest'. *The National Interest* (Summer (1992): 8.

Neo, Jaclyn C.L. 'Secularism Without Liberalism: Religious Freedom and Secularism in a Non-Liberal State'. *Michigan State Law Review* 2 (2017): 333–370.

Neo, Jaclyn C.L. 'Equal Protection and the Reasonable Classification Test in Singapore after Lim Meng Suang v. Attorney-General'. *Singapore Journal of Legal Studies* (2016): 95–117.

Neo, Jaclyn C.L. 'Secular Constitutionalism in Singapore: Between Equality and Hierarchy'. *Oxford Journal of Law and Religion* 5, no. 3: 431–456.

Neo, Jaclyn C.L. 'Seditious in Singapore! Free Speech and the Offence of Promoting Ill-Will and Hostility Between Different Racial Groups'. *Singapore Journal of Legal Studies* (2011): 351–372.

Rawlings, H.F. 'Habeas Corpus and Preventive Detention in Singapore and Malaysia'. *Malaya Law Review* 25 (1983): 324.

Sheehy, Benedict. 'Singapore, "Shared Values" and Law: Non East Versus West Constitutional Hermeneutic'. *Hong Kong Law Journal* 34 (2004): 67.

Sinnadurai, Visuvanathan. 'Singapore Citizenship Laws'. *Malaya Law Review* 12 (1970): 160.

Tan, Seow Hon. 'The Constitution as "Comforter"? – An Assessment of the Safeguards in Singapore's Constitutional System'. *Singapore Law Review* 16 (1995): 104.

Tan, Yock Lin. 'Some Aspects of Preventive Detention in Malaysia and Singapore'. *Malaya Law Review* 29 (1987): 237.

Tan, Kevin Y.L. 'Law, Religion and the State in Singapore'. *The Review of Faith and International Affairs (Special Issue)* 14, no. 4 (2016): 65–77.

Tan, Kevin Y.L. 'Defaming Politicians, Scandalising the Courts: A Look at Recent Developments in Singapore'. In *Democracy, Media and Law in Malaysia and Singapore*, edited by Andrew T Kenyon, Tim Marjoribanks & Amanda Whiting. London: Routledge, 2014, 105–128.

Tan, Kevin Y.L. 'Economic Development and Human Rights in East Asia: Legal Reforms in Singapore and Taiwan'. In *The East Asian Challenge for Human Rights*, edited by Joanne Bauer & Daniel A. Bell. Cambridge: Cambridge University Press, 1999, 264–284.

Tan, Kevin Y.L. 'Fifty Years of the UDHR: A Singaporean Reflects'. In *Human Rights Perspectives*, edited by Tan Ngoh Tiong & Kripa Sridharan. Singapore: United Nations Association of Singapore, 1999, 118–140.

Tan, Kevin Y.L. 'Fifty Years of the Universal Declaration of Human Rights: A Singapore Reflection'. *Singapore Law Review* 20 (1999): 239–280.

Tan, Kevin Y.L. 'Issues of Multiculturalism in Singapore'. In *Beyond Rituals and Riots: Ethnic Pluralism and Social Cohesion in Singapore*, edited by Lai Ah Eng. Singapore: Eastern Universities Press, 2004, 98–113.

Tay, Simon S.C. 'Culture, Human Rights and the Singapore Example'. *McGill Law Journal* 41, no. 4 (1996): 743–780.

Tay, Simon S.C. 'Imagining Freedom'. In *Imagining Singapore*, edited by Ban Kah Choon, Anne Pakir & Tong Chee Kiong, 2nd edn. Singapore Times Academic Press, 2004, 81–105.

Thio Li-ann, 'Contentious Liberty: Regulating Religious Propagation in a Religiously Diverse Secular Democracy'. *Singapore Journal of Legal Studies* (2010): 484–515.

Thio, Li-ann, 'Reading Rights Rightly: The UDHR and the Creeping Influence on the Development of Singapore Public Law'. *Singapore Journal of Legal Studies* (2008): 264–291.

Thio, Li-ann, 'Between Eden and Armageddon: Navigating "Religion" and "Politics" in Singapore'. *Singapore Journal of Legal Studies* (2009): 365–405.

Thio Li-ann, 'Singapore Human Rights Practice and Legal Policy: Of Pragmatism and Principle, Rights, Rhetoric and Realism'. *Singapore Academy of Law Journal* 21 (2009): 293.

Thio, Li-ann. 'Constitutional "Soft Law" and the Management of Religious Liberty and Order: The 2003 Declaration on Religious Harmony'. *Singapore Journal of Legal Studies* (2004): 414–443.

Thio, Li-ann. 'Control, Co-optation and Co-operation: Managing Religious Harmony in Singapore's Multi-Ethnic, Quasi-Secular State'. *Hastings Constitutional Law Quarterly* 33 (2006): 197–253.

Thio, Li-ann. 'Pragmatism and Realism Do Not Mean Abdication: A Critical Inquiry into Singapore's Engagement with International Human Rights Law'. *Singapore Yearbook of International Law* 8 (2004): 41–91.

Thio, Li-ann. 'Recent Constitutional Developments: Of Shadows and Whips, Race, Rifts and Rights, Terror and Tudungs, Women and Wrongs'. *Singapore Journal of Legal Studies* (2002): 328–373.

Thio, Li-ann. 'Religion in the Public Sphere of Singapore: Wall of Division or Public Square?'. In *Religious Pluralism and Civil Society: A Comparative Analysis*, edited by Bryan S. Turner. Oxford: Bardwell Press, 2008, 73–104.

Thio, Li-ann. 'She's a Woman But She Acts Very Fast: Women, Religion and Law in Singapore'. In *Mixed Blessings: Law, Religions and Women's Rights in the Asia-Pacific Region*, edited by Carolyn Evans & Amanda Whiting. The Hague: Brill, 2006, 241–277.

Thio, Li-ann. 'Singapore: Regulating Political Speech and the Commitment "To Build a Democratic Society"'. *ICON* 1 (2003): 516–524.

Thio, Li-ann. 'Taking Rights Seriously? Singapore and Human Rights Law'. In *Human Rights in Asia: A Comparative Legal Study of Twelve Asian Countries, France and the USA*, edited by Randy Pereenboom, Albert Chen & Carole Petersen. London: RoutledgeCurzon, 2006, 158–190.

Thio, Li-ann. 'The Death Penalty as Cruel and Inhuman Punishment Before the Singapore High Court? Customary Human Rights Norms, Constitutional Formalism and the Supremacy of Domestic Law in PP v. Nguyen Tuong Van (2004)'. *Oxford University Commonwealth Law Journal* 4, no. 2 (2004): 213–226.

Thio, Li-ann. 'The Impact of Internationalisation on Domestic Governance: The Transformative Potential of CEDAW'. *Singapore Journal of International & Comparative Law* 1 (1997): 248–350.

Thio, Li-ann. 'Trends in Constitutional Interpretation: Oppugning Ong, Awakening Arumugam?'. *Singapore Journal of Legal Studies* (1997): 240–290.

Selected Bibliography

Index

The numbers here refer to paragraph numbers.

Index